Elvis

and

Ireland

IVOR CASEY

First published in 2013 by Appello Press

Copyright © 2013 Ivor Casey

All rights reserved. No part of this book may be reproduced in any form or by any electronic or mechanical means, including information storage and retrieval systems, without permission in writing from the publisher, except by a reviewer who may quote brief passages in a review.

ISBN: 978-0-9573752-0-8

Cover art: "Elvis 1958" by Nuala Holloway
(www.nualaholloway.com)

For my parents

ACKNOWLEDGMENTS

For their support in helping me bring this book to fruition I would like to express a sincere debt of gratitude to Don Conroy, Jakki Moore, Nuala Holloway, Jerome Casey, Eoghan Harris, Jimmy Murakami, Kingston Gasteen, Stephen Totterdell, Peter Donnelly and the late writer and historian Leo Daly. I would also like to give special mention to the Gilbert Library, Pearse St., the National Library, Kildare St. and the National Archives, Bishop St., all of which are in Dublin City and all of which provided excellent facilities for research.

Buachaill óg bocht a bhí ann nuair a fuair sé giotár dá bhreithlá. Bhí sé fós ina ógánach brionglóideach gan mórán airgid nuair a thuill sé clú agus cáil ar fud an domhain. Amhránaí fuinniúil, iomasach agus paiseanta ab ea é le fuaim speisialta. Bhí na milliúin tóghtha leis an nguth binn álainn a bhí aige. D'éirigh leis meanma agus a misneach a ardú, ní amaháin lena ghuth ach freisin leis na hamhráin mhothúchánacha a chan sé. Is siombal mhór é do dhaoine óga agus tá meas acu air agus ómós acu dó go dtí an lá atá inniu ann, cé go bhfuil sé imithe ar shlí na fírinne le blianta. Ar ndóigh, ní bheidh a leithéid arís ann.

AUTHOR'S NOTE

It all began on a Saturday afternoon in August of 1997. As I glanced through the TV guide I noticed that Elvis Presley was getting a lot of media coverage for some reason. Anybody planning to sit in and watch TV that day could not have escaped reference to him. I soon learned that it was the 20th anniversary of his death and that the world was stopping in its tracks to honour him.

I remember his songs being played on the radio continuously while I made preparations for my return to school, as the summer drew to a close. The exciting and catchy rhythm of "Jailhouse Rock" ran through me as I faced the mundane task of getting a new school uniform. I had only briefly heard of Elvis Presley at this point, having been born six years after he died, but I had a faint memory of enjoying *Blue Hawaii* as a much younger child. This was enough to interest me into watching the tributes which flooded the TV that night.

Love Me Tender and *Aloha From Hawaii* stood out the most for me that evening, but the following days were like the days after Christmas. There seemed to be an "Elvis atmosphere" throughout Ireland at this time. This was especially due to the song "Always On My Mind" having been rereleased and riding high in the charts. I listened intently to that song and quickly learned that Elvis had recorded it after separating from his wife.

At thirteen it dawned on me that some singers sing songs about issues which affect them deeply, rather than just taking what's handed to them. My peers had their big modern day bands to follow but I had unwittingly never followed the crowd. I enjoyed lots of music but following one person or group was just something I never did and not something I comprehended doing, until Elvis.

I bought the new Elvis love song compilation with "Always On My Mind" leading the album and discovered a range of voices, moods and emotions which I had never found before. It has often been explained that Elvis had that indescribable something which drew people to him and that's what I was now discovering, without any influence of that fact. I loved every song and how it was sung and I knew I soon had to find more. As a teenager I collected a considerable amount of Elvis memorabilia, even going as far as to put lunch money aside to buy each new compilation released.

While I did go through a long phase of fan boy devotion, I found through Elvis a gateway to so many other styles of music. I also read up about his immense cultural impact. It seemed like every country in the world had an Elvis story to tell, whether it was his banning in communist Russia, his trips to Germany and France or his overwhelming fan base in Japan, including a Japanese prime minister (Junichiro Koizumi). There is even a replica of Graceland in Denmark and a square named after him in Hungary. The UK, right next door to us in Ireland, always appeared to have an Elvis story with most of their legendary performers having either met him or having been greatly influenced by him. I soon noticed how Ireland kept getting overlooked.

I learned more and more about modern day popular culture through books and TV and kept finding myself confronted with the same chain of events; that the '60s were the beginning of anything major. At least this was how it seemed as I read and viewed Irish accounts of pop culture. What I wanted to know was, what about Elvis and rock 'n' roll in 1950s Ireland? With a TV series like *Reeling in The Years*, the account of pop culture does not go back further than 1962, as Ireland's TV service didn't exist then. But I wanted to know what Ireland was like with regard to modern pop culture before this time.

Pre-1970s and most certainly pre-1960s Ireland is recounted accurately as a Church ruled and dominantly Catholic society. It first appeared to me that the pop culture at that time was the "stations of the cross" as anything remotely exciting or colourful was frowned upon, disapproved of or simply banned. However, the '50s was the time the showbands first formed and I knew Elvis and rock 'n' roll must have shone through the cracks of censorship. Knowing that Elvis Presley had an enormous influence around the world, the idea to look at the story of Elvis through Irish eyes emerged. I set out to discover his influence on Ireland and Ireland's response to him as well as the circumstantial links between Elvis and Ireland.

By my final year in school I knew writing was an area I was certainly going to pursue so I began writing this book in the Spring of 2002. The following year *The Sunday Independent* printed my first article as a journalist and Elvis was also the subject then as I covered the "Elvis The Concert" production at the Point Theatre in Dublin. I put the book on the back burner, touching on it occasionally as I pursued a career as a freelance journalist working on historical and cultural articles, as well as achieving a B.A. (Hons.) Degree in English, Media and Cultural Studies.

Nonetheless, with that great admiration for Elvis still lasting I returned to the book ten years after it was conceived. I finally achieved what I had set out to do and that was to write an "Irish biography" of Elvis Presley. It has been a tremendous ten years of research with the National Archives, libraries and Newspaper archives well explored for any mention of Elvis and countless hours of conversations and interviews.

Elvis and Ireland reflects the Irish side of his global appeal by journeying through his life story while picking up the Irish connections, links and stories along the way. Hundreds of Elvis books already exist but rarely does a new Elvis book have something to say from a totally different cultural stand point.

As I kept crafting the book it gradually started to simultaneously become a historical document of Irish popular music while still keeping in line with Elvis's story. I see it as a book for all music lovers and all Elvis fans, and not just the Irish ones. It has been an incredible experience for me, from the moment I discovered the magic of Elvis at thirteen to finding my passion in life and having Elvis's inspiration help pave the way.

CHAPTER ONE

Ireland's own international superstar, Bono, once explained that Elvis changed everything with regard to music, sex and politics. It is clear to see through the eyes of a later generation, whether it is Bono born in 1960 or myself, born in 1983, that after Elvis, the world shifted course, along with his resilient sound and performance style. Born into exceptional poverty in 1935 Elvis Presley would go on to conquer not only the music industry but celebrity stardom.

He would become the ultimate of phenomenal icons and this extraordinary status would reach all corners of the world as he infused musical and cultural inspiration. He would be the symbol for original and innovative styles and bring something new and exciting to the fabric of different nations as much as those nations had brought something new to the America in which he was raised. One of the major places in this mix of cultures was a little island to the far West of Europe.

During the 1930s Ireland and America were both in economic turmoil. 1930s America marked the height of the Great Depression which affected every part of America and stretched out to international countries including Ireland. In America some of the worst affected areas were the deep southern states such as Mississippi and Tennessee. Throughout this period over fifteen million American citizens lost their jobs as businesses and banks closed their doors. While America had The Depression as its down point in which to overcome, Ireland was only in the early stages of developing an independent republic with economic progression yet to prosper. While America gradually rose out of its economic woes, thousands of Irish citizens left their homes for the other side of the Atlantic Ocean.

Throughout the early years of an independent Irish nation, the country began adopting a sense of what it was to be Irish and highlighting what could make its culture distinguishable and separate to its former coloniser. While the Irish poet W. B. Yeats had spoken of a Celtic revival to embrace the Irish myths and legends of centuries ago, other Irish writers such as playwright Sean O'Casey focused on telling stories of the current age of struggle within Irish society.

With a growth in communications through cinema, the press, music and the Irish Diaspora sending back stories, American Culture began to be filtered more and more into the country. In Ireland, Hollywood cinema and American pop music had been finding a niche in Ireland from the earliest points of an independent nation, even if most of this was usually heavily banned or censored. Despite the dramatic attempts to keep Ireland self-sufficient and independent of outside influences, mainly due to the power of the Catholic Church, Irish people would prove to show their desire for foreign forms of entertainment.

Regardless of the influence on Ireland by American culture, there has been a revolving cycle of influential cultural input from other nations into America. This has in turn produced cultures which have been branded American. One of the most branded American icons is Elvis Presley and while he might be seen as encompassing much of what American culture represents, his background, life, music and career have not existed without touching or being touched by the allure of varying cultures around the world. Elvis Presley is not just a person and not just an American product but a major figurehead for the unification of modern world cultures in some form or another and Ireland is very much one of the stronger nations in this link. A lot of this unification comes from the struggle to rise from the depths of poverty and achieve at something in life and find fulfilment by using art as a form of expression.

As in Ireland during the 1930s, The Depression in America saw millions of people suffer and struggle with each breath to try and eke out a living. In a small Mississippi town named Tupelo a married couple with no qualifications and little education struggled to live comfortably. The husband, Vernon Elvis Presley, (born 10 April 1916), had grown up with few ambitions, eventually landing a job on a dairy farm. On 17 June 1933, aged seventeen, he married twenty-one year old Gladys Love Smith (born 25 April 1912).

Vernon built a little two room shack for himself and his wife in East Tupelo. Gladys Smith was a free spirit who became notorious for dancing and partying. She was independent within herself and enjoyed living in a way women weren't expected to at that time. Despite this, she liked to stay at home, doing chores such as feeding chickens. This was a task not so different from a young rural Irish girl of the time.

On the night of 7 January 1935 Gladys began to go into labour. A local doctor was called upon as the Presleys didn't have the money for hospital treatment. Then, in the early hours of 8 January, a baby to be named Jesse Garon was delivered stillborn. Gladys continued to feel pain and at approximately 4.35 A.M. Elvis Aron Presley was born. He was the survivor of twins, arriving about thirty-five minutes after his brother. Jesse was placed in a tiny coffin and buried at an unmarked grave at the Priceville Cemetery, not too far from where they lived. The Presleys were known for being an extremely polite and peaceful people who were always considerate of other people's feelings. This was something which Elvis would adhere passionately to all his life.

The only changes seen in their immediate family history was regarding their name, when Vernon's mother, Minnie Mae Presley, was responsible for dropping an "s", from "Pressley" to the prevailing "Presley". However, the variation on the family name was only minor in comparison to what the name had originated from. There has been a genealogical trace on Elvis's paternal side back to Germany. It has been uncovered that the name Presley originally derived from such German names as "Breslaar" and "Preslar".

In some traces of the Presley family tree, the names David Pressley and his son Andrew have surfaced with the information that they travelled from either Scotland or Ireland and settled in North Carolina in 1754. David is noted among some sources as being the great-great-great-great-great-great-grandfather to Elvis. Nonetheless, in other sources there is no link to Ireland but just to Germany. In more unofficial genealogical traces, the Preseli hills in

Pembrokeshire, Wales, have been cited as a point of origin of the Presley name.

What is also noteworthy is that the name "Elvis" is linked to both Wales and Ireland. In the sixth century there lived a Celtic Saint Elvis, who was the Bishop of Emly in the province of Munster. He would have been known as Saint Ailbe in Ireland and he lived in around the early to mid 500's A.D. This particular saint is also linked to Wales as there exists here a Neolithic burial chamber, bearing the name "St. Elvis Cromlech". A search of both the forename Elvis and the family name Presley trace back to Western Europe and to the Celtic areas, with a link between Ireland, Scotland and Wales.

Elvis's maternal genealogy has had more definite traces through history. Researcher and author Elaine Dundy discovered that Gladys's great-great-grandmother was a full blooded Cherokee Indian named "Morning Dove White". In 1818 she married a man named William Mansell, the son of Richard Mansell. The Mansells trace back to Western Europe. Starting out in Northern France, the family moved to Great Britain where they began travelling around for many years, landing mainly in Scotland. They eventually settled in Ireland. It was while in Ireland that the name multiplied immensely. Then in the early 1700s the majority of the Irish Mansells emigrated to the southern states of America where they were referred to as Scots-Irish. Most of the Scots-Irish settled in Alabama and were noted as being a compassionate community, a quality reflected in the Presley family personality.

A recent U.S. Census states over forty million Americans claim Irish descent. This can reflect on why some lifestyles are similar among both countries. In the state of Mississippi where Elvis was born and where most of his family going back a few generations came from, there are approximately 390,000 people who claim Irish ancestry. In Elvis's second home state of Tennessee there are a total of 875,000 citizens reporting Irish ancestry. Unfortunately there rarely are definitive family trees and for Elvis Presley there is none that leads much further back than the year 1800. What can be confidently said is that Elvis' descent from Ireland is strong, due to both parents' connections and the potent Irish connections in American culture in which the Presleys partook. Ireland and America shared some similarities in each other's rural districts. Employment came from crop and dairy farming. Similar styles of folk music entertained the masses. Farming related events added excitement to small towns. Religion ruled and church service was the major activity of the week. In more shady areas, strong alcohol was bootlegged with Irish *poitín* and American *moonshine* in their respective countries.

Vernon could never sustain a job for long and good paying work remained scarce. The battle to survive during the Depression went on. The Presleys often had small portions of food, consisting mainly of corn bread and water. In 1938, due to worsening financial circumstances, Vernon and two other men altered a cheque given to them for the sale of a hog. They were caught for this criminal act and Vernon was sent to prison for three years leaving his wife and son, aged three, to fend for themselves.

Gladys got a few odd jobs such as cotton picking but at the same time had to care for her only child. Gladys and three year old Elvis travelled the town asking people to sign a petition to have Vernon released early. In early 1939, after eight months, Vernon was released from prison on good behaviour. The Presleys moved from house to house and often moved in with relations as their financial status had not improved. The family moved to predominately black neighbourhoods where Elvis was raised within the culture, especially in the cotton fields. Despite legal segregation and racial tension in the South, Elvis became friends with black people and was introduced into a world of hypnotic blues music.

During the 1940s, Elvis was recognised as a quiet and shy pupil at school and caused little trouble. As Elvis had no siblings and his father was not often at home, his only real companion was his mother. While Vernon had failed to chase any ambitions in life, Elvis intended to do his best to succeed. As a child, he often said to his mother that some day he would buy her a big house and a car. Gladys's complications at the birth and the loss of Jesse meant that she was fortunate that Elvis survived. This was the main reason she kept such a possessive hold over her only son.

Elvis's singing talent first came to public attention at the age of ten. At a competition at the Mississippi-Alabama fair and dairy show (A rural American equivalent to one of Ireland's many Agricultural Shows, such as The Ploughing Championships), he gave a performance of "Old Shep" and achieved fifth place. Then for his eleventh birthday Elvis wanted a bicycle but as bicycles were too expensive he received a guitar instead. This would remain an historic gift and another symbol of his direction towards music.

The Presleys were a faithful but not strictly devout family who rarely missed church service at their local Assembly of God Church. Due to legal segregation, black people would go to their church and white people to theirs. In America's South many of the very poor communities saw each other as equals, as they both struggled through similar circumstances. It was at church that singing took more of an effect on Elvis. As a toddler Elvis would run up to the front of the church and start dancing and singing in rhythm to the gospel choirs.

At the age of thirteen in 1948, Elvis and his family moved to Memphis, Tennessee, as the chances of success in the city were greater for Vernon. This move added to Elvis's guidance towards music, as Memphis was the home of the blues. Elvis was sent to Humes High School but here he shortly began to get a rough time from city lads who tried to intimidate this country boy. As he grew into his later teens Elvis's long hair and side burns, among a trend of crew cuts, made him a target of bullying.

Again, moving around Memphis, the family got evicted from homes due to their inability to come up with full payments. The tough times never ceased. Eventually they moved into Lauderdale Courts, which was considered an upturn in their lives. At various locations in Memphis, Elvis was once again brought further into the culture of black people with whom he made friends. Between listening to them play the blues, which would inspire him to use his guitar, and singing at church, Elvis's passion for music was being further developed. He practiced his guitar on the steps of the homes he lived in and would play anything that came to mind.

Elvis joined the music class at school and imitated his favourite blues and country artists with his guitar. The music he imitated was a new style, strange for white people to hear. Some kids didn't like it but others told him he would be famous. Either way, Elvis never drifted from what he loved best, making music. Music became his only tool for expression due to his shyness. He was entranced by all styles, having been raised listening to Memphis radio which played country, blues and the mood music of Irish tenors. His dreams, ambitions and desires began and ended with music. He would play anything at all once there was a deep, intense outpouring of emotion involved.

His tastes ranged from gospel groups to ballad and blues artists to the pop styles of Dean Martin and even some classical and opera music. Music with Elvis saw no divisions and he admired tenors like Enrico Caruso and Mario Lanza. From constant listening to the radio he admired the great Irish tenor, John McCormack. McCormack, who was born in 1884, came from the town of Athlone in Co. Westmeath: "The heart of Ireland". He joined the choir of the Dublin Cathedral in 1903 and made his operatic debut at Covent Garden in London in 1907. In 1909 he sang at the Manhattan Opera House in New York City. McCormack's greatest success was on the concert platform, where his rendition of Irish folk songs achieved great popularity. In 1938 the great Irish tenor retired from the stage and died in 1945. Elvis would later express an appreciation and understanding of the works of such a noted Irish tenor in his later repertoire.

Despite a few guitar lessons from others, Elvis was largely self-taught. He played by ear and never learned to read music. The radio provided him with all he needed. Some of his favourites included "Mystery Train" and "That's All Right". Defying segregation, Elvis would often go to the "black" churches where he was accepted and sit at the back. Here the preachers were full of charisma, clapping and dancing in worship. The black gospel styles were probably the first type of rock music but in these times no white person would even think of professionally performing this due to racial tensions.

At seventeen, Elvis got a job as a cinema usher and this

gave him the chance to see films for free. He would try and see everything released including the Irish based, *The Quiet Man* (1952) with John Wayne and Barry Fitzgerald. On viewing *The Quiet Man* a number of times since its release and remarking to friends how beautiful he thought Ireland was, he probably never knew it would be one of many countries where he would make a cultural impact.

In June of 1953, Elvis received his high school diploma, making him the first member of his immediate family to do so. He had succeeded in school, had discovered a talent, had saved enough money to buy a car for himself and soon found a job working for a tool company. Then during the summer of 1953 Elvis took time out to record a song that he claimed was for his mother's birthday. He went into Sam Phillips's recording studio in Memphis, which was later called Sun Studios, where he paid to record a song. However, it was obvious Elvis was also there in the hope of getting noticed.

While getting ready to record, the studio secretary Marion Keisker asked Elvis who he thought he sounded like. Elvis replied saying, "I don't sound like nobody". The quiet, shy, soft-spoken gentleman gained enough self confidence to try and achieve in the music business. Keisker took note of this, next to his impeccable manners and politeness. His first recording was the ballad "My Happiness" which was followed by "That's When Your Heartaches Begin". Sam Phillips was not all that impressed by Elvis's recording but Marion Keisker noted how he was certainly different.

In January of 1954 he recorded the songs "I'll Never Stand In Your Way" and "It Wouldn't Be The Same Without You". Again there was little interest coming from Sam Phillips. His second attempt drew no success. Elvis then got a job as a truck driver for the Crown Electric Company. He also began to study to be an electrician. However, good luck prevailed for Elvis one day in the summer of 1954 when he decided to drop back to Sun to try out yet again. Phillips expressed an interest and got Presley recording a few songs including "Without You".

On 5 July, after a period of time which saw Elvis playing some talent shows while working for Crown Electric, Sam Phillips got back in contact with him. He was teamed up with local guitarist Scotty Moore and bass player Bill Black. They performed several songs including, "I Love You Because" but Phillips still searched for something distinctive. After mixing and jamming on songs, trying to discover what Phillips was in search of, Elvis picked the Arthur Crudup song "That's All Right" without any real intention of recording it sincerely. Suddenly something special happened. Phillips found what he wanted and everything came together. Within a few minutes it would become an extraordinary discovery and help change the face of music around the world.

Chapter Two

In the Ireland of 1954 R&B music was alien to most Irish listeners unless they chose to tune into foreign channels which could be accessed in certain locations around the country. There was only one national radio channel and no television. The only Irish radio broadcaster was Radio Éireann and modern forms of popular music were not played on it. The radio, known nationally as the "wireless", only played safe standards consisting of Irish traditional, céilís, classical and opera.

The alternative to this was Radio Luxembourg, which was the most popular foreign channel to play a diverse range of musical genres, having originally set up in 1933. It was one of the earliest pirate radio channels and would become an essential asset to the birth of rock 'n' roll throughout Britain and Ireland. It was here to which music lovers seeking advanced and modern sounds could turn, to hear the latest works from around the world and mostly from America, including jazz and blues.

The 1950s would see the emergence of a new and alternative sound with which most of the Western world was unfamiliar. Popular music was about to be greatly altered and while most national radio channels around the world adapted to it, Ireland was going to hold off on it a little longer than almost everybody else.

One of the most significant events in this musical change occurred in the summer of 1954 at Sun Studios in Memphis, Tennessee when Elvis Presley, Scotty Moore and Bill Black brought their skills together. The trio messed around on the R&B classic "That's All Right" jamming away and enjoying the performance. Their performance was solid and something of their own. Presley's vocals were loose and free and there was an undeniable freshness, exuberance and confidence over the simplicity of the arrangements in their performance.

There was an incredible chemistry among the musicians as they began to explore a new sound. This sound was something Phillips had been looking for and this session was the starting point for something, at that time undefined yet certainly extraordinary.

Irish broadcaster, author and journalist Joe Jackson found in Elvis and his version of "That's All Right" that "He tapped into the spirit of gospel music while singing. He tapped into his own spirit and in doing so he transformed a mournful blues into a song of celebration. That is the essence of how the most influential recording in the history of rock 'n' roll was created". Due to his interests in vast styles of music, Elvis instinctively blended the sounds which he loved and created something of his own.

"That's All Right" would stand the test of time as a revolutionary rock performance. It would begin a chain of many exciting and innovative recordings at Sun Studios which were soon to follow. Irish musician Eamonn Campbell, of legendary Irish folk group the Dubliners, remembers "Up until the age of nine it was a great wish of mine to play the accordion. However, one Saturday night I heard a record on Radio Luxembourg of Elvis singing 'That's All Right' and it totally changed my outlook on music for all time. I was so carried away by the vocal sound and the incredible energy and rhythm of the music that I decided there and then no matter what, I was gonna get a guitar. Elvis's voice was so unique and Scotty Moore's guitar playing, with slapback echo effect, was unbelievable, especially to a kid of nine in Drogheda".

That particular day at Sun Studios concluded with the ballad "Harbor Lights" and another uptempo recording, "Blue Moon Of Kentucky". On this song, Irish singer-songwriter Charlie McGettigan recalled, "When I became interested in bluegrass music in the 1970s, Bill Munroe's version was the one I'd have heard. Bill, it seems, wrote the song in 1946 and it was in waltz time. Elvis's version was recorded in Sun Studios and the most striking thing about it is not only his voice but his acoustic guitar sound. He was a great rhythm guitar player and it really shows on this track. Elvis's raw energy injects real feeling into the lyric. 'Blue Moon of Kentucky' sounds just as good today as it did all those years ago when it was recorded".

In the days of Elvis's first recordings, studios had very little technology. The studios could not alter sound and it was all up to the artists. The records were cut in mono and there was no mixing in stereo. Echoes were created by Sam Phillips to form an original sound. Microphones were strategically situated in different areas of the studio and the artists had to play the best they could. The sounds of the instruments were equally as important as the singer's voice and that is what Sam was interested in capturing. There were no backing tracks so if a song had to be recorded again, everyone involved recorded it again. Regarding Sam's technique and Elvis, Eamonn Campbell notes, "His Sun recordings are milestones in the history of the recording industry. Even today with all the digital effects available, the Sun sound still stands out".

On top of all this, it was Elvis's own distinctive style that made him special. He had blended an R&B song with a country rhythm and poured gospel into it. Sam Phillips gave artists the opportunity to express themselves, to let out their feelings, to have their voice heard, to free their emotions. The first song to convey Elvis's feelings and his own voice was definitely "That's All Right".

R&B originates from African influences and the roots of country music lie in the folk music that Irish and Scottish settlers brought to the Appalachian Mountain region of America's Southern states, in the 18th and 19th centuries. Irish ballads and reels in particular had a major early influence. Such music was performed from colonial times in both religious and social contexts, including church services, weddings and barn dances. In the early 1920s the first country recordings emerged, introducing the music of string bands. The string-band repertoire consisted mostly of traditional folk and gospel music and appealed mainly to people in the rural Southeast of America.

The Irish connections in the music are comprehensible given Ireland's heritage of storytelling and folk music. This was something expressed verbatim; especially by those in rural areas. One of the major influences on the country music front in America was *Sean Nós*. This was an Irish music genre that came from the deep inner soul of people who sought to asseverate everything they honestly cared about.

Irish traditional music inspired the modern ballad. Some songs were slow paced and others were a lot more energetic and remained ever popular in mostly rural areas of the country. From the 1960s onwards artists such as the Clancy Brothers, the Dubliners and the Chieftans brought it to a new level and they became some of the most popular performers of this genre. Traditional Irish ballads and Irish 'n' Western had a large influence on American country music.

The Country Music Hall of Fame in Nashville today records in scrupulous detail the musical contribution of Irish immigrants to the popular culture of America. Elvis used country music made up from folk and bluegrass combined with R&B and a voice executing gospel to form a rockabilly sound. Here we see how Elvis was indirectly influenced by Irish traditional music and how such different forms of music were fused together.

On 8 July 1954, the very first official Elvis Presley recording was played on live radio by DJ Dewy Philips (no relation to Sam Phillips). While his parents sat waiting to hear the performance, a nervous Elvis went to see a movie. The performance of "That's All Right" instantly became popular in the area of Memphis. Nobody could tell if he was a black or white singer. When the song first aired generating feral excitement, Dewy had Elvis come on the show for an interview and he arrived trembling with fear. His natural nervous personality remained intact but all signs pointed to him fulfilling his long time dream.

After the tremendous response to their first record, Scotty Moore became manager and agent to the trio starting a career for Elvis that looked to have a very bright future already. 17 July marked their first live performance in front of an audience. Only covering two songs, it still sealed a historic event in their lives. The event marked the beginning of one of the most important groups in music history.

Sam Phillips got Presley and the group to perform at the Louisiana Hayride and the continuation of gigs began to generate interest among music listeners for this group. Towards the end of July, Elvis signed a contract with Sun Studios which had to be counter signed by his parents because of his young age.

There has been much debate over who created rock 'n' roll music in the decades since. The term "rock 'n' roll" was first used in the late 1940s but who defined and perfected it has become the greater question. Bill Haley who recorded "Rock Around The Clock" is sometimes credited for having started it off, although there were other upbeat R&B performers previous to him, such as Big Joe Turner, Roy Brown and Fats Domino. Haley's songs were not rock as it would become known as, but rather a "razzle dazzle" dance form of country western bop. In 1954 Haley's movie, *Rock Around The Clock* saw music cross between jazz and country. It sparked a change in the emotional rhythm of young people. The youth crowded into cinemas to experience the change. It even arrived in Ireland where some Gardaí were assigned to watch over those who attended screenings of it. It was a sign of something massive that was about to arrive.

Since Presley helped introduce "black music" to popular culture, some critics have accused him of cultural theft even though "black music" was his culture, as he had been raised around it. In reality it is not possible to steal any music once you have an honest passion for it. Elvis's music is not applied mathematics, it's not black and white or technical, it's about feeling, it's about emotional intelligence. This was Elvis's natural skill. Elvis was Elvis. He was nobody but himself. Irish musician Barry Devlin of the Irish rock group Horslips, maintains, "Elvis started it all, on his own and against the odds - a true original".

Blues music spoke volumes to Elvis because that music based itself upon poverty and he knew exactly what being poor was like. He used something that could not be manufactured or directly copied, he used his heart and the passion he felt for the music. Many of his essential influences came from black artists and Presley was always open about his influences, becoming the first major white performer to express a debt to "black music".

As Presley sang music only associated with black people, a transition emerged in the segregated South. Elvis showed that colour didn't make a difference once a person liked the sound. Irish musician and producer B. P. Fallon, responding to the criticism that

Elvis was simply a white man singing black music, said, "That's not a criticism at all. Elvis showed the white folk how to do it. He helped break the race barrier by being himself". Fallon's music credentials include working with rock groups Led Zeppelin and U2. He also recorded a passionate blues song called "I Believe In Elvis Presley" in 2009.

With Elvis there was an emergence of unity between the races. Irish broadcaster and journalist John Kelly stated, "The most famous southern white man was Elvis Presley. And given the nature of the South, he is a riddle in more ways than one. It's worth remembering that when Elvis Presley started acting black, it was neither popular nor profitable to do so".

Elvis subconsciously put a hand in both sides of the border and brought them together. John Kelly, who made the 2002 documentary *Who Was Elvis Presley?*, noted, "What Elvis was doing was nothing to do with colour. He had transcended that". He follows, "Elvis Presley was a subversive. Rock 'n' roll was bringing white into contact with black, musically and physically in brand new situations. If there was a rope across the ballroom floor, people started to jump over it".

Elvis saw music as something for everybody to enjoy. Since racism was such a huge quandary where he grew up, he remained very different with what he had done. Irish music legend Bono of U2 has written on this area of Presley's impact, believing that he was instigating the change that the civil rights movement wanted by breaking down barriers. The fact that people generally do not see Elvis as a political figure is the subtlety of his persona. Elvis was very much a political figure whether he chose to be or not as he helped alter the way people view the world.

Before Elvis arrived rock 'n' roll was generally called "race music". Top white rockers like Elvis became responsible for diminishing this racist label. No one man invented rock music as it was rather fused together by an assembly of talented performers. The rock artists of the 1950s would go on to revolutionise the music business with their new creative sounds and with Elvis at the top. In the words of Irish journalist Barry Egan, "The landscape of popular culture would be a lot flatter without Elvis Presley". Elvis cut straight to the raw sexual energy in the music. He based all moves on instinct. He went straight to his heart and worked from there, not letting a fabricated construct of "prim and proper" America get in the way.

Around the middle of September 1954, Presley's first major recording session took place with a mixture of ballads, country and rock. Although he continued the fast paced concerts, rock music was not his sole choice in music. A few days before hand he recorded the ballad, "Blue Moon", which was a genre that impressed Presley as much as the other styles. His recordings continued with "Tomorrow Night" and "Good Rockin' Tonight".

Elvis shot through the songs he loved best. His mind was like a jukebox and Phillips was mesmerised by the amount of songs he knew. He was an expert on the words, styles and harmonies and with his own talents portrayed a method of introspective communication for the audience. Each song with mixed emotions needed a different attitude and Presley had the instinct to convey everything required within a song. Whether it was a growl, a hic-up or a sneer, he mixed sexuality and innocence together. Decades later, speaking on Ireland's *The Late Late Show*, Irish actor Jonathan-Rhys Meyers who would later portray Elvis, commented on him. He spoke about how Elvis "was very sexually provocative, at the same time vulnerable and that's what made him attractive to people. He was able to express this vulnerability in such a way that was controlled".

Throughout the rest of 1954, Elvis performed gigs anywhere and everywhere. These were early days and he had not hit the all time success regardless of his number three hit on the charts with "Blue Moon Of Kentucky". They played in high schools, fields and open air auditoriums. Day after day and night after night from Mississippi to Texas to Alabama, the shows moved on. Elvis would also make sure to send home the money he earned, explaining that it was to help his parents pay the bills. As the trio looked promising as up and coming stars, Sam Phillips tried on many occasions to get them to play on "The Grand Ole Opry" in Nashville. *The Opry* first went on the air in 1925 and the show, originally called *WSM Barn Dance*, featured amateur rural musicians. In Ireland *The Opry* could be heard each Saturday on the American Forces Network, which broadcast from Germany for American troops stationed there.

When Presley, Moore and Black eventually got an audition, they performed "Blue Moon Of Kentucky", but it was not appreciated well enough to give Elvis and his band a spot on the show. Many stories have come out that Elvis was told to go back driving a truck. However, other sources have stated the owner suggested he perform the music that got him off to a good start. Elvis was gravely disappointed as this show was renowned for having artists who showed a positive talent. Nevertheless, it was due to this rejection that Elvis became a constant performer on the Louisiana Hayride, which took risks and gave great opportunities.

Elvis and his group drew large crowds as their appeal grew. Contracts were negotiated between Elvis, the group and the Hayride and then as Scotty took a step back from manager, a man named Bob Neal took his place. Neal helped the group by booking them at venues while they worked on their music. Their last recorded songs of 1954 were "Milkcow Blues Boogie" and "You're A Heartbreaker". With a few dozen performances, several radio shows and many newspaper articles praising him as a possible new success, Elvis and his musicians went into 1955 hoping for better things. They were already securing a name for themselves in the Memphis area. Time would tell if this man now titled the "Hillbilly Cat" would become a success.

More gigs commenced throughout 1955 but nothing spectacular had happened. The three worked hard, travelling long distances, getting little sleep and then performing high energy shows. They were young and free and it was this that made their music special. There was an impulsive emotion conveyed in all the performances and emotion became Presley's most significant characteristic. He was a deeply emotional individual and the ambition to be a singer was driven by this factor, as singing could reflect all his feelings. This was why he would jump through so many different genres throughout his entire career.

The Dubliner's Eamonn Campbell explains, "As a singer the young Elvis was totally unique. There was a rawness, raunchiness and passion in his vocals never heard before. He'd mixed Blues, Gospel, Country 'n' Western and Rock 'n Roll into a completely new style of music".

All action, overwork and little rest had negative effects on Elvis as he fainted several times before and after shows. Even at this very early stage, hundreds of teenage girls were racing up onto the stage to grab hold of him. He not only had his own musical style but his own performance style too. Musicians usually stood still like cardboard cut outs but Presley swayed and moved to the rhythm, displaying the passion he incorporated. People got out of their seats screaming and dancing. There was no doubt that he had set the foundation for a revolution.

In February, the group recorded "Trying To Get To You" and "Baby Lets Play House". Signs of fine achievement showed as they gained single hits in R&B and Country music charts. While word was spreading about Presley's attraction towards a great number of people, a man named Colonel Thomas Parker began monitoring his popularity and saw something very special and profitable. He quickly introduced himself to Presley and explained that he could make him a million dollars as long as Elvis stuck to the music and Parker stuck to the promoting. After some time Tom Parker became an adviser to Elvis and Bob Neal. Neal stayed on for a while managing Elvis but by the end of July, Parker had full representation of Elvis.

Parker was born Andreas Cornelius Van Kuijk in 1909 in Holland. He illegally entered America in 1929 and worked in carnivals and circuses. The title of "Colonel" was bestowed on him by a Governor who he helped in a political campaign. From then on Parker insisted that everybody call him by that title. He went onto manage the country star Eddy Arnold. But after witnessing the performances of Presley he knew for sure that this new artist would be something extraordinarily unique.

In August of 1955 a new addition arrived to the group as they hired the drummer D. J. Fontana to add that extra beat to their work. By the middle of '55, local press, small time radio and TV shows explained that the new singer, Elvis Presley, was attracting thousands of young teenage girls. Everything was new and exciting about him. His music, unusual dress sense and how much of a sharp instinctive performer he was.

The new recordings of "I'm Left, You're Right, She's Gone" and "Mystery Train" added to his growing success and his appeal spread to further areas. Irish musician, producer and writer P. J. Curtis remembers being stunned on hearing Elvis for the first time. After hearing Presley's "Mystery Train" Curtis recalls, "It was like nothing I had heard before. I can only say I was completely floored by it, as if ten thousand volts had shot through our crackling radio to hit me right between the ears. The sizzling electric guitar and rhythm guitar driving behind this ghostly, ethereal voice that seemed to come from another planet".

Professional stars who had great experience felt Elvis would only last a short while but others thought he was sensational and would be a huge success. Colonel Parker knew for sure what would happen as long as he was behind the steering wheel. Throughout '55 the Colonel was encouraging Sam Phillips to let Elvis move with a large record label because it would mean better chances of success. It took some persuasion but in the end it worked as Phillips needed the money. Sam Phillips was paid $35,000 to let Elvis move to RCA. This would bring Presley from regional fame to chances of international success.

In November of 1955 the original trio went back to Sun Studios for the last time. They cut "When It Rains, It Really Pours" and it marked the very last Sun recording for this wondrous music group. These recordings would remain sacred and considered for years, still to this day, the best recordings by Presley. Elvis Presley, Scotty Moore and Bill Black had begun building the foundations of popular rock music, which would be the biggest influence on modern music in America and the rest of the world, including Ireland.

Chapter Three

When Elvis was signed with RCA Records on 21 November 1955, there was widespread anxiety throughout the company. There was $35,000 involved and a high chance that Presley would turn out to be a passing fad. Some saw Elvis as a messy, greasy kid. He was loud and boisterous. He didn't look pretty and polished but oozed sexuality and this was threatening and dangerous. Elvis was a walking contradiction to everything the establishment expected in their popular entertainers as he didn't concern himself with being groomed. Cut straight to today and these are the ingredients of a successful rock star.

After making eighteen radio show appearances, performing almost three hundred concerts in 1955 and starting a life for himself in the music business, Elvis went into 1956 to reach for new levels and to become the first rock superstar. A man named Steve Sholes would be the manager over Elvis's music at RCA and he worked with great efficiency to get studio sessions done. Presley's first recording session at RCA was between 10 and 11 January and he recorded the songs, "Heartbreak Hotel", "Money Honey", "I Was The One" and Ray Charles' "I Got A Woman".

In 2002 Irish jazz musician Mary Coughlan did a cover of "Heartbreak Hotel" in her own style. Mary remembered that it was her uncle who was a big Elvis fan and had quite a collection of Elvis singles. He styled himself like Presley and collected an Elvis magazine which came out when he had become internationally popular. She remembered his enthusiasm for Elvis, buying his latest records and gathering people to listen to them. These were her memories of Elvis taking effect on people.

Coughlan was born in Galway in 1956, and during the 1970s began singing in the area of blues and jazz. She recorded her first album in 1985 and achieved critical acclaim throughout Europe and America. Although Mary was born in 1956 when the sounds of jazz were diminishing she embraced the music and kept it alive in another age, which Elvis had done with R&B, which had hardly seen a wide audience. In Ireland throughout the 1950s jazz had been criticised while Irish tenors and classical music were accepted by the masses. This was the pop music at the time but many felt jazz challenged the mainstream which indicated how rock music was going to be considered hazardous.

During recording sessions Elvis dedicated himself to his work. He cut dozens of takes of the one song until he himself found the best one, which demonstrated perfect instrumental arrangements and vocal quality. He was devoted to his work, concentrating on it, listening closely and studying the acetates of his music before they were released. Recording a song over and over, he constantly repeated his performances until he had on record the sound that mirrored the one in his head.

Despite the myth, Elvis hadn't become a success over night, for it did take a whole year to even get noticed by Sam Phillips. Then it took many recording sessions and hundreds of concert performances to achieve a name. For those who believe his looks got him attention, his first recording had gained him great popularity for almost two years before most of America even knew what race he was. Elvis also had competition from many other artists both in his field of music and all the more commonly accepted styles.

Speaking to *The Belfast Telegraph* in 2007, former Northern Ireland politician David Trimble found in Elvis that, "If he was just a good looking singer with a good voice, he wouldn't have had the tremendous impact that he had". Trimble also claims, "Elvis in his early years, the changes he made to the music scene, to pop culture and many aspects of life were really significant".

On 28 January 1956 Elvis made his first television appearance, on the *Dorsey Brothers Stage Show*. This show was hosted by well known jazz musicians Tommy and Jimmy Dorsey who were born into an Irish community in Pennsylvania. Walking onto a stage dotted with shamrocks, Elvis's hair and clothes were designed and worn with flare and he went straight into bizarre songs with a sound alien to a wider world. Two days later that sound was again transported to record as his second recording session for RCA included songs that would define the early rock 'n' roll era including, "Blue Suede Shoes", "My Baby Left Me", "Lawdy, Miss Clawdy" and "Shake, Rattle And Roll".

The song "My Baby Left Me" was covered by Irish singer Imelda May during a memorial concert for Elvis in 2010. The Dublin-born singer began singing at the age of 16 in 1990 but finally had her debut album released in 2005. Her music is very much performed in the rockabilly tradition and her influences include Elvis, as well as Eddie Cochran and Gene Vincent. In 2010 she appeared on television in a dress made out of material bearing Elvis's image. Imelda has also covered "That's All Right" in her live performances.

On top of Elvis's hectic studio schedule, the shows went on, with sometimes four a day and by the end of February he had already completed about seventy-five shows that year. The TV appearances continued and on St. Patrick's Day he repeated his performance of "Heartbreak Hotel" along with "Blue Suede Shoes" and did his versions of "Money Honey" and "Tutti Frutti". One week later he made his last appearance on the *Dorsey Brothers Show* but was back on TV the following week when he performed on *The Milton Berle Show* in California. Appearing on TV like this was sensational for the time. America was only discovering the power of TV. He reached incredible audience figures within a flash but it was discovered that TV had the ability to shock people with something so new and different.

Elvis's movements on stage were strange for audiences to see. Elvis moved with the beat and introduced something new and daring to the performance stage. These gestures came naturally to him through the music. He let himself go loose and this added to the already controversial music. Strict, conservative parents did not let their children go see him and he was often not allowed to perform at certain venues, because it was felt he was a dreadful influence on young people. Everything about him said sex, as he threw the rule book out the window on how to present oneself, gyrating and twisting with the music's emotional feel, prowling like a sensual panther up and down the stage infusing a sexual charge.

Elvis rebelled when criticised and became a youth leader who, without a speech, expressed his feelings through the performance. It has sometimes been suggested that Presley's daring nature and determination was a clear indication of his Celtic roots as the Scots-Irish settlers in America originally ingrained such extreme fortitude.

Elvis's music and image set a divide between young people and adults and the "teenager" was born. Elvis's music challenged their repression, setting their world free by being a symbol of expression, setting the track for both popular and teenage culture. Ireland's P. J. Curtis shared the feelings of many young people at that time, such as future rock legends Lou Reed and Bruce Springsteen, when he felt the immediate urge to get a guitar. P. J. recollected, "In early 1956 such was my new found music passion I now had to get myself a guitar much to the disgust of my father. Yet when I tried to purchase one in a shop in Ennis they didn't even know what a guitar was. It was still such an alien instrument back then".

The spread of rock music, especially under the popularity of Elvis, became an inspiration for young people to discover their own voice and their own independence. His rock 'n' roll music and image taught young people about the world unlike any formal education. Elvis Presley helped unleash young people from the state of paralysis which beset societies across the world at this time. Some may say it was only music, but history proves it was a happening.

Irish musician Eamonn Campbell states, "To the young generation growing up in the aftermath of WW2 he epitomised the free thinking youth of the time and he was also probably regarded as a rebel against the ultra conservative views".

Rock 'n' roll was a revolution for teenagers who needed to find their own sense of identity. A new way of life was born but an extraordinary number of adults went out of their way to stop him. His methods were despised by older people, who were either racist against such black influenced music or people too conservative to feel an emotional spark. He was considered unfit for children's ears and eyes, was labelled as the devil and continuously put down for performing this "evil" music. Attempts were made to ban him from performing and appearing on TV. Parent groups made continuous complaints about him and TV specials denounced rock 'n' roll music. Records were literally broken and radio stations banned rock music from being played. Radio presenters were ordered not to play his music and many were fired for breaking the rules. He was branded a menace to young girls and tarred as the most obscene, vulgar influence on America.

After performing "Heartbreak Hotel" on his third TV appearance, the song became an instant number one hit, selling in excess of one million copies at a time when record players were not a common household item. While the song had very haunting lyrics and emphasised a modern sound for pop music, it was very strange for the charts at that time. The gloominess, depressing and suicidal mood of the song differed from such songs like "Hot Digity" by Perry Como, which in Ireland was knocked off *The Irish Times* list "Record Of The Week" in September 1956, by the new bizarre Presley sound.

While various countries around the world including America and Britain had set up an official music charts system to categorise the popularity of music singles, Ireland was behind and would remain behind for many years. Although "Heartbreak Hotel" could be heard in Ireland and struck a chord with some modern Irish youths, this particular song would not see an official Irish chart placing until a rerelease over fifty-one years later when it got to number nineteen on 16 August 2007. This was followed by a rerelease of "Blue Suede Shoes" which became an Irish number twenty-four hit on 23 August 2007.

Apart from Ireland's Mary Coughlan, "Heartbreak Hotel" was also recorded by the Irish group Blink. Dermot Lambert, Brian McLoughlin, Barry Campbell and Robbie Sexton make up the group that formed in Dublin in 1991. They have had success in both Ireland and America with their albums. The group covered the Elvis song for a tribute charity album in 1998. Some of their other recordings include, "Going To Nepal" and "It's Not My Fault".

Elvis Presley had risen from destitution and proceeded on his way to being a massive star. His first album *Elvis Presley* became a number one smash. The cover art-work made a statement, with a black and white photo of Elvis in performance stance roaring out his songs with his name in bright green and pink down the side. The bright colours emphasised the impact of his music and the world changing from its narrow black and white views. The album was the biggest pop success for RCA and it firmly established Presley as history's first rock star. He then received his first gold record award for the phenomenal sales of "Heartbreak Hotel" and many more were yet to come.

Off stage, Elvis worried about pleasing the public. The criticism did bother him but he tried to reject it. Nonetheless, Colonel Tom knew that any publicity was good publicity. Elvis's sensitivity gave in and often lead to a loss of sleep over the worry that all his good fortune would be gone.

In March of '56 Elvis purchased a home at 1034 Audubon Drive, situated in a middle class suburb and was the first house the Presley's ever owned. This was the sure sign that they could finally put the years of slaving through the Depression behind them. Although Gladys could not drive, Elvis bought a specially sprayed pink Cadillac for her. It was another sign of the flamboyant lifestyle and was an example of how he now had the money to get things they never could afford before. Vernon began working for Elvis, dealing with mail, paying bills and doing odd jobs.

One area Elvis was anxious to prevail in was the movie business. On 2 April, Parker contracted a deal between Elvis and Paramount Producer, Hal B. Wallis. Wallis had previously produced *Three Cheers For The Irish* (1940), *The Sea Wolf* (1941) with Irish actor Barry Fitzgerald and *Casablanca* (1942). He also produced seven pictures with Irish actress Geraldine Fitzgerald, including *Dark Victory* (1939) and *'Til We Meet Again* (1940). For his first picture, to be titled *The Reno Brothers*, Elvis was loaned out to 20th Century Fox.

As concerts and TV appearances throughout 1956 continued, Elvis's salary increased as Colonel Parker would not accept anything less than the charges he put up. Parker arranged a mass production of merchandising and this was where the exploitation of Elvis's name came in on a large scale. Ranging from Elvis lipstick, shoes and handbags to Elvis badges, posters and photos, much memorabilia was created and Parker received a great deal of the profits. This merchandising scheme was tacky but impressive and Parker proved to be a shrewd businessman. Elvis on the other hand was not a good business man, like many creative artists and let Parker manage all his business affairs.

For a break Elvis went out boating with his girlfriend of the time, June Juanico. They spent time fishing and water skiing, enjoying the life that he and his family had dreamed about, relaxing with no need for a care in the world. It was a great break away from the riots and roaring girls who chased Elvis, screaming after him during and after shows. This trip isolated him from any of that. Unfortunately, as June Juanico recalled on an Irish talk-show in August 1997, at the end of the day on arrival to shore, a boat pulled up alongside Elvis. A couple of reporters jumped up and started taking photos of him. It appeared no matter what he did, he could never escape the press. He was a major figure for the media and would be hounded as long as he was a huge star.

On 5 June Elvis made his second appearance on *The Milton Berle Show* alongside Debra Paget and actress Irish McCalla. Elvis performed an outrageous version of "Hound Dog", twisting, shaking and gyrating more than before on TV. Overnight outrage broke out across America. Critics ridiculed him for his actions on live TV and a huge amount of complaints and panic was generated because of this performance.

Angry people stated that nobody wanted to see someone move around on TV as it only influenced delinquency among minors. His music was influencing sex! Elvis had done something abnormal for the time by unintentionally performing as if it were a type of striptease. He explained how rhythm and blues was something you felt all over and throughout your body and how he would go into a complete trance when he sang.

Elvis was criticised by racists who appeared on TV saying they were doing away with Presley records in cafés and restaurants because it was "nigger" music. Local newspapers stated that Elvis was cracking Memphis segregation laws by attending functions for black people. He wanted to see and meet his black friends and musicians he so deeply admired. Members of the media were baffled by Presley's respect and admiration of such a vast number of black artists. His knowledge and understanding of their musical styles and persona was not common for white men in America.

In light of all the complaints about his movements and sexual presentations, Elvis decided to swallow his pride on his next TV appearance in order to please certain viewers. He was asked to make a more conservative presentation and he politely accepted the request. On 1 July Elvis was in New York to appear on *The Steve Allen Show* dressed in a tuxedo. He was asked not to move about and a dog was brought on stage to which he should sing "Hound Dog". This was in order to delete the sexual innuendo implicated in his performance.

Elvis was then asked to appear in a little western comedy sketch. It turned out to be extremely humiliating for Presley and although this style appealed to mainstream America, the real image of Elvis was lost. He later deeply regretted doing the show. Later that evening, Elvis gave a special televised telephone interview and discussed his life up to this point, emphasising that he could not understand how music could have a bad influence on anyone.

Following these shows Elvis reported into RCA to officially cut "Hound Dog", "Don't Be Cruel" and "Any Way You Want Me". By 8 August "Hound Dog", with the flip side "Don't Be Cruel", reached number one in the U.S. charts and became one of Elvis's greatest selling singles. Although Ireland did not officially compile music charts at this time, "Don't Be Cruel" became an Irish number twelve hit in 1978 after being rereleased when the Irish charts had been long set up.

"Hound Dog" made the top spot in *The Irish Times* "Record of the week" on 13 October 1956 and a rerelease in 2007 became an Irish number twenty-five in the Irish charts. "Hound Dog" is a quintessential rock 'n' roll classic. Ireland's Labour party minister, Pat Rabbitte, having once stated that Elvis was a childhood hero, explained that "Hound Dog" was the song that reminded him most of his school days.

Irish rock 'n' roll musician, John Keogh who would form one of the first major Irish rock bands, the Greenbeats, remembers having first discovered Radio Luxembourg. John notes, "I was now familiar with early Elvis and with an even bigger chart star in America, Pat Boone. A friend of the family was in London for a visit and knew I was playing piano and was interested in this modern music, so he brought me back a copy of NME (I'd never heard of it before then) which had a centre page feature. Elvis on one page and Pat Boone on the other with the headline, 'Which one is the biggest star?'. By this time I had heard 'Hound Dog', so for me, there was no question as to who was the biggest and the best. That centre fold of NME was also the first time I saw a photo of Elvis".

As time drew closer to the making of Elvis's first movie, new plans were arranged to change the title from *The Reno Brothers* to Presley's upcoming song "Love Me Tender". It was arranged that Elvis would now sing in the movie and this did not impress him as he wanted serious roles. Though this irritated Presley he did not challenge anything because he had agreed to look after the music while his manager looked after the business.

On 16 August 1956 Elvis arrived in Los Angeles to begin production on *Love Me Tender*, a Civil War era western. Elvis treated everyone on the set with utmost respect, referring to all his male and female co-workers as sir and ma'am. Elvis's main co-star, Richard Egan, had appeared in *The Flame Of Araby* (1951) with Dublin born actress Maureen O'Hara and later starred with Wexford born actor Dan O'Herlihy in *The Big Cube* (1969).

On 1 September 1956, with a break from film work, Elvis began recording a selection of new songs. In the three days of studio recording he came out with the numbers "Playing For Keeps", "Love Me" and "Too Much". 1956 was a year which established his status as a phenomenal hit-maker and was the year his music surpassed boarders as it spread through the global airwaves and onwards into Ireland.

Chapter Four

In 1956 rock 'n' roll music spread across the world. Sales of rock 'n' roll music outdid all other genres and it was rapidly becoming the most popular form of music of all time. However, even with its soaring popularity Radio Éireann refused to play rock 'n' roll. Without Radio Luxembourg Irish people of the time would have had little knowledge of who or what Elvis or rock 'n' roll was. Young Irish people listened to it and discovered this new exciting and energetic music. From this, the admiration for Presley's songs influenced a challenge to strict taboos in conservative communities.

P. J. Curtis explains, "The rural Ireland of the mid '50s remained as isolated as if we were at the edge of some distant galaxy. Radio Éireann only played safe standards and ballads so I felt I was the only one who was tuning into this strange music coming from these exotic stations".

However, an interest in rock 'n' roll took off slowly in a country adverse to outside influences. In late 1956, *The Irish Times* printed a story about the effect of rock music in Ireland, explaining, "Rock 'n' roll, which started life as a precocious child and has now grown into a sedate and popular adult in America, has not, as yet, shown much sign of life in Ireland". The article continued, "Although there are some bands with their own combinations, the average Irish dancer knows very little about rock 'n' roll dancing".

Young Irish people who were lucky enough to be in a location where foreign radio could be found, got to hear something different. Nonetheless, traditional Irish and classical were the adult genres, so this was what most young Irish people had to endure then. On the other side of the Atlantic, however, young American kids were having little difficulty discovering what was enjoyable and liberating, as Elvis continued to make highly publicised TV appearances.

On 9 September 1956 Elvis made his first appearance on *The Ed Sullivan Show*. Ed Sullivan was an Irish-blooded New Yorker who was a legend in his field. He was the most powerful and triumphant of all TV hosts and appearing on his show meant success. Ed often had Irish and Irish-American acts on his show including, the McNiff Irish Dancers, the Emerald Society Pipe Band, the Irish Steppers and the Friendly Sons of St. Patrick. Sullivan also had as guests, the Irish Hollywood stars Barry Fitzgerald, twice in 1952 and Maureen O'Hara, three times between 1955 and 1962.

Sullivan was very hesitant about having Presley appear as he felt his show was good clean family entertainment. Nonetheless, he was convinced that having Elvis on the show would boost the ratings. On this particular occasion Sullivan didn't host Presley's first appearance due to a car accident and was replaced by the actor Charles Laughton. Charles introduced Elvis among other acts and also promoted the upcoming Broadway performance of the play *Major Barbara*, by Irish playwright George Bernard Shaw.

Elvis gave his first performance of "Love Me Tender" and the song received one million orders before it was released, making it another number one smash. This was the first time a song got such a volume of pre-orders. Elvis completed film production on *Love Me Tender* and the title song went on release. Over eighty percent of America's TV audience saw his performance on Ed Sullivan's show and many more got to see what all the commotion was about, regarding this new controversial star.

His sexually charged performances stood out completely from the straight forward conservative show. Such appearances on TV were breaking incredible boundaries not only for TV ratings but for the massive exposure of rock 'n' roll music to the world. A continuous string of singles had Elvis knocking himself off the top position. By the Autumn of '56 the single "Love Me Tender" knocked "Hound Dog" and "Don't Be Cruel" off their number one spots. Later on "Love Me Tender" would be knocked down the charts by his latest song "Love Me".

Presley's "Love Me Tender" never received an opportunity in the Irish charts but the song would become a Top 30 hit in 1990 for the Irish pop group, Gina, Dale Haze and the Champions. The group originally from Cork, formed in 1973 and have had hits with their own songs "Minnie Minnie" and "Do You Wanna Do It".

On 26 September 1956 Elvis made a triumphant return to Tupelo where he gave two shows and was welcomed fondly by the local governor. Despite this honour, criticisms had not diminished, but he gradually failed to be intimidated anymore. He had appeared on TV several times, had chart topping hits and continued to perform around the country. Elvis then returned for a fair in Memphis where he met and bowed on stage with who was called "Americas favourite Irish tenor", Dennis Day. Dennis was not from Ireland but was born in New York in 1917. His career was formed from performing famous Irish songs and therefore he became known as an Irish tenor. Dennis died in 1988 in California.

Presley performed to an enormous crowd on 11 October 1956 in Dallas, Texas. 27,000 fans converged at the "Cotton Bowl", which according to a local newspaper had not experienced such an equalled frenzy since the favoured "Fighting Irish" of Notre Dame had been heavily challenged in a game of American Football in 1949. It was the largest paying crowd to turn up to watch a performer in the history of Dallas. This was an everlasting indication of how Elvis was becoming America's most popular performer. For the youth he was a tough guy, a "greaser". However, Elvis's style transcended this as he wore eye shadow, mascara and pink shirts and broke the rules of heteronormative male convention. He also had his hair dyed jet black from his natural sandy blonde.

Success kept coming his way as on 19 October 1956 Elvis's second album, simply titled *Elvis*, went straight to number one. The album included songs cut in early September with "Rip It Up", "Long Tall Sally" and "Reddy Teddy". In a pictorial section of *The Irish Times* around this time, images showed excited fans at an Elvis concert. It was one of the first reports on rock 'n' roll music and Elvis Presley in the Irish media stating, "this is hysteria. This is the kind of scene that makes many wonder where all this rock 'n' roll business is going to end". However, Elvis also showed Irish music listeners that there was more to him than rock 'n' roll as his mellow "Blue Moon" topped *The Irish Times* "Record of the week" in late November.

Plans were made for Elvis to re-appear on *The Ed Sullivan Show* and on 28 October 1956 he appeared in a line-up which included The Little Gaelic Singers. This was a cheesy, stage Irish production made up of a large group of young boys and girls from Co. Derry, who sang "She Didn't Dance The Day" and "Believe Me If All Those Endearing Young Charms". They performed in front of a set designed with replicas of the Irish harp and Irish flags. Right after them, Elvis appeared and this indicated how diverse Sullivan's show could be and how diverse America was. This particular programme ended, advertising the staging of a scene from Irish playwright, George Bernard Shaw's *The Apple Cart*, on the following week's show.

In November, *Love Me Tender* premiered in New York City to a street crowded with screaming enthusiasts. Although rock 'n' roll was considered "sinful" music, the fans ignored criticisms and expressed their love for Presley. While Frank Sinatra was considered a heart-throb, Presley's sex symbol status surpassed anything before him. Irish music journalist and *Hot Press* editor, Niall Stokes, said, "I think he did have a kind of sexual energy which elevated popular music to a different level". The sight of Elvis triggered orgasmic squeals from teenage girls and young women. Orgiastic sensations ran through their bodies. They touched themselves passionately in deep love for this young boy. This was their first discovery of sexuality, sensuality and heart throbbing erotic power.

Sexual awakening helped free Western society as it was taken out of the darkness. The backwards society which ridiculed it as something "dirty" was kicked aside. This potent sexuality mixed with rock music lead to other forms of excitement. Young people needed a reason to go crazy and because of Elvis they went wild. Some fans took many risks so that they could experience the excitement of being part of the rock 'n' roll blast. Girls climbed fire escapes to get into Presley's hotel rooms. Many climbed walls to get into his house and all of them scratched their names, phone numbers and love messages into his cars and chased him before, after and between concerts screaming his name and tearing his clothes.

Fans broke through police barriers to grab hold of him. Girls had to be dragged from the stage as they screamed, pulling their hair and wailing indefinitely. Nothing could compare to the fidelity expressed for him. As fans screamed before doors opened to admit them into the movie, a forty foot picture of Elvis was unveiled above the cinema. The film became a huge success but the reviews tried to bring it down. Despite the negativity, his films drew massive sales and became top grossing pictures, but creativity was a key factor he sought after.

In early December Elvis dropped into Sun Studios to see Sam Phillips. By chance Carl Perkins and a new artist on the scene, Jerry Lee Lewis, were recording. Country singer Johnny Cash, another "Sun" artist who had got his break playing support at an Elvis concert, also made a brief appearance at this time. The group chatted and began jamming and singing old songs and some gospel numbers, with Elvis taking turns on piano. The session at Sun with the top four popular artists of the time became known as the "Million Dollar Quartet" and was an historic moment.

Irish journalist Joe Jackson, speaking of Elvis's eclecticism stated how "he could slide so easily from gospel to rhythm and blues, from holy to horny music". This transition was clear at this session but also at other stages in his life. Both styles had an equal share of passion. Jackson explained how Elvis must have felt, "If God means all good and sex comes from God, then sex must be good". Presley felt "Guilt is not of God" and Jackson added "that's why he sang in such a guilt free way about sexuality".

1956 marked a year of success for Presley, as he achieved adequately to establish a serious and triumphant career. Eleven TV appearances, up to three hundred concerts, a movie, three number one hit singles and two number one albums. Elvis became a national celebrity and was becoming famous throughout the world. He had set a trend to be followed and imitated and inspire millions who looked to him as their greatest influence.

Elvis crossed the lines of culture, language, race, politics and class. Despite the campaign by conservatives to rip him apart he fought those masses and stood firm as a symbol of youth, progression and discovery. In the words of Irish artist, writer and broadcaster Don Conroy, "Elvis was like a force of nature. He did to the music industry what Picasso did for the art world. Like a tornado he cut through the established music, first bringing both excitement and devastation and in its wake allowed the light to penetrate which enabled the growth of new musical concepts".

* * *

The first highlight of 1957 was Elvis's third appearance on *The Ed Sullivan Show* on 6 January. With controversy over his performances still looming about, it was arranged Presley would be censored on the show. He could only be seen from the waist up as the TV cameras zoomed in towards his head and shoulders to cut out the "obscenity" of his suggestive movements. In a state of good humour and total rebelliousness Elvis performed the song "Don't Be Cruel" and ended it using his hands and arm movements to imitate his gyrating legs. It turned out to be a harmless but effective two fingers to those who were devoted to criticising his style of performing. This display of backbone in public cemented his culture changing liberalism.

Elvis performed several songs on the show, but his last performance was a change of pace as he sang the gospel tune "Peace In The Valley". He was risking his image as a bad mean "greaser" by performing a spiritual tune but no hesitation was expressed from Elvis and the song was well accepted. Sullivan bid farewell to Presley as this would be his last TV appearance before heading off to Hollywood to continue his movie career. Mr. Sullivan had accepted Elvis at this stage as he got to know the real guy behind the image. He stated to the audience and TV viewers that, "Elvis is a real decent fine boy and we never had a pleasanter experience on our show with a big name".

Shortly before his twenty-second birthday Elvis reported into Paramount studios for work on his second movie, *Loving You*. Hal Kanter, who wrote the script received hate mail for writing a story for Presley. Kanter was told not to encourage this "anti-Christ". A similar response to the previous year when Elvis appeared on

The Milton Berle Show when Milton received approximately half a million pieces of hate mail from those who were disgusted that he host a show with the symbol of rock 'n' roll "evilness" making an appearance.

The story of *Loving You* was another with which Elvis was not too pleased. In this case, a plot was created which would be repeated for years; a young man whose singing talent is accidentally discovered rises from small town success to national fame. Elvis's original band from the Sun Studios teamed up again on 12 January 1957, along with the backing harmony group the Jordanaires, for the recording of the *Loving You* soundtrack. Some of the songs recorded included, "Got A Lot O' Livin' To Do" and "Mean Woman Blues".

As well as recording songs for the movie, Elvis worked on songs of his own choice. He recorded the future chart breaking hit "All Shook Up". Also cut were "Peace In The Valley", "Take My Hand, Precious Lord" and a new recording of his classic Sun Studios cut, "That's When Your Heartaches Begin". The studio executives expressed frustration with Presley when he was spending valuable time singing gospel songs, when "serious" work had to be done. When Elvis found out about this he stormed out of the studio. Some producers were ignorant of the fact that Elvis singing gospel was his way of warming up. As an artist it became his method of setting his mood in order to give his best at his work.

With another session on 15 January Presley did the numbers, "Teddy Bear" and "Party" among others. "Party" would become an Irish number twenty-seven hit on 13 September 2007 through a rerelease and this was its first placing on the Irish charts. Recording sessions continued and by the end of February he had cut "I Need You So" and the risqué R&B number "One Night Of Sin". Fears of controversy over the use of the word "sin", which was too suggestive an innuendo for a night of passionate sex, lead to the song being re-cut as "One Night With You". Irish journalist Barry Egan remarked, "When he sings 'One Night' - the animal desire barely kept in check by his romantic idealism - we don't have to be reminded that he was the purest embodiment of rock 'n' roll".

Everything he recorded meant something to him or represented his youthful emotions. Every session embodied a feeling of energy, amusement and stimulation and while each artist never lost his or her focus on the music, the exciting atmosphere always stayed intact. Elvis's attitude and approach to each person and session resembled a party milieu rather than a serious job and it was that environment that came out on record. There was a guileless emanation of ebullience centred at the heart of what each song illustrated.

Elvis's first number one hit of 1957 was "All Shook Up" which became the best selling single on 3 April. It became the "Record of the Week" in *The Irish Times* in August '57 and a re-issue of the song forty-eight years later received its first placing on the official Irish charts, becoming an Irish Top 25 hit on 6 January 2005.

In early 1957 Elvis searched for a new home as his current house had become too open to the public and was invaded by fans. He eventually discovered a house, on the outskirts of Memphis. It was a country house built around 1940 and named "Graceland". Surrounded by trees with a long drive, this was a beautiful but modest mansion. A few weeks later, after the purchase was finalized, the Presleys moved in along with his collection of Cadillacs and motorbikes. Questioned about his large collection of cars, Elvis answered that he could open a used car lot if he ever went broke. The truth was that he was getting these cars as gifts for friends and family. All his life the main gift anybody would receive from Presley was a car. Giving away all sorts of vehicles became demonstrative of his generosity.

The move to Graceland was a symbol of the rags to riches fairy tale and the often over glorified fantasy of the "American Dream". Throughout this never ending roller coaster, Gladys stood in the background feeling miserable. She felt like a prisoner and although Elvis offered her anything in the world she just wished to return to the simple life of being poor, living in a shack. Gladys feared for her son's life. She rarely saw him and believed he was being trapped by Hollywood and The Colonel, of whom she was clearly suspicious. In the early months of '57, Gladys was admitted to the local hospital as she was beginning to have health problems. She began to drink heavily and started taking diet pills. Gladys couldn't come to grips with this new glamorous lifestyle. She relied on her son for strength and while Elvis has been accused of being a "mamma's boy", he loved his mother like any compassionate human being would.

When Gladys was released from hospital, Vernon and herself went to Hollywood to visit their son. They also got a chance to appear as extras in his current film. While Elvis was performing the song "Got A Lot O' Livin' To Do", they were seated in an audience clapping and cheering along to the tune. This was considered one of the most sexually provocative performances filmed for a musical at that time as the movements, more daring than ever, represented sexual activity.

The legendary Irish group the Pogues covered this particular song in tribute to Elvis decades later. The Pogues, who originally formed in 1982, artistically mixed Irish traditional music with the sounds of punk. Critically acclaimed singer and songwriter, Shane MacGowan, from Tipperary, was the group's front-man. Some of their noteworthy songs have included "Sick Bed Of Cúchulainn" and "Fairytale Of New York". With their radical attitude and support of working-class liberalism, the band has been one of the greats to come out of Ireland.

Between 1956 - 1957, small pockets of Irish rock 'n' roll fans, mostly in Dublin, began to emerge and be recognised. Groups of young adults began combing greasy quiffs and wearing their collars up. They became known as "Teddy Boys", originally a British phrase and were to be seen hanging out in groups outside chip chops and cafés. They made sure to see Bill Haley when he performed in Ireland and even caused a riot when his movie *Rock Around The Clock* was screened in Dublin. They all seemed to be waiting for some bigger culture to emerge which was being suppressed by the major authority figures of Ireland.

CHAPTER FIVE

In April 1957 Elvis travelled to Canada to give five concerts, which would be his first and only shows outside of the U.S. His first four performances took place between Maple Leaf Gardens in Toronto and the Ottawa Auditorium in Ottawa. Then suddenly his fifth scheduled show was cancelled due to pressure from the local Catholic officials ordering that Presley be stopped. Prior to this, leading up to the day of his fourth show, one Catholic school in particular insisted that their students were forbidden from attending Elvis's concert.

The Notre Dame Convent in Ottawa instructed that the girls at their school make a pledge that they would not go. A notice was written on the blackboards which the girls were to copy down and to which they were to sign their names. Despite having signed the pledge under pressure, several girls, ignoring such oppression, took hold of their lives and dared the trip to see their rebel hero Elvis Presley in concert. It was subsequently reported that eight girls were expelled from this school for attending the performance, or as the school put it, for disobeying their rules. One "perpetrator" explained that a nun called her from class into the hall, told her she was no longer welcome at the school and that "her soul was condemned to hell".

In Ireland the Catholic Church also gave Elvis and rock 'n' roll fans a tough time. Many priests howled their condemnations from the pulpit and criticised, in ferocious anger, their disgust with rock 'n' roll music. They roared that Elvis was slouched at the left hand of Satan with a distinctive plan for the corruption of young people. They shouted to the masses in the churches and schools if there was anybody who liked this Elvis Presley? Naturally, nobody responded, and this again encouraged a demonisation of this symbol of expression.

The Dublin Archbishop, John Charles McQuaid, demanded a report on Irish people who were listening to and attending events involving rock 'n' roll. According to John Cooney's biography of

McQuaid, he set up a vigilance committee which involved spies targeting rock 'n' roll fans, in what were reported as "mad houses". "Indecency was the order of the night", one spy reported and McQuaid asked his spies for information on over one hundred individuals, involved in what was considered "un-Catholic behaviour".

Northern Ireland journalist, author and political activist Eamonn McCann recalled a time in the late 1950s, a Catholic priest named Flanagan standing firmly at his altar instructing Catholic boys to stay clear of rock 'n' roll music and "most especially of Elvis Presley who was evil". "Elvis Presley", the priest continued "is singing these songs for one reason only, to madden young women so he might rape them". The priest claimed that all of Elvis's band and those associated with him were drug addicts and sexual degenerates. Flanagan, a spiritual director at the school claimed to the pupils that Elvis has been "unmasked by properly qualified theologians as an agent of the devil".

In the Ireland of the 1950s the Catholic Church had total persuasion over the government and the country's decisions, even though the Church and State were supposed to be officially separate. The Irish government gave the Catholic Church extreme power to do and say as it pleased without hesitance and their views were unquestioned. The Catholic Church was given majority control of both primary and secondary education. It was their opinions that held sway and consequently this increased their power to do as they pleased. Legislation on divorce, contraception and censorship gave legal power to Catholic moral teaching.

This type of domination remained in Ireland until human and civil rights and a sense of individuality, fused by rebels, changed such a culture. As a dominant religion Catholicism lead and guided the people of Ireland with dogmatic rule. During a time when Ireland was void of vibrancy the Catholic Church used its power to try and direct the outcome of potent social influences such as Elvis and rock 'n' roll, which represented colourful facets of Western life. Fortunately Elvis and other American rock stars, living in a more diverse society, ultimately did not have to take much notice of religious ridicule. Their social rebellion contributed to a trend that would change modern society through the coming decades.

Looked at here is the conservative culture that was firmly in place in Ireland before a daring and liberal culture took the world by storm. Also examined are the changes rebellious rock music and Presley's liberal lifestyle would bring to a strictly religious country. With Bill Haley's movie *Rock Around The Clock* becoming a success, there was an obvious market for rock 'n' roll in Ireland. Although the Catholic Church indicated that Ireland was not to embrace such a "threatening" figure as Elvis, his music would still trickle into the country. This unearthing would have influence on Irish history in regard to religion, politics and entertainment.

Foreign entertainment was seen as a threat to the cultural traditions. Bishops denounced dance halls, theatres, movies and popular music and this continued for decades in Ireland. Visual or verbal references to any type of sex or sexuality, affairs, virginity and divorce were strictly deleted from movies, including Elvis's movies, which we will later see in the book. Roman Catholic influence insured that Ireland never discussed such issues as sex, abortion or suicide. The Catholic Church kept a firm stance in the bedrooms of Ireland. An atmosphere of silence on critical matters became part of Irish culture.

The Irish Censorship Board gave precedence to Catholic moral ideology and one major area of censorship was the censoring of literature. Books with any reference to sexuality were banned. Catholic groups vetted books underlining what they saw as "indecent" passages and submitted them to the censorship board. Some of the most important literary works of the twentieth century from across the world were censored including works by Irish writers Frank O'Connor, George Bernard Shaw, Brendan Behan, Sean O'Faolain and Kate O'Brien. Liam O'Flaherty and Samuel Beckett, who also had works banned, stated that the Irish Catholic Church took hold of the reins of power. Irish people were kept ignorant of sexual matters and of artistic developments around the world.

The Council of Irish Bishops in Maynooth warned, "The evil

one is ever setting his snares for unwary feet. At the moment his traps for the innocent are chiefly the dance hall, the bad book, the indecent paper, the motion picture, the immodest fashion in female dress, all of which tend to destroy the virtuous characteristics of our race". Irish culture, mainly before the 1970s was in the grip of cultural isolation which would be challenged by internationally popular artists and the radio airwaves.

Rock stars bent the rules of such authority and their music and image symbolised the rebellion against such rule. However the grasp of this authority in Ireland was so firm it meant that Ireland was not going to rapidly produce any rock 'n' roll stars. America and Britain would lead the way and eventually a growing indifference emerged in Ireland to Catholic thinking on such issues as rock 'n' roll and dancing. Rock musicians and celebrities firmly became the new figures of reverence surpassing a position once held by bishops and cardinals. This move of deep felt admiration towards the performing arts did increase tremendously with Elvis's arrival, but longevity has proven him to be far more than just a singer but also a symbol of social change.

Elvis Presley and rock 'n' roll were a break-through in a society that was ignorant of individuality. Rock 'n' roll was a liberal art and form of free expression. As Irish writer Oscar Wilde put it, "Art is the most intense mode of individualism that the world has known". Elvis and rock music reached out to neighbouring countries and fused ideas, dreams, hopes, goals and ambitions. The 1950s introduced rock 'n' roll and while it was first seen as obscure and hazardous, in the long run it helped change society. Rock 'n' roll was a fast paced, upbeat, motivating sound that sent adrenaline rushes through the veins of the world. Rock music was the definitive response to a society that repressed individuality.

In Britain there was also a strong protest against rock 'n' roll music and its influence, by the Church of England. The same tired story continued that his music was satanic but in Britain he achieved number one hits in his early days. It was also not too long until an Official Elvis Fan Club was set up there as well as the quick emergence of rock 'n' roll singers and bands.

In the Ireland of these times religious rules and rituals took precedence over rights and refuge. The importance in noting this Irish history of religious fervour is to pin-point how rock 'n' roll could not make an immediate impact here. However, it indicates how the increasing liberalism in entertainment culture would make an enormous and essential transition over the latter decades of the twentieth century. This liberalism lead to the uncovering of all kinds of horrific crimes carried out by those previously considered infallible. Hence came the realisation that a "position" can never be trusted but an "individual" has a noble chance. Rock 'n' roll was a force that helped highlight the concept of the "individual".

With the rebel music in rock 'n' roll form becoming more powerful, social life world-wide progressed. Nevertheless, with changes, Elvis quickly got a wide range of Irish fans and his film *Love Me Tender* was released here in 1957 without any cuts. However, when Presley started to release more films, nuns banned girls from going to see him. In one particular instance Sister Columba of the Presentation Convent in Mullingar, Co. Westmeath, warned the pupils that "attendance at the Presley film would result in them being expelled".

Elvis's music was played in city clubs and available to buy at various stores and while he did entertain many Irish people, this was challenged by the poverty and the condemnation. In Ireland, many became amazed by the presence of this young singer. Irish music journalist and producer Shay Healy recalled going to see an Elvis movie and said, "Elvis was young, good looking, vibrant, rebellious, sexy - everything we weren't in Ireland in the '50s". This indicated Presley's ability to open doors in different cultures and societies.

Irish journalist, broadcaster and sports correspondent, George Hook, a teenager of the 1950s who grew up in Cork City, found himself drawn to the music of Bill Haley and Elvis Presley. As recalled in his autobiography, living right through these alternating times he remembered, "In Cork, like everywhere else, priests denounced rock 'n' roll from the pulpit as the Devil's music, which made it even sexier in our eyes". However a lot of Ireland wasn't sure how to deal with Elvis, as rock 'n' roll music seemed too dangerous for any revolution to take place here.

Irish musicologist P. J. Curtis states, "Radio Éireann at that stage still didn't feature Elvis. Catholic Ireland just could not be exposed to such 'filth' from some 'sex-mad, satanic, degenerate', as Elvis was viewed at that time". Dubliner's band member Eamonn Campbell also notes that "The Catholic Church in the '50s would've viewed Elvis and rock 'n' roll as agents of Satan, promoting sex and wickedness".

Before any liberal society fully emerged in Ireland, an expression of sexuality was considered a morally sinister act. Everything Elvis tended to do and stand for was, on his part, unintentionally against the protests of conservatives, from the unashamed sexual suggestiveness and fast music to the bright, flashy dress sense and dancing. In Ireland, a serious ignorance towards sexuality was part of regular life. Changes that did come along arrived partly because of rock 'n' roll and the individuals who took advantage of this liberation.

Irish musician John Keogh explains, "In Ireland, and worldwide, extreme conservatives saw the whole rock 'n' roll movement as subversive and generally immoral. Elvis, because he had immerged from the pack, head, shoulders and particularly hips above the others, was singled out for more bad press than any of the others. Whether deliberately or unconsciously he terrified the establishment with his magnetic sex appeal".

Long before Elvis, in 1933, the Archbishop of Tuam, Dr. Thomas Gilmartin warned, "a terrible judgement must await those who organise immodest dances". The Church saw dancing as the tantamount to fornication and in order to stop this, Catholic priests destroyed dance platforms and threw instruments into the ditches. Dance bands were strongly criticised during the 1930s and this kept the progress of modern forms of music to emerge in Ireland at a slow pace. By the 1950s R&B records pushed the walls a little further ahead but when Elvis Presley arrived a rebel streak within teens was given the opportunity to be unleashed.

Condemnations of Elvis from the pulpit have continued, even

long passed his time. Historian and writer Leo Daly recalled in the 1990s that there was one particular case in a Co. Westmeath church where a priest informed his parishioners that "Elvis was responsible for destroying the culture of Ireland". This priest failed to realise that it is up to the individual to take or leave what they want from the society in which they live. The inability to do this reflects a serious education problem and points at those running the majority of Ireland's schools, which happened to be the Catholic Church itself. If Elvis's influence was responsible for changing Irish culture, the Irish people were obviously unhappy with its limits. What this midlands priest did succeed in doing, however, was confirming Elvis's almighty status as the supreme rock star who inspired a change to international cultures.

Despite the early lambasting of Elvis, rock 'n' roll music and dancing by the Roman Catholic Church, it eventually softened its views due to the survival and unequalled power of popular rock culture. Popes have subsequently hosted pop acts, breakdancers and rock stars at the Vatican including meetings with the rock star Bono. Despite the denouncement by the Catholic Church, rock 'n' roll would not fall, but constantly surge in popularity, eventually becoming a conventional form of music.

In spite of ridicule towards Elvis from Catholic or any other religious hierarchy, Presley eventually took their condemnations of him nonchalantly. Presley is known for never making any return criticisms to those sections that struck blows at him. However, Presley did give generous donations to Catholic charities. Later on in his life, as we will see, Elvis Presley opened his mind to many religious and spiritual groups, without conforming to one organisation.

American democracy was one of the many influential symbols of Presley which eventually latched onto other Western countries on a broad scale. Elvis was an example of somebody who could think for himself regarding the search for an intellectual understanding of spirituality. Despite being born into a certain religion Elvis never failed to explore other religions. Presley loved the Christian God but didn't put his God before people.

His image of rebelling against the establishment, intentional or not, was a tremendous influence to international societies. It would turn out that many years after this point in Irish history, his ways would become very influential on Irish society also. Elvis Presley is an example for people to supervene the route of being eager to triumph, while still signifying rectitude. Anybody can walk through a window once it has been smashed by one of courage. In time, controversy over rock music would fade due to the rock artists of the 1950s making such an impact. Chances of success for future artists in Ireland and abroad had been paved by the first rock stars, the main one being Elvis.

Such an increase in liberalism, next to an expansion in communications, a growth in democracy and the fortitude to express oneself, eventually helped to free the country from a repressive, Church ruled society. Chain reactions gradually occurred and eventually a feeling of liberation and sex and any kind of reference to it became second nature to Irish youth and no longer could a religion torture them for it.

From the days of Elvis Presley the youth developed their own culture, their own conscience, their own lifestyle. This was the beginning of it. Rebellion would begin. It would be the new attitude and atmosphere of every generation. The '60s were around the corner and those who absorbed Elvis and his fellow rock 'n' roll artists were getting ready to introduce him to the Irish mainstream. Rock would land in Ireland in a very big way, as a country with much to discover and rebel against.

Chapter Six

At the start of 1957 *Love Me Tender* began screening at the Capitol Cinema in Dublin. *The Irish Times*, briefly commenting on the release, asked, "Is Presley human?" followed by the statement, "Dublin audiences will have a chance to judge the hip-swinging singer for themselves in the Capitol this week". In a subsequent review of *Love Me Tender*, the film correspondent for *The Irish Times* noted, "the famous frenetic 'wiggle' leaves me cold. The younger members of the audience, however, seem to react only to this St. Vitus routine. When Mr. Presley is just singing or going through the motions of acting they are as quiet as mice, but let him get one of these spasms and every jerk produces roof lifting squeals". An unnamed film critic for *The Irish Independent* stated, "The plot is a reasonably good one and it certainly gives the glamorous Elvis an opportunity to show that he can do other things besides sing".

Towards the end of April 1957, Elvis met the songwriters Jerry Leiber and Mike Stoller for the first time. He had recorded a few of their songs including "Hound Dog" but this was Presley's first encounter with the writing duo. Some critics target Elvis for not writing his own material. What has to be recognised is that a great deal of admirable singers never wrote material, including Frank Sinatra, Dean Martin, Enrico Caruso, Luciano Pavarotti or the Irish legend Luke Kelly. Like an actor, their art was to communicate other writers' work.

Elvis, as did all these musicians, became a master of interpretation, with his own incredibly distinctive style. He presented the feelings and emotions of the music in the most intrinsic manner. His way of giving his best as a performer was to approach everything from the heart. It was the performance that counted most. Singer and songwriter Steve Wall of Irish rock group the Walls commented, "I don't think Elvis needed to write songs. I don't think it's anything to detract from him that he didn't write songs. So many songs were being offered to him and everybody wanted Elvis to do their songs".

As a superstar recording new tracks on a regular basis, the possibilities for writers to achieve success were opened. Elvis's liberal approach to songs influenced the ambitious notion of testing, discovering and fearlessly performing new kinds of music. At one point early in his career Elvis said that he would like to write some of his own work but only made brief attempts. His major skill was an acute hearing of the sound he wanted. He added or took away from the original format of a tune to what he found best. Presley was an explorer and at the recording sessions he took full control and nobody told him what to do. As a true artist he made all the decisions and never let time be a hindrance in the studio, starting and finishing at his own leisure, refusing to conform to the commercial assembly line. The music freed him and this was the original intention of his rock style, pure escapism.

Leiber and Stoller were prepared to write music for Elvis's next movie which at this point was changed from *The Rock* to *Jailhouse Kid* to eventually *Jailhouse Rock*. The film was set to be directed by Richard Thorpe, who had previously directed Irish actress Maureen O'Sullivan in *The Voice of Ann Boyle* (1936), *The Crowd Roars* (1938) and a series of *Tarzan* movies between 1936 and 1942. In *Jailhouse Rock* Elvis played Vince Everett, a truck driver who ends up doing eighteen months for manslaughter. It gave Elvis a new chance to test his acting ability and again he proved he worked well in scenes involving tension. Suspenseful and intriguing, it still is a rock music classic.

One of Elvis's costumes in the film was a woollen knitted sweater which became the topic of a 2005 Irish language documentary titled, *Elvis 'Aran' Presley*. Screened on the Irish language TV channel TG4, the programme set out to discover whether the sweater was one of the famous "Aran Island" produced woollen tops. Irish actor Tom Ó Suilleabháin hosted the search which brought him from the Aran Islands off Co. Galway to Memphis, Tennessee in a determined quest to find out if it was in fact of Irish origin.

Recording sessions for the *Jailhouse Rock* soundtrack included "Young and Beautiful", "Treat Me Nice", "Baby I Don't Care" and "Jailhouse Rock", which epitomised Elvis's own loud and boisterous rock 'n' roll style. Irish music producer, songwriter and journalist Shay Healy remarked, "when he sang 'Baby I Don't Care', for me it created an adrenaline rush that was irresistible. He was helping me to kick the last vestiges of 'squareness' and timidity into submission". The title song "Jailhouse Rock" was re-issued forty-eight years later and on 6 January 2005 it went to number twenty-three on the Irish charts for the first time.

"Jailhouse Rock" was also covered by Northern Ireland group Ash in 1998. Ash formed in 1992 and was made up of the musicians, Rick McMurray, Tim Wheeler, Mark Hamilton and Charlotte Hatherly. Some of their songs include "Petrol", "Kung Fu" and "You Can't Have It All".

Once again in his latest recording session Elvis incorporated his usual techniques of artistry and expertise remaining focused on all technical and emotional aspects. Throughout all his sessions he embodied an air of professionalism by never getting mad or offending anyone. No matter who made a mistake or messed up a performance he only blamed himself. This was an aspect of his proficiency that would continue on as a defining factor of his persona for his entire career.

During the *Jailhouse Rock* period, Steve Sholes wanted Elvis to record more music. The opinion that Elvis would just be a fad caused the company to put pressure on him to record as much as he could while he was still popular. Everyone was profiting from Presley's work and although Elvis was making a lot of money, others were trying to squeeze him dry. For his work on *Jailhouse Rock* Presley received $250,000 plus fifty percent of profits. This salary was unheard of and gradually made him one of Hollywood's highest paid actors, but Parker got a massive percentage of all income which ranged from twenty-five to fifty percent throughout Elvis's career.

On 25 May 1957, *The Irish Times's* "Record of the week" was Elvis's "Playing For Keeps". In America the *Loving You* soundtrack was released in July and shot straight to number one. It was his third album release and his third number one album hit. Elvis constantly proved to be a larger than life success. By fans and critics he was crowned "The King of rock 'n' roll" but he never liked getting any title. Yet, releasing hit after hit, he truly dominated the rock music business.

The single "Teddy Bear" with its flip side "Loving You" became Presley's third number one hit in 1957, making a total of six number one hits so far in his career. This song first received an Irish chart entry half a century later through a rerelease which saw it become a number twenty-four Irish hit on 6 September 2007. The movie of the same name was a great success and went on release around the world. It managed to be passed by the Irish censor and had its premiere in late October 1957 at the State Theatre in Phibsboro, Dublin.

Elvis was already breaking record sales and was most definitely a phenomenon. These songs became hits across the world and Radio Luxembourg continued to help introduce his persona to the youth of Ireland. Elvis had become the ultimate rock star. Entertainment was an occupation he adored, not just for financial reasons but for the satisfaction felt from entertaining people. In his spare time Elvis would go to all-night gospel sessions. He was deeply in touch with gospel music and knew off by heart every major gospel recording. When somebody hummed a tune briefly, Elvis knew right away what that song was.

Elvis went on performing live concerts and at the end of August he played Washington where he drove into the stadium in his Cadillac and gave another power charged performance in front of 12,500 fans. After these shows Elvis travelled to L.A. where work on his new album began in Hollywood. He finished off a song for the *Jailhouse Rock* soundtrack and in September began work on the new project titled *Elvis' Christmas Album*. The previous April, an EP was released titled "Peace in the Valley" containing a recording of the title song and the other gospel tracks, "It Is No Secret", "I Believe" and "Take My Hand, Precious Lord". It was Elvis's first spiritual release. Although he had performed the song "Peace in the Valley" on *The Ed Sullivan show*, displaying his love of spiritual songs, this EP was a definite indication of his beliefs.

This gospel release was a blow in the face for those who dictated against him, especially the religious advocates who protested the supposedly "anti-Christ" rock music.

Putting aside his depth in music and becoming music history's greatest success, Elvis helped set out a widely popular and incredibly fashionable image. In the 1950s white guys from ordinary backgrounds generally didn't wear flamboyant clothes. Whether or not it would have evolved with or without him, Elvis's popularity helped bring this style to the forefront for the world to imitate. Often daring in his attire he wore black shirts with cream suits, without ties, which was unusual then. Even keeping top shirt buttons open to sleeves rolled up made an impact. Elvis wore clothes with colour, unusual designs and flare.

A young Irish Shane MacGowan, explained, "I was a greaser, I wore my hair long and quiffed up and I wore a black leather jacket, sort of James Dean, Elvis Presley kind of look". Elvis epitomised the rock 'n' roll image of slicked back hair, loose, casual and flashy clothes, motorbikes, cars and flirtation. After Elvis came along, many teenagers' lives began to solely revolve around music, looking good and having sex. Long before any hippies, Elvis helped push forward a sexual liberation.

Elvis had a stance like nobody else. From the curled lip to the sway in his movements he had a deep-rooted rhythm. Elvis kept levelheaded and knew it was possible he could lose everything. He watched his weight, rarely smoked and banned alcohol from his house. All the moving about and high energy concerts were his constant exercise. At a young age he was already a major idol to millions of teenagers worldwide as the "hip" rebel image made an international impact. Presley also built a small group of bodyguards and right hand-men to assist that tough image, some of whom would be around him all his life.

In the Christmas song sessions of 1957, Elvis first recorded "Blue Christmas", a laid back track oozing rhythm and blues. Other Christmas tunes recorded were "White Christmas", "Here Comes Santa Claus", "Santa Bring My Baby Back" and "I'll Be Home For Christmas". Through many of his Christmas performances Elvis lost himself within the feel of the blues' outpouring of emotion.

Suggesting what made him an everlasting star, Irish artist Jim Fitzpatrick, stated, "Charisma", adding, "lots of people can sing but so many do not have the animalistic charisma that he had". The Dublin born artist is internationally famous for his Celtic designs and creating album covers for Irish rock group Thin Lizzy. He remembers being a fan at Elvis's prime. As a teenager, Jim drew pictures of Elvis as his successful method of attracting the girls. He remembers how difficult it was to be a rebel but so many teenagers kept on trying, through the influence of Presley and the condemnation by priests. On one occasion at school, Jim heard his name being called over the intercom, being instructed indoors to have his Elvis inspired "duck tail" shorn off. It was an example of the new social attitude arriving with rock 'n' roll in Ireland. Fitzpatrick explains that he would have loved to have seen Elvis, at this stage in his life in concert, noting that Elvis may never have known that he lead a cultural impact in Ireland.

Shortly after the Christmas song sessions Elvis travelled to Tupelo for another benefit show in front of 12,000 people in support of a youth centre. Then there was a string of shows in California including L.A., which provoked new uproar. This was his first concert here, which had become like a new home due to the movie business. His performance created outrage once again as Hollywood celebrities watched in shock as he twisted his body to the beat of the music. His dancing and music had been denounced on TV and in newspapers for almost two years now but yet these stars turned up despite all the procrastinations. It was ludicrous for anyone to go to the concert without knowing what to expect.

The next day there were headlines saying Elvis would face jail if he didn't clean up his act. Even the L.A. Vice Squad warned Parker of this. The L.A. Police Department even filmed Presley's concert. In fear of a riot possibly breaking out, this film would have been evidence of what Elvis's stage acts were influencing. Presley ran the risk of going to jail and having his life destroyed by all the protests against rock music, simply because his music made young people feel free for the first time.

The concerts, the music and the movies saw Elvis involved in and promoting a new style of show business, shaped and fitted for a young audience. Although many films for years had been made especially for a younger generation, his movies were like the music, something young people could identify with and follow alone without the company of adults.

In October 1957, *Loving You* had its Irish premiere at the Theatre Royal in Dublin. The Theatre Royal was famous throughout these years for hosting variety shows and being a centre of entertainment. Around the same time as the new Elvis movie premiere, a new variety show was being hosted at the Royal. It was listed for including several singers, among them, Peter Edgery who was featured as "Dublin's Elvis Presley". According to reports, the singer received a cool reception from the audience.

In November 1957, Elvis made his first trip to Hawaii to perform three concerts. The third show, which took place on 11 November, would prove to his very last performance of the 1950s. This concert brought an end to an important phase in his life. The 1950s of live performances for Elvis meant reaching to the crowd with his own special magic. These concerts also gave him some of his greatest publicity. After the '50s had passed by, the controversy, complaints and outrage over his performances tended to fade, as new acts came on the scene under his influence.

In December 1957 *Elvis's Christmas Album* went to number one and stayed at the peak position for three weeks. This made his fourth album release his fourth number one album hit. A rerelease of the single "Santa Claus Is Back In Town" would crack the Irish Top 25 on 14 December 1980.

On 16 December 1957, the Memphis Draft board announced that Presley would soon receive his draft notice to join the United States Army. Plans for Elvis's fourth movie were underway and this project had to be completed before the star would leave for army duty. With a clear conscience Elvis entered 1958 set and ready for his final movie before giving up his freedom and career for his country. Elvis boarded a train for L.A. where he began production on his next movie, *King Creole*. Soundtrack work began on 15 January 1958, with the recording of "Hard Headed Woman" and "King Creole". These songs made their first Irish chart entries at number twenty-six and number twenty-two respectively as rereleases between 27 September and 4 October 2007.

The soundtrack session was followed by the songs "Trouble" and "Crawfish". "Trouble" was covered in 1998 by Irish singer Jack L. Jack L. (Jack Lukeman), was born in Athy, Co. Kildare in 1973. He is a singer known for his strong haunting vocals. Early in his life he travelled to Germany and met the Black Romantics who became his backing group. Influenced by the work of songwriter Jacques Brel he returned to Ireland as a soloist, discovering his own voice. Success came his way with the 1998 song, "Georgie Boy".

Also from the *King Creole* soundtrack to be covered by an Irish group is the song "Crawfish" for which the Walls added their own original slant. The Walls were formed by Steve and Joe Wall, previously of the rock band the Stunning, whose memorable songs included "Brewing Up A storm". Carl Harms and Rory Doyle joined the Walls and they did their first gig in 1998. Their popular songs include "To The Bright And Shining Sun" and "Passing Through". In live performances the Walls have also covered the other Elvis classics, "Mystery Train" and "My Baby Left Me". On how he admires Elvis, Steve Wall remarked, "for me it was his voice. The early recordings, all the stuff that was done in the Sun studios. When I started listening to music, getting influenced by music, by listening to the early R&B men, Elvis got thrown in amongst that. His Sun recordings just blew me away for the pure energy".

In Presley's fourth motion picture he took the role of Danny Fisher, a troubled school boy whose singing talent is discovered by the owner of a small club called King Creole. Competition in nightclubs leads to the young talent getting mixed up in a game of cat-and-mouse which leads to tragedy. The film was well-received by many critics and *King Creole* proved Presley's acting ability, going down well with most audiences. He was dedicated and focused and sought tips from everyone on the film sets. He in return was helpful to everybody and interacted with all cast and crew members, even singing songs when requested during breaks or holdups on production.

King Creole is still considered Presley's best film. With Hal Wallis back as producer, Hungarian born Michael Curtiz (1886-1962), of *Casablanca* (1942) fame, directed. Co-stars included New York-born Academy Award winner, Walter Matthau (1920-2000) who soon after starred in a TV production of Irish playwright Sean O'Casey's *Juno and the Paycock* (1960).

The last non-soundtrack recording session before army induction took place on 1 February when Elvis recorded the tracks "My Wish Came True", "Doncha' Think It's Time", the Hank Williams classic, "Your Cheatin' Heart" and "Wear My Ring Around Your Neck". "Wear My Ring" was covered in 1998 by the Irish alternative rock group An Emotional Fish who collaborated with musician Seanie Fog on the performance. An Emotional Fish formed in the late 1980s, gradually gaining attention after 1989. The band was made up of Gerard Whelan, Martin Murphy, David Frew and Enda Wyatt. Some of their hits include, "Lace Virginia" and "Rain". "Wear My Ring" also became a number twenty-five Irish hit for Elvis on 18 October 2007 with its first time on the Irish charts through a rerelease.

As film production on *King Creole* came to an end, Elvis attended a party in Hollywood with the rest of the cast and crew before it was time to give up his career due to his country's obligations. Elvis wanted to do his time in the army and passed no judgement on the fact it could possibly damage his career. 24 March was the big day. Accompanied by his parents and a string of girls, Elvis reported to the Draft board where he was sworn in as Private 53310761 and appointed squad leader with basic training beginning right away.

Elvis was given his army uniform and what became a legendary haircut. The dyed black mop of long blonde greasy hair was chopped off as he was given the regular G.I. treatment in front of fifty reporters. When parents waved goodbye to their sons Gladys was visibly distraught. Although there was little to worry about she was concerned about something happening to him. This whole ordeal was damaging to her, as at the young age of forty-five her health was beginning to deteriorate. She was overweight and had an alcohol problem which only brought her mood down.

7 March 1958 saw *Jailhouse Rock* open at the Adelphi Cinema in Dublin City. Ireland's Shay Healy remembered, "*Jailhouse Rock* was the first time I really connected with Elvis. I was heading for my Leaving Cert and Elvis was heading for stardom. He was cool and beautiful, totally handsome to men and women. When I later discovered that Elvis had choreographed the dance for *Jailhouse Rock*, my estimation jumped another two notches".

The Irish censor passed the film with just one cut, in a scene where a showgirl's legs fill the screen, a scene "too sexy" for Irish eyes. *The Irish Times* reported that *Jailhouse Rock* was "a lower form of entertainment" and that Adelphi Cinema were "giving us the ineffable Elvis Presley". The reviewer of the film stated how MGM presented Elvis for "about 90 of the films 95 minutes as a completely unlikeable person and, for my money, a close approximation of his real self". *The Irish Independent* noted that those "who consider his contortions and the peculiar teenage background with which he is surrounded rather unwholesome, wince and suffer in silence".

Ann B. Murphy, reviewing the film for Ireland's *Evening Press*, commented, "It starts out to be another study in sociology but quickly deteriorates into a plethora of swimming pools, beautiful girls and flashy cars". Teenagers rushed to see it and the film established the beginning of an Elvis craze in Ireland, despite the powerful authority of the country warning people off him or cynics ridiculing rock music as mindless immaturity. Murphy finished her review of the film explaining, "The fans will just love it and judging by the screams which echoed through the cinema, they will certainly get their money's worth". This film would prove to be Presley's first visual introduction as the rock 'n' roller to an Irish audience.

CHAPTER SEVEN

In March 1958, *The Irish Times* ran a whimsical column asking readers what they would do if they were millionaires. One reader, 13 year old Kevin O'Malley from Terenure, wrote that he "would hire the biggest theatre in the world and engage Elvis Presley and Little Richard and others to give the biggest concert ever staged". It expressed the feeling of the modern Irish teenager at the time and highlighted the gap between the generations as the adult columnists frequently put him down. Nonetheless, despite the boys dream, Elvis was currently no longer able to do concerts as he gave up his life for the armed forces.

A few days before Elvis entered the army, in March 1958, an LP was released of his best hits to date. This would be the first of an endless line of Elvis Presley greatest hits releases. Titled *Elvis's Golden Records*, the album reached number three and stayed for fifty weeks on the U.S. LP charts. Previous to that release, his first single of the year, "Don't", which made its chart debut on 27 January, went to number one. A rerelease of this track made its first Irish chart entry, fifty years after its first release, becoming a number twenty-seven Irish hit on 20 September 2007.

In his first few weeks of service, Private Presley took on all the strenuous tasks every solider has to endure such as the daily hikes. He was well acquainted with guns, tanks and rocket launchers and he soon received a marksman's medal with a carbine and achieved sharpshooter level with a pistol. After two months in the army the soldier got time off and went straight to Graceland. On 10 June 1958, wearing his army uniform, Elvis went back to Nashville for the first time in nearly two years to record a few tracks. A distribution of creativity with remarkable new guitar styles was poured out on such songs as "I Need Your Love Tonight", "A Big Hunk O' Love" and "Ain't That Loving You Baby".

Elvis was delighted with the session. He messed around in the studio doing one liners from songs and playing jokes. After one take of "I Got Stung" he sang a quick line of "When Irish

Eyes Are Smiling" for no apparent reason other than his casual messing about. This was an American produced song written by Chauncey Olcott and George Graft Jr. and published in 1912. It has become a traditional folk song of Irish tenors ever since. Elvis often repeated singing a line from this particular song at further sessions. Perhaps subconsciously he was interested in recording the song earnestly, as he tried out everything and would later cover other popular Irish based songs.

Shortly after, Presley headed to his army base and had his family stay at a mobile home nearby. Elvis was treated like any other soldier, got all the normal training and was given all the standard tasks. Exceptions were not made because of his fame and wealth, but he could have very easily had this if he entered into the entertainment corps division. Presley never considered asking for exceptions and in fact had a tougher time than any other soldier because all eyes were upon him. While soldiers have a right to complain Presley did not because he was aware any general frustrations on his part would be used against him. There were also no decisions made to have him perform music for the other troops.

At this time Steve Sholes was persuading Parker to get Elvis back into the recording studio once again before his army duty brought him abroad. This was not to be as the 10 June recording sessions would be his very last sessions of the 1950s. The golden era of rock 'n' roll in Elvis's life would now take a rest. His army duty took over and he left his future career in the hands of Parker and Steve Sholes. It became their job to keep Elvis's name in the public eye. The first single was "Hard Headed Woman" which, released on 30 June 1958, reached number two. This release also began the special promotion campaign for *King Creole* which hit the cinemas on 2 July. The movie was an instant success and it peaked at number five in the weekly cinema charts.

The Irish film censor for the time, Liam O'Hora, ordered eight cuts to *King Creole* on preparing its release for Ireland. Scenes cut included one that took place in the school Principal's office, which involved a description of Danny's (Presley) family circumstances.

Such a cut deleted the attempt to justify Danny's rebelliousness. One other scene cut involved Danny tricking Nellie (Dolores Hart) into going to a hotel with the objective of having sex with her. References to this scene were also cut at another point in the film so that audiences wouldn't realise they were missing something.

The Irish censor also sliced out a scene where Maxie Fields (Walter Matthau) asks his mistress, Ronnie (Carolyn Jones) to lift up her skirt and show off her legs. The scene which shows the exploitation of Ronnie leads to a fight between Danny and Maxie. Other parts cut away from the film included two musical performances, one with the obvious reason of Elvis's gyrations and the other by a scantily clad woman singing about bananas.

O'Hora complained that "this picture is a tough one for me, particularly so because it features the controversial Presley who has such an appeal for uneducated adolescents". When the picture was brought before the appeals board, O'Hora revealed how much trouble he had "particularly from Headmistresses of girls' schools' regarding Elvis's most suggestive abdominal dancing". However, he did add that Presley's gyrations were much more restrained than in previous pictures. Despite this, the Appeals Board rejected the appeal towards the cuts and banned the film altogether. *King Creole* would not be allowed to be shown to an Irish audience.

Throughout the summer of 1958 Gladys Presley was becoming quite ill. She had often lost her appetite, had irregular eating habits and lost her facial colour. She also had an increase of severe depression. Elvis decided to have her and Vernon travel home to Memphis and contact their personal physician. From an early age Elvis had always felt alone and it was his mother who helped his survival. It was due to this platonic love being so strong that when a dark cloud began to form, it was as if lightning struck a deadly and powerful blow at him. His life would dramatically change forever from this moment on.

On the Saturday morning of 9 August 1958, at approximately 11.30 A.M., responding to an emergency call, an ambulance transported Gladys Presley from Graceland to Methodist Hospital. When notified, Elvis was not too worried because her recent sickness had recently raised false alarms. Nonetheless, her condition suddenly became critical. Her health rapidly grew worse and doctors diagnosed her with hepatitis. As soon as Elvis found out about his mother's worsening condition he panicked and threatened to go A.W.O.L. from his base, if he didn't get clearance to go, which was not granted forthwith.

On 12 August in an exhausted state, Elvis was finally given leave and was on his way to Memphis. As soon as he arrived he raced to the hospital to be beside Gladys. Vernon had been with her all along and once Elvis arrived they both stayed either side of her hospital bed. Elvis was in shock and he lamented by her bedside as they spoke together. The next night Vernon suggested Elvis go home to rest, while he stayed at the hospital. Nothing but worry went through Elvis as he tried to sleep. Doctors did what they could do but all was too late.

In the early hours of 14 August 1958 Gladys Love Smith Presley passed away from a heart attack due to hepatitis, with her husband beside her. Elvis was contacted right away but he knew what had happened before he answered the phone. He was completely inconsolable - everything he truly cared about vanished within a flash. As he showed up at the hospital the tears cried out in extreme devastation. His mother was more essential to him than anything else and now she was gone.

The funeral commenced on 15 August. It was the worst day of Elvis's life and he collapsed at several different occasions. The pain was unbearable for him knowing that his mother was gone. Her body was brought to Graceland and Elvis stood by her coffin speaking to her as tears streamed down his face. As the gospel group the Blackwood Brothers were her favourite singers he had them fly in from their concert tour to perform at the obsequies. The group were set to sing three to four songs but Elvis would not let them finish as he didn't want this moving moment to end.

After the body was taken to Forest Hill Cemetery, a short distance from Graceland, Elvis fell upon his mother's coffin weeping without shame. It was a heartbreaking and incredibly emotionally disturbing display of affection. Gladys had proven the importance of a loving mother. He regretted not devoting his time to her in her last years and his heart ached with grief. As the funeral came to an end he now realised that she was gone forever. This was the starting point of deep emotional pain which lay ahead.

On 16 August, Elvis went to his mother's grave and spent the day by her graveside. Elvis was in a total state of trauma and this resulted in a period of deep depression. He received over 100,000 sympathy cards and letters but had to dry his tears quickly and return to his army base. In the early part of September it was reported Elvis would be stationed in Germany. This would be the first time he left for overseas.

After reaching New York before departure by ship he gave a press interview and seemed to be in a steady mood. In the past Elvis was always charming, funny and in perfect humour during his interviews but what appeared to be a calmer, quieter, darker Elvis emerged. With a more serious outlook he had come from seeing the pits of extreme sorrow to facing a more challenging life. A life without the person he loved most dearly. Carrying his duffel bag and a present of a poetry book from a fellow soldier, titled *Poems that Touch the Heart*, Elvis boarded the USS General Randall that would embark on its voyage to Europe. One thing that went with Elvis on his trip was the worry of his career. Would it be still there when he returned home or was this venture into the army the final marking point?

On the morning of 1 October 1958 the USS General Randall arrived and docked at the port of Bremerhaven in Germany. Over 1,500 fans showed up. Fans raced up to him for autographs and hundreds of girls screamed, waved and cheered for him. The Elvis phenomenon had clearly spread throughout the world as coming to Germany was like stepping outside the gates of Graceland. A reporter for RCA arrived with a large bouquet of flowers for Presley but she was told that no flowers were to be given to the soldiers. However, just as Elvis boarded the train to take him to his new base, the flowers were forced into his hand. Obeying army rules, but in an act of kindness for the gift, he threw the flowers to the crowd as a thankful gesture and it was the perfect departure.

Elvis's first assignment was to be a jeep driver. Photographs were taken continuously and he never seemed to get privacy as the press and the fans couldn't get enough of him. In the event that the barracks wouldn't be continuously surrounded by spectators, Elvis was given permission to live off base at a hotel in Bad Nauheim with his father, grandmother and a few friends who had accompanied him. Press conferences still took place with hundreds of people gathering to get a glimpse of the star. An army of reporters showed up with note pads, tape recorders and cameras.

In a new interview with the media he was asked about different music and he explained he had an interest in a wide variety of sounds. Germany's traditional music had been made up of many classical composers and opera singers but this was an area Elvis was only discovering. After stating this, he explained how he loved mood music and had a very keen interest in Irish tenors.

Popular Irish singer Sinéad O'Connor once referred to the most famous of Irish tenors, John McCormack as "the Elvis of Ireland". This suggests that John McCormack is as much a legend for Ireland as Elvis is for America. Both performers once dominated the music business in each other's respective countries. Sinéad O'Connor herself is a singer and songwriter. At a young age she became lead singer for the Dublin group, Ton Ton Macoute before establishing her solo career. She is an extremely passionate performer who, like Elvis, bares her soul in her work. With an eclectic sound, ranging genres such as hard rock and Irish folk, she has always sung songs true to her heart. One of her most well known performances is "Nothing Compares To You". Sinéad, admiring Elvis commented, "I thought he was an angel, he was one of those human beings who isn't quite human".

Back in the U.S.A., Parker worked out new strategies in marketing Elvis and came up with an idea for an EP Titled *Elvis Sails*, consisting of the press conference Elvis gave before leaving for Germany. In it, Elvis was heard talking about his future ideas after the army and his ambition in becoming a good actor. He told reporters his scheduled release date from the army and his surprise that he was not bothered by any of his fellow soldiers due to his fame and reputation. After these general questions, up came a question about his mother's death. With an obvious change of tone in his voice he spoke about her, explaining that since he was an only child, that was what had brought them closer together. He stated everyone loves their mother but as a result of being an only child his mother was right there with him and helped him with his life. The loss of Gladys was not only the loss of a family member but the loss of a friend and companion with whom he could talk freely.

In September Elvis's soundtrack album to *King Creole* was released reaching number two. Steve Sholes got anxious about needing new material for release. He even suggested Parker go to Germany and have Elvis do a few recordings. Under no circumstances would Parker leave America and he informed Sholes that they should not over flood the market and space out their releases.

Elvis's time overseas opened new areas in his life and he became friends with many American G.I.s and German people. Travelling to Germany opened his life to meeting new people and seeing a different culture from his own. Although hundreds pressured him to perform, he could not do so as he was here to work for his country.

Towards the end of November Elvis was promoted to private first class. Still staying at a hotel, the Presleys and their extended family of friends got ready for Christmas. With the wild party bringing fun and good cheer, Elvis entered 1959, a whole year which would keep him working for his country. In the early stages of the new year Elvis had his family pack up and move to a new five bedroom house at Goethestrasse, Bad Nauheim.

It was also not long until Parker was in contact with Elvis, suggesting to him to make some recordings while in Germany. He said that other instruments didn't have to be present and that Elvis singing while playing piano would be enough, as the fans just wanted to hear his voice. A few home recordings were made but appear to be just casual private recordings with poor sound quality. However the excitement, interest and enthusiasm was certainly present as Elvis randomly went through a selection of his favourite songs, including "Irish" songs "Danny Boy" and more than one version of "I'll Take You Home Again, Kathleen".

Chapter Eight

Throughout 1959 and 1960 Elvis was referred to on more than one occasion during Dáil and Seanad debates in Leinster House (Ireland's house of Parliament). Politicians discussed the issues of broadcasting and popular music not having any output on Irish radio services. While some politicians in a country guided by religion scorned Elvis and rock 'n' roll it was being realised that Elvis was no passing fad. Elvis and rock 'n' roll music had turned the tide and had gone against the grain. This made some politicians sit up and realise that Ireland was not providing for its modern youth.

On 22 July 1959 Thaddeus Lynch, a Fine Gael TD, spoke of the diversity of taste with the generations and how Radio Éireann should try and cater for the youth of Ireland. In his presentation, Thaddeus Lynch explained, "The programmes on Radio Éireann should be suitable for young people. The young people like modern dance music and popular classical music. I am speaking from very great experience. I have been collecting records for a lifetime". Lynch continued to explain, "There is a gramophone shop in the street where my office is situated and I see the young Irish boys and girls buying Elvis Presley and rock 'n' roll".

The debate over the output of modern styles on Radio Éireann was slowly referred to now and again and almost a year later the issue resumed. This time, on 31 March 1960, James M. Dillon, a member of Fine Gael, who appeared to be more in favour of Radio Éireann, explained the differences in taste and was aware of the youth tuning into such foreign radio as Radio Luxembourg.

Dillon stated, "There is a continued dissemination of advertising programmes on Radio Luxembourg and I often have to make the choice between Radio Luxembourg and Radio Éireann in the middle of the day. My son likes Radio Luxembourg; I like Radio Éireann but then, I must admit that Radio Luxembourg usually has 'Elvis The Pelvis' and Radio Éireann has not. I am not at all sure the comparison is unfavourable to Radio Éireann".

However, despite some cynicism, Dillon was well aware of the financial positives of having Elvis broadcast on Irish radio.

In a further Dáil debate on the issue, held on 19 May 1960, he explained, "It is usually a passionate desire to listen to 'Elvis the Pelvis', and I cannot pretend to enjoy that buck. I recognise freely that there are others who do, and every man is entitled to enjoy what he likes best in the form of music, whether it be Elvis or Ludwig van Beethoven. Certain it is, however, that the net result is that Radio Luxembourg gets immense advertising revenue. If we could command a tithe of the advertising revenue Radio Luxembourg enjoys, we would be able to achieve what I think is the ideal: we would be able to cater on one wavelength for the fans of 'Elvis the Pelvis' and, on another, for the enthusiasts of Mozart and Beethoven".

While Elvis was away from his homeland protecting the Western world and while the well being of ordinary Irish people suffered in silence, Irish politicians were up against the incredibly complex decision of whether they should play Elvis's music or not. It was a decision which seemed to lack a rapid conclusion as the debate loomed over to the following year, eventually sparking the public's interest. Nonetheless, it was clear Ireland was building up an immense group of Elvis fans and popular music was becoming more popular than ever. Diversity and change were maturing and some alternatives for the culture of Ireland were underway.

While rock 'n' roll music was causing "tricky decisions" for the Irish government, Irish fans of popular music saw the first compiling of music sales appear in the *Evening Herald* on 12 February 1959. While these were not, and are still not considered an official charting of music sales, it was giving an Irish audience a rough idea of what the Irish music buying public were pursuing. Under the column of "Rick O'Sheas Record Player, Herald Top Ten", the very first number one chart entry went to no other than Elvis Presley, for his release of "One Night" and its flip side, "I Got Stung". This release stayed for no less than two months in the Irish Top 10. A rerelease of "One Night" became a Top 15 hit in the official Irish charts forty-six years later.

On 23 March 1959, Elvis's single "A Fool Such As I" entered the American charts, reaching number two, followed by "I Need Your Love Tonight" one week later. On 30 April, the single of "I Need Your Love Tonight" entered the "Herald Top Ten" at ten and climbed one place the following week. Shortly after, "A Fool Such As I" entered these unofficial Irish charts at number four on 14 May 1959. The single climbed to three and then to two over the following couple of weeks. By 4 June, both "I Need Your Love Tonight" and "A Fool Such As I" were side by side at numbers three and four, respectively. A rerelease of "A Fool Such As I" entered the official Irish charts for the first time in 2005, reaching number twenty-eight on 3 March that year.

Meanwhile in Germany, Elvis received another break from duty and travelled to Munich and then continued on to Paris. As the trip to Paris was not reported, this gave Elvis a brief chance to travel about the city. At his hotel in Paris, staff noticed a long line of women going in and out of his room. Elvis took all the adulation in his stride and enjoyed the experience of life in a new city. For entertainment in Paris, Elvis travelled about the town, attending regular tourist locations. A theatre named The Lido provided the entertainment of semi-nude chorus girls.

By the time Elvis had returned to his station and settled in, his single "A Big Hunk O' Love" went on sale and became Elvis's next number one hit. This track would make it to number twenty-three on the official Irish charts on 12 October 2007. With Elvis's army departure arranged for March of 1960, the Colonel set up a TV special with Frank Sinatra and a new movie was arranged which would parody Presley's actual time stationed in Germany.

As 1959 continued, several events occurred which would play a major part in Elvis's life. The first of these was his meeting with a young girl by the name of Priscilla Beaulieu, the daughter of an army major. At the age of fourteen when visiting the Eagle Club in Bad Nauheim, where stage shows were performed, Priscilla was offered the opportunity to meet Elvis. Priscilla was very enthusiastic about meeting the star and met him for the first time in Goethestrasse.

After their first meeting Elvis was intrigued by Priscilla. For her age she came across as mature and he found her a great person with whom to talk. He was also enthralled by the young girl's beauty. Often spending time in his bedroom they spoke for hours and she began to notice the very sensitive side of Presley as he talked about the loss of his mother. She got to know the side of him of which the general public were not aware.

Priscilla connected with Elvis and became quite aware that he was becoming a very lonely person. He may have had people surrounding him morning until night but there was an unreachable loneliness in him. Elvis was aware of her age and although her step-father gave Elvis permission to meet her, he saw her as a great friend. He knew what an outburst the media would create on finding that he was friends with this girl but he became concerned about protecting her.

The second event of 1959 that would have a later effect on Presley was his first heavy use of medicine. A drug called Dexedrine was introduced to Elvis by another G.I. and was used to keep the soldiers awake throughout the night while on manoeuvres. The drug gave Elvis more time awake in order to keep up the job expected of him by his country. Convinced the drug was completely harmless, he took it frequently.

The final event which became important to Elvis was his introduction to the art of karate. This came about after Elvis began to focus on philosophy and the concept of reincarnation. The connection between martial arts and the spiritual interest was the involvement of discipline and meditation as he held fascination with higher perception. Presley took his first lessons in Germany and became very enthusiastic and excited about the art, developing a deep passion for it.

In early January 1960, Presley was promoted to acting sergeant. He received his full sergeant stripes and celebrated the achievement. With his finishing date approaching, a farewell party was held. Irish journalist Bryan Kelly, covering a *Sunday World* article about Elvis in 1977, wrote of how he was at this party in Germany and how "Elvis drawled, 'some day, I'm gonna visit Ireland'.", a dream which would sadly go unfulfilled. On 1 March 1960, Elvis got ready to leave for America. This was it, it was all over and it was back to business and to try and establish a secure name again in the entertainment industry.

Elvis took his last steps in Germany and waved goodbye to all the people he had spent over a year with, people who became part of his life during his stay there, most of whom he would never see again. One person in the crowd was Priscilla and she wondered if she would ever see Elvis again. She waved and looked on as Elvis boarded the plane to take him back home.

En route to New Jersey, the plane stopped at Prestwick Airport in Scotland. This brief stop would also mark a noteworthy addition to the history of Elvis, as they were his only footsteps on Great Britain and it was the closest he ever got to Ireland. When the plane took off from Prestwick for America, its flight path went over Ireland, most likely above the hills of Co. Donegal. As the plane came over the Atlantic Ocean Elvis Presley's physical closeness to Ireland and the rest of Europe would fade into the distance forever.

As the snow fell and as America's most famous soldier arrived in New Jersey, a press conference was held. Nancy Sinatra, daughter of Frank, greeted him as well as hundreds of fans. On 5 March 1960 Presley got his official release from the U.S. army along with his pay cheque, which marked the end of his stint in the army. The following day he took the train back to Graceland. Arriving in the snow he was greeted by all his friends and family and a special welcome home party was thrown. Another press conference was held in Elvis's office and he talked about his time away. He was also asked about a young girl with whom he had been seen. He downplayed the acquaintance and laughed about being careful speaking to the press.

On his return to Memphis he visited his mother's grave at Forest Hill Cemetery and a special order of flowers was to be delivered every week. Elvis wandered about the grounds of Graceland knowing for definite that his mother was never coming back. He looked into the distance sombrely and silently grieving.

Not long after returning home Elvis was presented with the award for having sold fifty million records. Little time was granted for rest as work on the Sinatra special and his new movie was to begin. These were new exciting times for Elvis. He was given the chance to experience the great feeling of being back and being able to make a fresh start.

20 March 1960 in Nashville saw his first recording session and the humour was in place to do what he loved best. During his time away, others were given a chance to try and pass him out, such as Pat Boone who covered blues songs in pedestrian fashion. Irish actor Dermod Lynskey remembered the time when Boone arrived. Dermod commented on the era which saw Boone and Presley compete, stating, "With Elvis's hip wiggling, his performance was suggestive. No 'respectable' girls were seen dancing to his music. When Pat Boone came on the scene he was referred to as the "respectable" girls Elvis Presley".

The golden era of rock 'n' roll existed during the 1950s but major artists of this period were no longer rock music royalty. Jerry Lee Lewis's name was damaged by his marriage to his thirteen year old cousin and with Little Richard entering religion, two important rockers were gone. There was also the death of Buddy Holly, and Chuck Berry was in prison and Carl Perkins and Bill Haley could not command the same interest as before. The only one left who survived this historic period was Elvis Presley and he had gone at the point when the music business was taking a sharp turn. Having been away for two years he was ready to conquer the entertainment industry once again.

With most of the regular crew it was as if nothing had changed except the new technical upgrades. The only original member to leave was Bill Black who had no interest in returning after gaining his own successful career. Black never worked with Elvis again and tragically died from a brain tumour in 1965. Scotty and D. J. had been very successful working for other artists but they were still interested in returning. The first two songs recorded, with Elvis on vocals and guitar, were, "Make Me Know It" and "Soldier Boy". As Elvis got back into his old mood he cut more tracks over the next nine hours. These included "Stuck on You", "Fame And Fortune" and "A Mess Of Blues".

With the Sinatra TV special drawing closer, Elvis headed to Miami by train. Getting into his private carriage he greeted thousands of fans, waving to crowds as he set out for his televised welcome home. While rehearsing with Frank Sinatra, RCA's pressing plant worked over time to release Presley's new single. Over one million copies were made of "Fame And Fortune" in forty-eight hours and were shipped out immediately.

At the end of March the taping of the Sinatra show took place. An hour long programme, it introduced Elvis's return and featured Frank and Nancy Sinatra with Sammy Davis Jr. singing songs and presenting acts. The show ended with the re-appearing of Elvis singing two songs and then concluding with a duet with Frank. The show went out on ABC television throughout America on 12 May 1960 and gained over forty percent of the regular TV viewing audience. Elvis wanted to be back in the studio soon again and on 3 April set up for work on his new LP, *Elvis Is Back* - his first post army album. There had been over one million pre-orders for anything by Elvis Presley so he went into the studio and followed his instincts.

CHAPTER NINE

Starting his new session with "Fever", Presley's sensual version proved his voice could enter into different areas. Another tune he also recorded was a specially written version of the classic operatic song, "O Solo Mio". The famous Neapolitan folk song's rhythm and sound was re-used with English words and titled, "It's Now Or Never". It tested Elvis's vocals and emphasised a powerful singer as he reached operatic pitch.

Other songs from this particular session included "Dirty, Dirty Feeling", "Such A Night", and one of Presley's best R&B tracks, "Reconsider Baby". One other song recorded during the session was "Are You Lonesome Tonight?" Like "Fever", it tested his diversity regarding styles. It became another exquisite performance. Irish manufactured girl group Bellefire later gave their rendition of "Are You Lonesome Tonight?" on an Irish tribute to Elvis in 2002. Another abstemious version was performed by American jazz musician Norah Jones, who covered the song at the famous Windmill Lane Studios in Dublin for another star-studded Elvis tribute, also in 2002.

Presley went on to do the music he had always wanted to record. Although the majority of fans wanted him as a rock artist, he had a fanbase that wanted anything from him. Despite the decline of most of the 1950s rock stars, rock was still popular and it was Elvis's trademark, but he had now fully established himself as a diverse artist. "Stuck on You" with its flip side "Fame And Fortune" entered the charts and went on to achieve another number one victory for him.

Over two weeks later he went out to Hollywood to begin work on his fifth film, now titled *G.I. Blues*. With fans rioting once again on first sight of Elvis, he had to be protected in his train compartment on his way to Hollywood. Soundtrack recording included "Pocketful of Rainbows", "G.I. Blues" and "Wooden Heart". Ireland, still without an official music chart in 1960, would have to wait until a 2005 rerelease of "Wooden Heart" got an eventual Irish chart entry. The song got to number twenty-two in Ireland forty-five years after it was recorded. Elvis's recording of "Pocket Full Of Rainbows" was resurrected almost fifty years later and used by the Irish National Lottery for a television advertisement promoting their lottery games. The *G.I. Blues* recording sessions also includes the second known occasion of Elvis suddenly singing a brief line of "When Irish Eyes Are Smiling".

The first day of recording went from 9 A.M., which was too early for a nocturnal Elvis. He enjoyed the night life and although he was not interested in the regular Hollywood lifestyle, he briefly went out clubbing. Elvis never got caught up as a typical Hollywood society celebrity. He didn't attend movie premieres or other A-List celebrity events and despite being nominated for countless music awards, he wasn't pushed to attend most of these ceremonies.

The second day of recordings included the usual amount of time and effort but Elvis was disappointed with the material. The songs were not his own choice and not something with which he could experiment. Elvis enjoyed re-arranging songs and making them his own. Some of the previous film songs had been more suited to Elvis's rebel image but it was *G.I. Blues* that started a clean cut Elvis for the eyes of the world. The rebellious greaser was out and the soft hearted romantic comedy was in. *GI Blues* was aimed predominately at a family audience.

The Colonel wanted to invent a new image of Elvis. He was a patriotic man who gave up his time for work in the U.S. Army. It was something many people had thought would "straighten" him out and make him "grow up", to put aside the delinquent greaser image. To a certain extent some of this came true. After appearing with the crooner Frank Sinatra and starting to record more adult songs, the public found a new side to Presley. Tom Parker saw this as an opportunity to try and clear away any of the negativity surrounding his client. He wanted to conform to conservative ways and *G.I. Blues* was another step towards this. Motivated by money, Parker saw no concern to keep true to Presley's original teenage following and made way for an image which could attract a universal audience.

After appearing on almost every magazine in America and around the world it was clear that Elvis was the most famous entertainer worldwide. Nobody could surpass him. To free himself from Hollywood, he and his entourage went to Las Vegas. It was becoming a major holiday destination for Elvis and he loved the atmosphere of glamour, glitz and gambling. Elvis's entourage began to wear black suits and dark sunglasses. It was a little fad that ran for a short time and after being seen by the press in this attire Elvis's group became known as "The Memphis Mafia".

Towards the end of July 1960, the single "Its Now Or Never" entered the charts and became another number one hit for Elvis. This song reached the Irish charts at number six, forty-five years later. "It's Now Or Never" was an inspiration to an underprivileged teenager named Barry White who was in prison for stealing tyres. The song hit him like a thunderbolt and it influenced the young man to clean up his act and do something special with his life. Thereafter Barry White became one of the world's most cherished love songwriters and singers.

"It's Now Or Never" also managed to leave an impression on Dr. Iognáid G. Ó Muircheartaigh, former President of the National University of Ireland, Galway, who found it to be the song that reminded him most of his school days.

The song was not too inspirational, however, to many Irish parish priests who continued to preach from alters around the country that it was a mortal sin to listen to Presley's music. The song referred to kissing and holding the singer tightly and some Irish Elvis fans at the time witnessed priests "flipping their lid" over such lyrics. The strict rule about keeping silent on sexual matters was still the dominant way in Ireland. The sexual liberation in rock 'n' roll form was long overdue.

At the end of July 1960, plans for Elvis's next movie were completed and he was to commence work on it right away. In August Presley was at 20th Century Fox for production of his new movie tentatively titled *Flaming Lance*. This new film was somewhat of a relief and brought a serious role for Elvis. Although there was a plan for four songs to be in the soundtrack the rest of the movie gave him a chance to prove his acting ability. This project opened new areas for his film career. Given the chance, Elvis could act but the chances would not often come his way. While Elvis has certainly never been considered a great actor he proved to perform well in scenes involving anger and sustained good comic timing.

With a change of title from *Flaming Lance* to *Black Star* a few days into production, Elvis played the part of Pacer Burton, a half breed Kiowa Indian torn between two races. After taking special horse riding lessons for many scenes, Elvis went on to check out the soundtrack material and while the four songs were recorded, two ended up being dropped from the film. The movie's title was again changed in September to *Flaming Star*, thus bringing Elvis back to the studio to change the title song.

In mid September Elvis saw a special showing of *G.I. Blues* and the movie became a huge hit. In Ireland the film was cut in several places. Liam O'Hora who continued to be an extremely conservative film censor, was deeply concerned that one of the characters was an unmarried mother. Although the child's parents, Marla and Rick, are intending to get married, O'Hora made cuts to make it appear that they were already married. Lines such as "We're gonna be married" and "Do you want me to be best man" and then "we already have a marriage licence" were sliced out in order for Irish viewers not to be scandalised by characters who obviously had premarital sex. A later reference to their "licence" was left in as it was felt an Irish audience would only assume it could mean a driving licence.

Another separate cut involved a soldier named Cooky, who is kissing his girlfriend on a couch and according to O'Hora appeared to be "on top of her". A further cut was ordered where Elvis and his friends arrange a bet that he can stay until the morning in the house of a woman they met earlier. The cut ensured that Irish viewers would not be corrupted by the notion of a man hoping to have sex with a young woman he just met. O'Hora also requested that the distributors "tone down the love making a little" and added "this picture will be seen mostly by teenagers in this country because of the presence of Elvis Presley. I have to be particularly careful on this account". *G.I. Blues* was screened at the Capitol Cinema in Dublin in January 1961.

Just before finishing production on *Flaming Star*, drafts were being arranged for his next movie, *Wild in the Country*. It was another opportunity to star in a more serious role. Then, as the month of October came to an end, Elvis planned to get back to Nashville. His first plans were set for the recording of a gospel album. After great success with his return album, which included music of his own choice, he took another step into the music field with material that suited him best. It was quite a risky decision as it was a major change from rock 'n' roll. It wasn't a genre for teenagers and although the love songs were a step away from rock, this was the ultimate leap in the other direction.

With his career more secure than ever he chose to record gospel as he was passionate about his beliefs. This would prove to be an early example of a "roots" album for a rock 'n' roll singer. The album was to be titled *His Hand In Mine* and work began on 30 October 1960. The regular musicians took part, along with Millie Kirkham who, with the Jordanaires, worked on backing vocals. Entourage member Charlie Hodge who had previously worked on Elvis's April session also added harmony on various performances.

With songs like "Milky White Way", "I Believe In The Man In The Sky" and "Known Only to Him" Elvis covered all his songs of worship with total perfection. Much of his gospel work was done with his own distinguished style. The music truly was his sole passion with no special expectations or requests from anyone. With a completion of fourteen songs recorded in this short period, two were kept back from the album. One non-gospel love song, titled "Surrender" and another gospel track called "Crying In The Chapel".

"Surrender" was based on the Neapolitan song "Come Back to Sorrento". It was another invigorating performance by Elvis, emphasising the influence great tenors had upon him. It became a U.S. number one a few months later. It eventually had an opportunity in the Irish charts through a rerelease on 10 March 2005 when it became an Irish Top 25 hit.

The *GI Blues* soundtrack hit the charts in November 1960 and became Presley's fifth number one album success. Spending ten weeks at the top position, it remained for a phenomenal one hundred and eleven weeks in the charts. It was his most successful album and it went to show how the movie business was the perfect promotion for the music. Parker was certain of this and also used the music releases to promote the movies.

On 6 November Elvis flew out from Memphis to L.A. for preparation on *Wild in the Country*, which was based on the novel "The Lost Country" by J. R. Salamanca. Directing was Philip Dunne, who had directed Irish actress Geraldine Fitzgerald in *Ten North Frederick* (1958) and who had written *The Luck of the Irish* (1948). The cast also included John Ireland and Hope Lange who had recently starred in *The Best of Everything* (1959) with Northern Irish actor Stephen Boyd.

Wild in the Country added to a list of several good movies starring Presley, which made him raise his expectations to what he would finally get. He knew this was just early days and the perfect role would eventually come his way. The original plan for the movie was to have absolutely no songs, but as usual that changed and much to his exasperation five were planned and added.

The following week after his new soundtrack session, the single of "Are You Lonesome Tonight?" went to number one. The song stayed six weeks at the top slot. With still no introduction of Irish music charts at this stage, a rerelease of "Are You Lonesome Tonight?" would give Presley an Irish Top 20 hit in 1982 and another rerelease made the Irish Top 25 in 2005.

Some critics have taken for granted how impeccable Presley's singing was. He trained his vocals everyday and took breathing exercises to hit the high notes and broaden his octave range. However it wasn't just the technicalities that existed. Elvis could change his voice. He had a multiplicity of voices, a voice which matured. It can be argued that what often makes a great singer is not just the technicalities of range, like a tenor, but the ability to communicate feeling, to convey emotion, to sing sweetly but yet with passion. After that, range is a wonderful addition and for

Elvis, a singer in the pop market, which consists of average range, he shone brighter than an overwhelming majority.

Irish singer John Spillane explained, "His voice was impossibly beautiful. How could any human being sound so good? And have such control and power? Definitely there were angels in Elvis Presley's voice, definitely there were angels there". For many hearing him sing was as if he was singing for you and you alone. Irish music star Bob Geldof pointed out, "There are millions who argue, it was one of the greatest voices of the century, without question". With this exceptional voice for portraying an emotional situation told through a song, his ballad work was quite spectacular. This is why such songs as "It's Now Or Never" and "Are You Lonesome Tonight?" became such enormous hits and would remain in history as two of the greatest love songs Presley ever made.

As December of 1960 approached, Colonel Parker set plans for a return to live performances. Elvis had not performed live since 1957 and nothing had been planned for 1960. With news spreading of fund raising for a special memorial at Pearl Harbor Parker decided this would be a good time to get Elvis back to concerts. After discussing the event, Elvis agreed to Parker's idea of doing a special concert that would raise money for the memorial. Apparently the fund raising was in trouble as the set target could not be reached. It was kept quite low key to save any embarrassment but now Elvis was coming along to save the day. The concert was planned to take place in March of 1961. Another charity gig was also arranged to take place in Memphis for 25 February of the coming year.

On 22 December 1960 *Flaming Star* opened to fair reviews which suggested that Elvis was coming to grips with his acting ability. Unfortunately the movie only gained moderate business, compared to *G.I. Blues*. It wasn't a family movie and it didn't have many songs. Although it was his best movie since *King Creole*, it was not what people wanted anymore after witnessing the fun packed musical, only released one month previous to this. *Flaming Star* premiered at the Capitol Cinema in Dublin on 30 June 1961.

As Elvis's first Christmas at Graceland without his mother drew closer, Priscilla Beaulieu arrived for a short visit. She was well protected from the press while on her visit and stayed with Elvis's friends. It was in that time that Elvis really grew to admire her more. She was becoming a loveable companion and a close friend. Her presence at Graceland for Christmas distracted the bad vibes that could have been generated from Elvis's fond memories of Gladys.

1960 had come and gone and it remained one of the most important years of Elvis's life and career. He had nearly completed three movies in a seven month period. He had returned to a career that had just been given a two year intermission, a career that could have, in that time, completely diminished. However, it did not fade away, and he returned to conquer the music business once again.

With three U.S. number one singles and two albums which charted at number one and number two, 1960 was a success in many ways, the success of not losing his career and the success of achieving so much extra on return. *GI. Blues* had also entered the Top 10 grossing films of the year. Elvis was on a roll. He had remained popular and things were looking brighter regarding love. He was beginning to live life to the full again, or at least so it seemed. Most importantly he was getting back to making music which would always be his path in life.

1961 was around the corner and more plans were in operation; the concerts, the movies, new albums and new singles. Could he keep all his success clenched firmly in his fist, so it would not disappear? A whole new music scene was on the horizon and Ireland was on the verge of fully embracing the modern sounds in the shape of showbands.

Chapter Ten

On 22 November 1960 Radio Luxembourg began airing *The Elvis Presley Show*, a fifteen minute programme featuring updates and music of the singer. Scheduled for every Tuesday, the show would run for several years at the peak of his popularity. This radio station's programme schedule could be seen in the Irish print media below the listings for "Vatican Radio", which highlighted the diversity which had now been created abroad in the shape of rock 'n' roll, and was drifting into Ireland. While this radio station gave rock 'n' roll fans what they craved, broadcasting in Ireland continued to present a different attitude.

Towards the end of 1960 and early 1961, a light debate opened up in the "Letters to the Editor" segment of Ireland's *Evening Press*. The topic, titled "Music for the young", discussed how Radio Éireann, which was Ireland's only radio station, should try and broaden their music output to tie in with the music of today. The issue, which had been raised in Leinster House, spilled over into public discussion and the idea of young people tuning into foreign radio was seen as a threat to the Irish broadcasting service.

Many Elvis fans agreed that Ireland's radio service should begin to play modern music but some fans suggested that rock was out, that it had been a passing fad and that the softer ballads were becoming more popular with the young. The suggestion that rock music was a fad had been going on for years but some felt the need to state it had at last diminished. An article had appeared in this same Irish newspaper, on 12 February 1958, stating, "After three years, rock 'n' roll is on its way out". Rock music had declined among Elvis's post-army albums but it would most definitely make an everlasting revival a few years down the line.

One Irish individual suggested that rock was "violent music, sex music, brainwash music. It is a manifestation of a mislead and confused society. Are we going to become just a facile, thoughtless, plastic-minded people?" However a thirty-three year old mother wrote in, siding with rock music, feeling that Radio Éireann should play it, as she found it quite enjoyable. There was certainly a mix of opinions as Elvis and rock music took a grasp of Ireland. No matter what, Elvis was no longer at a stage where anybody was going to take him down and the Irish rock fans were no longer going to be intimidated. The economic situation was taking a turn for the better and the freedom in rock music represented a modern and forward moving generation on the horizon.

At the beginning of the 1960s, Ireland's economy was starting to slowly progress. In 1958 T. K. Whitaker, Secretary of the Department of Finance, had drawn up a document titled "Economic Development" and this contributed to influencing important advances in the country. Ireland up to the late 1950s was a very oppressive place to dwell. There was a poor economy and most people worked for low wages. Up to 40,000 people were leaving the country each year in search of a better way of living. Ireland was fast becoming a breeding ground for exiles.

Entering *An Dáil Éireann* in 1959 Sean Lemass arrived as the new *Taoiseach* (Head of Government) with a vision of modernity and change. The country's social and economic everyday life needed to take a dramatic turn. Eventually more jobs were created as more businesses were set up. The education system also made vast improvements as more co-ed and non-denomination secondary schools were opened.

With Lemass as leader, he and his party put economic development into practice. With an improved economy, in which people had a little extra money for entertainment sources, there was a new found freedom. Part of the economic development resulted in a larger market for modern music and alas, rock 'n' roll records became more accessible around the country. School children of the 1950s who had to sneak a listen to Radio Luxembourg were now in a better position to buy an occasional rock 'n' roll record.

However, Presley was not getting the opportunity to appeal on a phenomenal level to the young people of Ireland, as he had in other countries. While there was a great amount of Irish fans there had not been a substantial development of rock culture in Ireland. Many of the big Irish rock 'n' roll fans wanted to join in with the new sound but Ireland was only at the very beginning of embracing modern popular music. The growing fondness for light pop songs was enough for Ireland to deal with at first and from this, the "Showband" era was born.

While Ireland in the early 1950s saw light entertainment in the form of big band orchestras, an added beat began to emerge towards the late '50s. This first began with a Northern Irish band named the Clipper Carlton, a group of eight musicians from Strabane in Co. Tyrone who decided to stand up and add rhythm to their music. Although the concept of the popular showband was yet to be developed, a group of men set up what would be one of the most popular showbands in 1957.

The Harry Boland Danceband was a group of seven young musicians from Co. Waterford. The musicians included Michael Coppinger, Brendan Bowyer and Tom Dunphy, who was also the band leader. After a musical instruments salesman named T.J. Byrne from Carlow witnessed the band, he made his way to become the manager of the group. With a change of name to the Royal Irish Showband, this group's main idea was to introduce the music of Elvis Presley and Buddy Holly to Ireland.

Brendan Bowyer, born 12 October 1938 in Waterford, became known for his ability to perform American rock 'n' roll music for the interests of an Irish audience. Brendan based his concerts on Elvis Presley with energetic and high spirited stage performances. It was this impersonation of America's top rock stars that made him by far the most popular singer of the showband era in the 1960s. Although the band had formed in 1957, it was not until the early '60s that they hit the all time success.

The 1960s was the main decade in Ireland which introduced a long line of musical showbands which became the countries very first pop music groups. Even though they covered some rock tunes of the '50s in a rather softer tone than the originals, some of the music was still restricted in those days. It was these showbands that played a major part on Ireland's live entertainment in the '60s, appealing to thousands of young people. They performed pop hits, novelty songs and plenty of sentimental country 'n' western tracks.

Later on as Irish traditional music found new popularity many showbands also added reels and jigs to their repertoire. In the early '60s, the showbands created major stars in Ireland and over the years up to seven hundred groups set up around the country. The one that remained the most popular was the Royal Irish Showband which had been an Irish pop music trend setter.

Some of the other Irish showbands and singers that dominated dance halls across Ireland throughout the late 1950s and '60s included the Capitol Showband, the Miami Showband and Dickie Rock, the Drifters and Joe Dolan and the Black Aces Showband, who had been printed in the media with the caption, "featuring Ireland's Elvis Presley". There was also the Victors, the Bachelors, the Fontana, the Ohio and many more.

The typical showband musicians came from every part of the country and each group had professional performers who were inspired by the pop music from outside the country. Most of them who played popular sounds with ballads and rock 'n' roll represented Bill Haley rather than Presley because the raunchy and provocative appearance was still a sensitive issue in Ireland.

The rule was to wear tidy suits and neat hair, look polished and stand still. Those who were more daring didn't play along with convention and took the risk. This minority played naturally, dropped the clean cut look and displayed the eagerness in the music that had made many teenagers take notice of their hormones to greater effect. It was these musicians who eventually helped the transition from the showband image to the beat group styles.

As Ireland continued to be dominated by Roman Catholic views, rock music was still not accepted on the mainstream and dance halls were often controlled by priests and nuns. No alcohol was allowed during performances, there would often be a break to say the Rosary, dancing was strictly forbidden during Lent and it was considered a mortal sin to get overly excited on the dance floor. The basic line was not to enjoy yourself to stimulating levels.

The sexual suppression in Ireland went as far as priests walking around the dance hall pushing apart girls and boys, who he felt were dancing too close to each other and "causing scandal". Authority within this Church even allowed its priests to search for courting couples up lanes, behind ditches and hedges, in farm outhouses and behind dance venues. Such ignorance over sex and invasion of privacy would diminish bit by bit but this sometimes made the Church come down harder with its condemnations. Yet, like the racists and bigots who slandered Elvis in America, religious ridicule only made it all the more exciting for a lot of people.

In 1960 some concerned devout Irish Catholics wrote to Canon McCarthy of Maynooth declaring that they had heard, "that the vast majority of modern dances are seriously immoral and suggestive and therefore are to be regarded a dangerous occasion of grave sin". The Canon, responding to a series of questions on sexual matters in a two volume publication, explained that, "Some modern dances are seriously suggestive of sexual intercourse". This was the same Catholic clergyman who warned that kissing was fraught with danger and "will often be at least venially sinful" and that the danger is that it will arouse "venereal pleasure".

While some of the new showband stars did present what old fashioned types didn't want, many showbands were quite mediocre. Their job was to basically be live jukeboxes. A great majority of the showbands' most memorable tunes were usually just safe cover versions of hits made famous by established performers. Although some of Elvis's songs were also covers, he had re-invented forgotten tunes and set a trend of altering great songs for a modern market.

From a financial point of view there were some positive aspects to this success as it has been estimated that up to 4,000 jobs were created and fortunes were made. Soon enough showband managers and performers adopted Elvis Presley's fashion of exposing a glamorous lifestyle outside of the performing. Young men involved in the showband scene were catapulted from poorly paid jobs to massive earnings but often showbands did not get the full earnings they were due. Promoters of big venues, which often included priests and politicians, held back large payments and this would later cause major disputes.

Showbands are often criticised for having been an extremely basic form of popular entertainment. However their original emergence in Ireland reflected the desire of the Irish to take hold and grasp something more than what was there already. Artistically they lacked a great deal, comparing very much to the boybands of today, but yet sustaining a greater reason for their presence than boybands, which was the introduction of popular songs to a nation primitive in communications. Eventually, from this period, beat groups emerged in the mid 1960s which were a sharper product of popular music, stretching further from the vapidity of the showband styles. Some of the great names which highlighted this separation would include Van Morrison and Rory Gallagher.

With the growth of entertainment in Ireland, one new area was television. Beforehand, anyone with a television set could pick up Britain's BBC, mainly on the east coast, but there was no Irish TV station. Although television has often been ridiculed for coming along and challenging the old fashioned social cultures, it opened many minds to world issues. It became a new form of education and introduced people to other world cultures. It was in 1960 that the government planned to bring the exciting entertainment source to Ireland. On 1 January 1962 RTÉ (Radió Telefís Éireann / *Radio Television Ireland*) began broadcasting for the first time and this broke new ground for the country's way of life.

One of this new channel's leading and most popular shows was *The Late Late Show*, hosted by Gay Byrne, which brought topical debate and new music to the homes of Irish people. It was fairly liberal, new and intriguing and marked a large step in modern Ireland's development. This sort of television programme opened eyes and broadened the minds of those imprisoned from a comprehensive world. Through the source of TV and the influence of the new effective pop music, many young people felt the desire to be more independent. Over time the Churches say on world issues did not hold maximum ground anymore and this was the clear sign of progression and the emergence of a more open minded society.

Independence came in the early 1960s when rock music made ordinary people feel free. Rock musicians would influence a stand up attitude where people gradually decided that they were not going to take any sort of dictatorship. Modern music in Ireland at this stage did not preoccupy the minds of many adults. Nonetheless, younger people did not find it as superfluous, as it quickly became a part of their lives. Elvis and other rock 'n' roll stars provided everybody with a new outlet. By the 1960s young people worldwide discovered this freedom and a larger revolution would soon arrive. The inspiration and freedom in rock music took hold of the conscience of youth.

Although Sean Lemass helped set a path for a positive outlook, progress was slow, for it was a delicate process. Fortunately the youth of the country did take interest in the entertainment sources and this was one area which progressed. However, Elvis was gradually backing away from rock culture by entering the movie business.

Elvis would remain successful, but Ireland would be widely introduced to him as a movie star, rather than that revolutionary rock star. Calamitously that would take a bad effect on his image in an Ireland that was changing its culture to adapt with more modern times. Unlike in Britain, Ireland passed by the rock 'n' roll revolution of the 1950s. The top artists of the 1960s would take the spotlight originally dominated by Elvis Presley and this would be when rock truly began in Ireland.

New artists during the years of a new Ireland would be given indefinite chances to make an impact on Irish people, most of whom had missed the original rock revolution. Fortunately, 1961 saw Irish audiences get the eventual release of the rebellious *King Creole* which had been banned in Ireland on its original release. The film was passed with just two cuts this time and Irish fans got to see the true Elvis Presley up on the big screen.

CHAPTER ELEVEN

On 18 January 1961 two important letters from Elvis were sent to a couple of Irish fans. These letters were written for a young married Irish couple who were living at an uneasy moment in their lives. It was in 1957 when Maurice Colgan first heard Elvis Presley sing. The song was "It's Playing For Keeps" and as he listened for the first time he found Elvis and the song quite strange but captivating. Like many others, it was such a new sound to witness in those times. Maurice was not put off by this young rock star and while living in England began to purchase his music. It was during these years that he met a seventeen year old girl named Maureen, after being drawn to a club that was playing Elvis's music. From this meeting, it wasn't too long until these two Elvis fans were married. It was later when they were about to have their second child that Maureen was faced with a major problem.

Suddenly in late 1960 Maureen became critically ill from a liver complaint. She was hospitalised and the couple were incredibly worried. It was a major down point in their lives and they didn't know where to turn. Finding comfort in this state was quite a tough chore. Then it occurred to Maurice one day that he should write a letter to the man they both truly admired. This was the man who had originally brought the couple together. Sitting down in his home in Salford, England, Maurice put pen to paper to tell Elvis about the problem his wife was faced with. He explained how tough it was for them and the great worry which had beset them. He kept this letter to Elvis quiet from his wife and hoped that there would be a reply from the man who was at a busy point in his career.

For days Maurice was in and out of the hospital doing what he could for his beloved wife as they hoped for her to get better. Then suddenly one day a letter arrived at the hospital addressed to Maureen. Another one arrived addressed to Maurice at his home. Both had U.S.A. postal stamps on them and the senders address in the top left hand corner read, "Elvis Presley, 3764 Highway

51 South, Memphis, Tennessee". Completely ecstatic, Maureen's spirits were lifted on seeing the envelope handed to her from the hospital nurse. The letter read; *Dear Mrs. Colgan, just a short note to say I hope you are feeling much better. Take care of yourself and don't worry - everything will be all right. Sincerely, Elvis Presley.* The other letter sent to Maurice said; *Dear Maurice, I sent your wife a get well message. Take care of her and yourself. May God bless you both. EP.*

One letter was a great thing to get, but two was beyond belief. For Maureen it was an incredible moment in her life. She was full of joy, for herself and for her husband and so delighted with Elvis Presley for sending this letter. Maureen recovered shortly afterwards from her life-threatening illness. Had having her spirits uplifted by Elvis's kindness contributed to her convalescence? Elvis had taken a short time to help an Irish life. The couple later returned to Ireland to live in Dublin. Maurice also campaigned for a statue of the young Elvis to be erected in Tupelo and his suggestion was honoured in 2002. The Colgans have remained devoted fans of Presley and have received much publicity in Ireland and abroad, not only for their special letters but for their efforts in commemorating "The King".

Aside from making sure his fans got letters from him, Elvis faced the year 1961 with many achievements in the waiting. His spiritual album *His Hand In Mine* entered the charts reaching number thirteen. Production completed on *Wild in the Country* by the middle of January and Parker held a press conference in Honolulu, Hawaii regarding the upcoming memorial concert. He then performed his Memphis concert. Much had transposed since 1957 and getting up in front of an audience to perform solo would proceed in an utter adrenaline rush. The concert in Memphis was performed in aid of twenty-six Memphis charities.

A few days later it was back to business at Nashville's RCA Studio B. These recordings aimed for a new album titled *Something For Everybody* and songs included "Give Me The Right", "Sentimental Me" and "Put The Blame On Me". The music, again chosen by Elvis did not take benefit of his rock success but was rather mellow. It was from these recordings that people were suspecting he had abandoned rock music. With its laid back nature, his music was not as hard hitting as before. His expression for love songs and soft adult contemporary work shone through.

Elvis soon reported into the Paramount studios for work on *Blue Hawaii*. The cast included Joan Blackman and Hollywood star Angela Lansbury, daughter of Irish actress Moyna MacGill. For its time the picture was quite sensual and in one scene Elvis's girlfriend lost the top half of her bikini while out swimming. The scene would later be cut by the Irish censor but overturned by the appeal board. The deeply conservative world frowned upon this fun but time moved with Elvis. In fact, something of a similar nature happened throughout the early '60s when a Galway priest witnessed a young woman from his parish sprawled on a beach wearing a bikini. The priest sent the woman a note asking her to wear a one-piece bathing suit in future. With a quick response she asked, "which piece do you want me to take off?" - a daring sign of changing times.

Towards the end of March 1961 *Blue Hawaii* soundtrack work began but most of the music was very much lightweight. The only tracks to generate a spark were "Rock-A-Hula-Baby" and "Can't Help Fallin' In Love". "Rock-A-Hula-Baby" received its first Irish chart entry on St. Patrick's Day 2005, when it got to number nineteen on rerelease. "Can't Help Fallin' In Love" is one of Presley's most cherished love songs and has been covered by many successful performers including Irish musician Luka Bloom.

Luka was born Barry Moore in Newbridge, Co. Kildare. He first went on tour to English folk clubs with his brother Christy Moore at the age of fourteen in 1969. It was while in America in 1987 that he signed with Warner Music in Los Angeles and became known as Luka Bloom. He has performed internationally and recorded the album *The Acoustic Motorbike* in which "Can't Help Fallin In Love" appeared on.

Blue Hawaii was the main instigator for a long line of similar films, made for a teenage audience. *G.I. Blues*, which was based along similar lines, had been a superb success while the serious *Flaming Star* didn't come close in box office receipts. As most of the audiences were young, the tropical style was a lot more suitable and remained a Presley trend. It was the first of the special "Elvis Presley formula" films. These were lively, exotic, fun loving beach movies for kids. Yet, the concept of the beach movie became quite common throughout the 1960s among many movie companies. The beach became a symbol of Presley in the '60s. This was noted in the Irish movie, *Last of the High Kings* (1996), written by and starring Irish Hollywood star Gabriel Byrne, when a group of Elvis fans pay tribute to Presley with a beach party.

Another Irish movie, *The Snapper* (1993) included a cover of the song, "Can't Help Fallin' In Love" during the end credits. *The Snapper* was one of a series of novels by Dublin author Roddy Doyle known as the Barrystown trilogy. The other films in the series were *The Van* (1996), where Graceland gets a mention, and *The Commitments* (1991).

In the movie of *The Commitments*, set in a working class suburb of North Dublin, actor Colm Meany plays the father of a young man wanting to manufacture a soul music group. The father is an obsessive Presley fan who has a picture of Elvis above one of a Pope. He has his hair shaped in a quiff, is occasionally heard singing "Can't Help Fallin' In Love" and gullibly believing tales from an old musician about his meeting with "The King". The film helped to project a stereotype in Ireland from some haughty sections in society that Elvis's popularity rests strictly among the "working class" or the simple anti-intellectual.

In the course of researching this book, I came across an Irish actress explain that she didn't take to Elvis because it was the kind of music her mother's maid liked. Other "middle class" individuals claimed that "Elvis was for the lower class" and sniggered that "only janitors like Elvis". Elvis does have quite a large following among the working class as he was the quintessential "working class hero". He was the man who made dreams become a reality and proved that anybody, no matter from where they came can be successful.

Despite his descent from poverty, Presley was more royal than royalty because of his integrity as a human being, completely earning the title of "The King" in more ways than one. His music has equally transcended all "classes". Elvis was inspirational and that is why his music is listened to by everybody, whether it's a janitor or a President, with Ireland's Michael D. Higgins and America's Bill Clinton just two examples of Elvis fans from different backgrounds. Presley appeals to those who feel the rhythm of such soul stirring music, which leaves the fact that he intrigued anybody with rhythm in their veins, no matter what the "class".

Elvis being used as the subject of deep interest for a main or amusing character has popped up in other places too. The sitcom *Father Ted* saw a modern middle class Irish Catholic priest, played by Dermot Morgan, often expressing much interest in Elvis Presley throughout the series. This included impersonating him for talent contests, dreaming about being him and sleeping on an "Elvis pillow". Although fiction, this show did include parodies on modern thinking priests which exist within the Irish Catholic Church. Despite the Churches early condemnation of Elvis and his music, that view slowly diminished with less fanatical worshippers, especially when his true personality was made public.

Two days after completion on the *Blue Hawaii* soundtrack, Elvis flew out to Honolulu. The time had eventually arrived for his charity concert to raise money for the Pearl Harbor Memorial. After several interviews, after meeting thousands of screaming fans, Elvis got ready for his performance at the Bloch Arena. With performances of his earlier hits and such recent songs like "Such A Night", "It's Now Or Never" and "Are You Lonesome Tonight?", the show raised over $62,000 and an incredible amount of awareness for the project which was finally constructed. After the concert, production began on *Blue Hawaii*.

On 15 June 1961, *Wild in the Country* premiered in Memphis. The reviews and the box office were only lukewarm. This was enough for Parker to realise that Elvis's roles in reasonably good movies was proving less profitable. In reviewing the film for an Irish release, the Irish film censor Liam O'Hora felt he was being lenient by passing the picture. He ordered over sixteen cuts, which were mostly dialogue. Some of the cuts requested included references to divorce which the censor stated were "most cold-blooded". Other dialogue deletions were ordered on the implications of sex, temptations, getting a woman drunk and references to Jesus. The film was released at the Capitol in Dublin on 2 October 1961.

With the usual team of musicians, the next recording session took place on 25 June, again in Nashville. Once again most of the songs were easy listening and Elvis had not returned to his earlier style yet. This time songs included "Kiss Me Quick", a whimsical tune and "That's Something You Never Forget", a haunting ballad. The session also formed the song, "His Latest Flame", another up-tempo tune that became the highlight of these recordings.

The next song "Little Sister" was closer to his rock 'n' roll days and stood alongside "His Latest Flame" as the jewel of the session. Shortly after, the album *Something For Everybody* was released and marked Presley's sixth number one album. A single release of "His Latest Flame" got its first shot at the Irish charts in 2005, which saw it get a number twenty-one placement in Ireland on 10 March that year.

Another movie was soon in the works titled *Follow That Dream* and the title song was the only reasonable one among a total of six. After a break in Vegas, Elvis decided that it was time once again to go back into the recording studio and cut a few more songs. After doing dull movie tunes, it turned out that Elvis's new choice in music was not of a much higher standard. Songs such as "For The Millionth And The Last Time" and "Good Luck Charm" differed only slightly to his movie music, but the voice was always beguiling.

"Good Luck Charm" was later covered by Irish singer, Juliet Turner of Co. Tyrone. At the age of fifteen Juliet was given a guitar and began writing her own songs. In 1996 at University of Glasgow she was offered the chance to record her own work. Juliet soon began opening shows for musicians such as Bob Dylan and U2. Some of her songs include "Pizza And Wine" and "Indian Summer".

In September 1961, Elvis travelled to United Artists for production on *Kid Galahad*, a remake of the 1937 film. It was that very day that his album *Blue Hawaii* went into the U.S. album charts at number one and stayed on the charts for a total of seventy-nine weeks. Preproduction on the new movie involved six weeks of working out and training, as the movie was centred on boxing. The story involved the character of Walter Gulick (Elvis), a soldier who returns to his birthplace after serving time in the army. Seeking work as a mechanic he also gets a job as part-time boxer with a local club titled "Grogans Gaelic Gardens", run by Willy Grogan. The theme of the movie was quite Irish based as some of the characters were of Irish descent, including a Catholic priest. Elvis also wore a boxing robe embroidered with an Irish shamrock.

The actors included Oscar winner Gig Young as Willy Grogan and *Blue Hawaii* star Joan Blackman played Rose Grogan. Another cast member was the only Irish actor to hold a main part in an Elvis movie. The part of the Irish Catholic priest, Father Higgins, went to Liam Redmond. Liam was born on 27 July 1913 in County Limerick. He joined the famous Abbey Theatre in 1935 and made his stage debut in Sean O'Casey's *The Silver Tassie*. Redmond starred in many productions between America and Ireland, including a 1962 film version of John Millington Synge's *The Playboy of the Western World* and a 1975 film version of Brian Friel's *Philadelphia, Here I Come*. He died on 31 October 1989 in Dublin.

On the day *Blue Hawaii* opened nation-wide, Elvis bought a new home in L.A. *Blue Hawaii* was an extremely popular film and became one of his most famous works. The Irish premiere took place at the Adelphi Cinema on Middle Abbey St. in Dublin on 28 March 1962. The Irish release saw various scenes cut. These involved a seventeen year old girl, named Ellie, attempting to seduce Elvis's character. The scene cut showed her running into his room, jumping into the bed and saying "I'm in bed".

Another scene cut included Ellie implying that she did not wear underwear and Elvis referring to her as "Miss oversexed". A further scene deleted showed the same young actress disrobing on a beach for Elvis. O'Hora reported to the appeal board, stating, "Ninety-nine per cent of the viewers of this picture will not be more than nineteen years of age". He continued, that various delegations which included the Catholic Women's Secondary Schools Federation had approached him because of "the suggestiveness of every single picture in which Presley figured".

Despite the cuts and abhorrence from conservatives, Irish girls completely roared the cinemas down on first sight of Elvis. Irish radio presenter and singer, Maxi, of musical trio Maxi, Dick and Twink, recalled, "My teenage years were filled with his magic. Upon trips to the cinema we'd hold competitions to see who could scream the loudest or spot him first in his movies. In the end we settled for screaming at his name on screen in the opening titles. No artist has managed to command that adulation since".

Entering 1962, trips to Vegas and shopping sprees with girlfriends took up the time. The song "Good Luck Charm" was released and on St. Patrick's Day it entered the charts gaining Presley yet another new number one hit. Returning to the recording studio between 18 and 19 March eleven songs were recorded by Elvis. The best recordings included "Something Blue", "She's' Not You" and "Suspicion". Irish group Engine Alley recorded a cover of the famous Presley tune "Suspicion" in 1998. Engine Alley were formed in 1989 in Co. Kilkenny. The core musicians include Canice Kenealy, Brian Kenealy and Eamonn Byrne. Some of their songs include "Infamy" and "Switch".

A song recorded at Elvis's latest session, titled "You'll Be Gone" was one in which Presley is known to have contributed most of the writing. Despite this, Elvis's music was failing to match up to his earlier work. The days when he was a young boy absorbing the blues music in the early '50s and going with full force, aiming to be like his blues heroes, seemed to be disappearing. Elvis expressed magnificent vocal talent and this distinct quality continued.

The beauty in his singing was displayed with even greater clarity with these easy listening ballads but some were mostly forgettable tunes. He began drifting away from that rawness and perfection he began with in 1954. The sound was getting better as far as the technology in studio went and his voice improved but he was nowhere near those earlier days when he proved to be a musical genius, creating a new world.

CHAPTER TWELVE

The year of 1962 marked the first year in which Ireland finally began an official compilation of music chart hits. These Irish charts were first compiled on 2 October 1962 by broadcaster Jimmy Magee. The very first number one hit was Presley's "She's Not You", lasting six weeks on the charts. Equally as impressive is that the very first number one hit by an Irish artist was a Presley cover. Arriving on 16 August 1963 the Royal Irish Showband took the top spot with their version of Presley's "Kiss Me Quick", which remained in the charts for fourteen weeks.

Ireland having its own music charts was another step forward for a country to provide the youth with entertainment. The music charts in Ireland were more or less equal to those in Britain and usually when Presley had a number one hit there, that song was a hit in Ireland too. Elvis's following grew vastly around Ireland, especially during the '60s when most of his works were not as sharp edged as in the '50s. His style in the '60s, leaning more towards the conventional pop sensation rather than the greaser, did tend to make him more acceptable. Nonetheless, while the showbands were lighthearted amusement, Elvis Presley was like something completely alien.

Shortly after his last session, Elvis was on the set of *Girls! Girls! Girls!* but history repeated itself over and over. A movie was made, songs were recorded for it, Elvis would then record songs of his own choice and following a short break, the same thing just happened all over again. Elvis waited for that dramatic role he had always wanted but this showed signs of never arriving. He never used his star power to get his way and while people expected so much from him, he got little of what he wanted in return.

The movies were now already set to a certain style; a man appears, usually gets a job as a part time singer, beats up a few nasty fellows and gets the girl. Behind all this there was a hardly noticeable, but sometimes interesting plot, not worked on to full capacity. In *Girls! Girls! Girls!* Elvis played a shrimp boat captain and night-club singer. His objective is to raise enough money for a boat his deceased father built. Unfortunately a man with more money deliberately gets in the way, resulting in a fight to win it over. A slight resemblance could be made to that of the plot to the later Irish play *The Field* by John B. Keane, which also involved a struggle with an adversary to get some sentimental property. Although the Presley film was on a far lower artistic level, it was an example of a good idea not put to full use. The movie based itself mainly on several relationships and had a variety of songs popping up every so often.

Norman Taurog directed and Presley's co-stars included Jeremy Slate who went onto star in *The Lawnmower Man* (1992) with Irish actor Pierce Brosnan. The soundtrack again featured much atrocious material but one song stood out particularly well from the collection. Written by Otis Blackwell, ("Don't Be Cruel", "All Shook Up") the song "Return To Sender" made a major impact in the film. "Return To Sender" proved to be Ireland's very first Christmas number one hit, reaching the top spot on 10 December 1962. *Girls! Girls! Girls!* was later released in Ireland on 19 April 1963 at the Adelphi Cinema.

During this time *Follow That Dream* was released to cinemas with roaring followers racing to get their seats. The movie became the fifth most successful movie of its time, making Elvis Presley one of Hollywood's most popular stars. While the films were not fantastic, they suited their era. The beauty and vibrancy of the settings proved to be an enormous escape from a dull and repressive Ireland where, for a great many, hope in something celestial in life seemed nonexistent. The film was passed by the Irish censor and went on release in Ireland, as was *Kid Galahad*, which was released at the Savoy Cinema on O'Connell St., Dublin in January 1963.

Shortly after production was complete on the latest movie, Priscilla Beaulieu returned once again for another visit. Elvis discussed her stay with her parents and came to an agreement. Their journeys took them from Elvis's L.A. home to Las Vegas. He wanted to spend time with Priscilla and apparently they never encountered a sexual relationship. Her good cheer and compassion appealed to Elvis on an equal level to her exquisite good looks. However, his relationships with many women indicated that Elvis just couldn't seem to settle down and he found no reason to leave the exciting life of a bachelor.

Elvis's next assignment was *It Happened at the World's Fair*. The cast included an early role for Kurt Russell, who was eleven years old when given a part to kick Elvis in the shin. Kurt went on to play Presley in *Elvis* (1979). Elvis had Irish chart success with "One Broken Heart For Sale", a song from this film, reaching number five for four weeks on 11 March of 1963. The release of this film in Ireland took place on 16 August 1963 with *The Irish Times* claiming, "even Elvis Presley's nearest and dearest fans will be disappointed".

Towards the end of 1962 Elvis grew anxious about doing more live performances. However, this low exposure concept was important for Parker's strategy. The subversive days of "The King" had now diminished for a more relaxed, adult entertainer. The movies were enjoying great success because the fans were not seeing Presley anywhere else. Elvis was happy about the film success but was hesitant about making future pictures with the same plots as they left much to be desired. While the films lacked, Elvis was proceeding on his way to becoming one of Hollywood's highest paid actors.

Elvis's high earnings became known to such an extent, they even managed to get a mention during Ireland's government debates. On 11 December 1962, Fine Gael politician James M. Dillon made the statement, which involved and criticised Elvis Presley's finances. During a Dáil debate he stated, "It may seem incongruous that 'Elvis the Pelvis' enjoys an income ten times as great as the Prime Minister of England and five times as great as the President of the United States. The fact is that the public are prepared to pay more for the gyrations of 'Elvis the Pelvis', than they are prepared to pay for the wisdom, experience and fortitude of President Kennedy". Dillon's irreverent attack on Elvis and the general public could be seen as an indication of a greater concern for money rather than the necessity and obligation of a public servant to carry out their job.

* * *

The year of 1963 saw Ireland produce its first music magazine by John Coughlan under the name of *Spotlight*. Coughlan was a junior reporter for the *Cork Examiner* and with the support of dancehall owners, Peter and Philip Prendergast, the new magazine was launched initially for Cork music fans. Irish journalist Shay Healy, who notes that "Elvis was of primary importance to Spotlight", wrote for the magazine and explains that, "its popularity grew and it wasn't long before it hit the rest of the country and along the way it became the The Bible of Irish show business". The magazine brought to Ireland news coverage of all the latest music happenings in Ireland and abroad for over ten years.

At this time Elvis was about to set foot on a new film set. *Jailhouse Rock* director Richard Thorpe returned for Presley's next picture, *Fun in Acapulco*. At the end of January 1963 Elvis recorded a total of twelve songs for the film, including Leiber and Stoller's catchy pop tune "Bossa Nova Baby". Presley's female co-star was Ursula Andress, who had risen to fame in the 1962 Bond movie, *Dr. No*. Speaking to Irish talk show host Graham Norton, Ursula joked that she was forced to do the movie with Presley and she only had seen him as a wiggling, bumping and grinding kid. But after they first met she was completely astonished. Andress stated that he was one of the sweetest and most wonderful young men she ever met.

Presley's new session in Nashville was of his own choosing and presented, for the first time in a while, some quality tracks. These included "Memphis Tennessee" and "Devil In Disguise", which, originally intended for a new album, ended up only becoming soundtrack album fillers. The song "Devil In Disguise" was covered by Irish singers Shane MacGowan and Camille O'Sullivan on *The Late Late Show* in 2007.

On 9 July 1963, reporting into MGM, production and soundtrack recording for the new movie *Viva Las Vegas* began.

The film was originally released in Ireland under the title *Love in Las Vegas*. It was an amusing musical, co-starring Swedish actress Ann-Margret and would reach an apogee in the middle years of Elvis's movie career. The time spent with Ann-Margret brought the two musical stars together. Their relationship became one of most talked about entertainment news items. On the soundtrack, love songs such as "I Need Somebody" and "Today, Tomorrow And Forever" emphasised the tenderness of Elvis's vocals.

The best song included was the catchy title song, which Irish group the Thrills covered forty years later. The Thrills covered "Viva Las Vegas" with Presley's 1970s guitarist James Burton at "The UK Hall of Fame" awards in 2004. The Thrills include Daniel Ryan, Conor Deasy, Padraic McMahon, Ben Carrigan and Kevin Horan. The band set up in Dublin in 2001 and have had international success with the hits "Santa Cruz" and "So Much For The City".

By the middle of September *Viva Las Vegas* was in the can and Elvis was on his way home to Memphis. It was not long until he was in the door of Graceland that more plans were being discussed for his next movie, *Kissin' Cousins*. At the exact same time, producer Hal Wallis was arranging his next Paramount production, *Roustabout*. Full of obscure and silly songs *Kissin' Cousins* was a large step backwards from the movie he had just finished. Filming began on 7 October and location shooting took no longer than two weeks. From this, the producers, film executives, as well as Colonel Parker and other promoters realised how they could profit largely from such little work.

Not long after *Kissin' Cousins* came to an end, Christmas had arrived. With another donation of $55,000 to over fifty different Memphis charities, Elvis celebrated the season with Priscilla and the regulars. Parties at Graceland were exciting and nobody ever had a dull time. They would joke and enjoy the usual horseplay and a lot of people fell or were thrown into the swimming pool. Elvis arranged risky fireworks fights with his entourage. Jackets caught fire and some escaped serious injury but in the end everybody was left laughing.

Elvis kept up a great spirit even though moments of depression could lead to anger of considerable measure. It happened on various occasions that his mood swings resulted in him lashing out at people but he would often regret and apologise. Elvis continued to use the medication he had been introduced to in the army. He was now being encouraged to use diet pills by the studios when he started putting on weight. His increasing insomnia then lead to him becoming addicted to sleeping pills and it appeared this medicine altered his personality at times. He fired people on a whim and re-hired them shortly after again. No matter how often he got angry at someone, he would later have a calm conversation with them or take them for a drive or just hand them some expensive, elaborate gift.

1963 drew to a close. While Presley proved to be having great chart success in Ireland, even the popular Irish performers were having success with covers of songs Elvis made famous. Dickie Rock and the Miami Showband did a rendition of "Suspicion". They would also go on to gain a number one hit with Presley's "I'm Yours" the next year, followed by "Just For Old Times' Sake" which got to number two the year after that.

The Royal Irish Showband also had a number one victory with the Presley song "No More", hitting the top spot in mid-December. Another Irish singer by the name of Pat McGeegan recorded "Hawaiian Wedding Song" from Presley's *Blue Hawaii* and got a number seven hit in November of 1963. The following year was to introduce a very challenging time for Elvis. While his movie success was on an even keel, his music was on a slide. Could he or would he last much longer? The clock was ticking until someone else would take a leap ahead of "The King's" current success.

In the first month of 1964, Ireland's two top pop stars, Brendan Bowyer and Dickie Rock were interviewed for the Irish *Evening Press*. They were first asked about Elvis Presley and his importance on their careers. Bowyer claimed that Elvis was over the hill, having finally reached his peak and that his recent work had been "fairly weak", but added, "I've been influenced by him to a generous degree". Dickie Rock felt however, that Presley "wasn't over the hill as it was impossible to get a seat at his movies". Referring to Presley's influence on him, Rock stated, "I hold that virtually every pop star is influenced by Presley".

By this time in Ireland the beat groups were growing bigger. These groups differed in their method, skill and in their approach to music than the usual showbands. They were sometimes referred to as showbands in concept, but their musical style varied. One of the earliest examples of this new emergence on the Irish popular music scene was the Greenbeats, who began under the name the Caravelles. They originally formed in 1960 and featured musicians John Keogh and Paul Williams. They stood out for adopting more of an edge to rock music. While the Greenbeats appeared during the more famous showband era, they proved to be much different to the standard incarnation of what a showband was.

One of the most successful and renowned Irish beat performers was Van Morrison. Born in Belfast, Northern Ireland in 1945, Van was a singer and songwriter who became one of the world's leading rock stars of the 1960s. He joined the Monarch's Showband when he was fifteen and toured with them until 1963 when he joined the Gamblers. They later became known as "Them" and recorded the rock classic, "Gloria". Like Elvis, Morrison had a mixture of musical styles, blending jazz, R&B and Celtic folk music with traditional Irish ballads. Later on, in 1967, Van gained a solo recording contract which took him to New York. This then lead to his first U.S. hit, "Brown Eyed Girl". Morrison has enjoyed a career spanning over four decades and has worked with the traditional Irish folk group the Chieftans as well as being inducted into the Rock 'n' Roll Hall of Fame.

By 1964, not many foreign singers had sprung into the major spotlight in the U.S. but in Britain, one group was forming and achieving success. The Beatles who had originally got together in 1959 suddenly stepped in. Outside of the U.S., Britain was the country where sales of artists like Elvis, Little Richard and Jerry Lee Lewis had been astronomical. However, the golden era of rock 'n' roll music was coming to an end. The important artists who had founded and made the music appealing were either dead, retired or had left the genre. Elvis was still billed as a rock star and continuously known as the undisputed "King of rock" but his latest music in these years was far from rock 'n' roll. Elvis, who had dominated the music business through the late '50s into the early '60s was now fading away into a tedious movie career.

While Elvis now faded into Hollywood obscurity new musicians brought forward the work he had started. "By the coming of the beatgroups", John Keogh suggests, "Elvis had become more middle of the road and fifteen to twenty year olds were looking for their own music icons. So what made the Beatles and the rest of us do what we did?. Rock 'n' roll of course and it's greatest influence was Elvis".

The Beatles idolised Elvis and stated many times on radio shows and interviews that they looked up to him as their inspiration. On their first arrival in America they resembled an Irish showband with the tidy suits and clean look. In fact, Irish showbands had already been performing in their hometown of Liverpool, which had direct connections with Ireland. The Beatles had also played as a support act to the Royal Irish Showband on one occasion.

It was 7 February 1964 when the Beatles arrived in America to swarms of roaring fans in New York. Elvis wished the group great success and hoped that the people of America would be as kind to them as the people of Britain had been to him. Like Elvis, they were booked for the popular *The Ed Sullivan Show*.

The show had hosted many popular talents since Elvis, such as Cork born actor Edward Mulhare, three times between 1957 and 1959, the renowned Irish playwright Sean O'Casey in 1960 and Irish actor Peter O'Toole, twice in both 1963 and 1964. It had and would host the traditional Irish folk groups, the Clancy Brothers with Tommy Maken, four times between 1961 to 1966, the Chieftans in 1964, the Dubliners in 1968 and Limerick born actor, Richard Harris, twice in 1968. While performing on the show Parker and Elvis sent the Beatles a telegram congratulating them on their appearance on *The Ed Sullivan show* and their visit to America.

Elvis had not had a number one single in America in almost

two years. A long string of releases were still popping up on the market but each new single failed to chart at the top. Regardless of this, he still had many successes. The song "Return To Sender" which was released in October of '62 rose to the number two slot. Presley's "Devil In Disguise" got to number three in June of '63 but following this, as each single was released, the positions slipped. Nonetheless, it was astonishing for a man who was originally considered a fad to have his career going strong all these years later. While single sales slightly slowed in America, Ireland rushed for Elvis's pop songs as "Devil In Disguise" hit the Irish number one spot on 15 July 1963.

With regard to his albums, music lovers tired of the banal material as the standard of his work fell. Colonel Parker was just delighted that the movies were earning him easy money. *Fun In Acapulco* went to number three but the success of the movie soundtracks slowly waned. *Fun in Acapulco* was the first of Elvis's albums to share America's Billboard Top album chart with an Irish group. This group's album being *The Clancy Brothers and Tommy Maken In Person at Carnegie Hall*.

On 26 February 1964, Elvis began work on Paramount's *Roustabout*, playing a singing drifter who gets a job at a carnival. During production on *Roustabout*, *Kissin' Cousins* opened to the public. It became the eleventh top grossing movie on its release and the twenty-sixth most successful film of the year in the U.S., plus the title song made it to number six on Ireland's music charts. This was quite an amazing feat as these movies were up against the competition of more serious and dramatic pictures. This tripe made him millions of dollars but his talents were not used to full advantage. There were many frustrating moments during film making and Elvis became fed up easily as he desired a serious role but he had no say on each of the projects.

A scene in *Roustabout* included a "wall of death" where motorcyclists have to build up enough speed to ride sideways in a circular direction. This segment of the film influenced an idea used in the 1986 Irish movie, *Eat the Peach*. The film, starring Stephen Brennan, Eamon Morrissey, Niall Tóbín, Tony Doyle and Joe

Lynch told the story of two men who decide to build their own "wall of death" after been made redundant. Sitting in a pub where *Roustabout* is being played on TV they get their inspiration from the Elvis film to do something daring and different.

Around this time Elvis's ever growing interest in philosophy and faith reached a level higher than ever. Since the time of his mother's death he became very determined to understand the whole concept of finding reasons, truths and fundamental principles for the world and human existence. Purchasing many books, he studied and read about the particular field of philosophy in a desperate attempt to broaden his knowledge. His love of people and sensitivity over family deaths had urged him to educate himself on the situation of life and death. He began to broaden his mind further than general Christian preaching.

Elvis became more and more inquisitive about the mysteries of life and why he had been chosen to be this huge success. With special guidance he began reading books about spirituality. Elvis began to research and privately study numerology, cosmology and metaphysics. Not before long Elvis had a library of books on these subjects. Elvis also learned about Judaism and showed an interest by studying its beliefs and wore a Jewish "chai" around his neck. His increasing mission to find meanings for all actions became essential to his life.

Often staying up into the early hours of the morning reading, he would glide through each book as they kept him engrossed with fascinating theories. However, Elvis didn't let his studies completely consume him. He once profoundly explained to a friend, "Love is the bottom line. It's not religion, it's love and that's where we should work from always". This indicated his ability to see the extreme difference between religion and humanity.

During the early part of 1964 a Las Vegas newspaper ran a story headlined, "Elvis helped in success of Burton-O'Toole movie". The story told of how Elvis Presley was responsible for the current success of actors Richard Burton and Irish star Peter O'Toole. It claimed that the profits from Presley's pictures were being put forward to helping the completion of more serious pictures, including these two actor's new picture, *Becket*. This infuriated Elvis as he came to realise that he was not being taken seriously as an actor and while his movies were not the greatest it seemed as if nobody was ever going to give him a chance.

He not only expressed immense anger but much inner hurt too as he realised how things were not going his way in an area in which he was eager to accomplish. Presley didn't express a problem towards Burton or O'Toole but rather towards Parker and Wallis for doing nothing for him. Elvis actually admired the Connemara, Co. Galway born O'Toole for his roles in *Lawrence of Arabia* (1962) and his later part next to Peter Sellers in *What's New Pussycat?* (1965).

On 17 June *Viva Las Vegas* opened across America and instantly became a smash hit. *Girl Happy* then went into production in late June. The next movie after that went into production in October 1964 under the title *Tickle Me*. One of his co-stars in this was Irish born Angela Greene who starred as Donna. Angela was born on 24 February 1921 in Dublin and at a young age moved to New York. She became a model and also gained parts in a wide variety of Hollywood classics throughout the 1940s and '50s including *Mildred Pierce* (1945). She died from a stroke at the age of fifty-six on 9 February 1978.

For 1964 the Irish had given Elvis a number five victory with "Ain't That Lovin' You Baby", a number eight success with "Viva Las Vegas" and a number nine hit with "Such A Night". "Ain't That Loving You Baby" landed in the charts again in 1987 when it became a Top 30 hit on 30 April in Ireland.

The sun set on 1964 and the year had brought more success but few challenges. At this stage the name "Elvis" had become a household name across the planet but there were worries of decline. The new year would bring new ideas, new films and songs and wishes remained for concert performances. Elvis remained the biggest star in the world but the movies were what kept him famous. It was the only way for people outside America, such as his Irish admirers, to get a chance to see him.

Portrait of Elvis by Don Conroy

Elvis 56 by Nuala Holloway

Elvis in the Army by Nuala Holloway

Elvis in the Army II by Nuala Holloway

Elvis 68 by Nuala Holloway

Elvis 72 by Nuala Holloway

Elvis 73 by Nuala Holloway

Gods of Rock: Elvis, Phil and Rory by Jakki Moore

Chapter Thirteen

By 1965 Ireland had opened up a little further to the modern music industry. It was this year that the country first entered the *Eurovision*, which gathered singers from European countries to compete in a song contest, beamed across the continent. Although the quality of songs could have matched most of Presley's movie soundtracks, Ireland turned out to be the most victorious in the contest, winning it seven times throughout the next thirty years. The show did create fame for some singers but it usually maintained a garish standard with only a few possible exceptions.

Years later, in 1994 with a change of pace from the typical whimsical pop songs, Irish musicians Paul Harrington and Charlie McGettigan performed "Rock 'n' Roll Kids" - a nostalgic song which solemnly reminisced on how a group of youngsters were devoted to the early rock 'n' roll songs they used to listen to on the radio. It was a song which showed how Ireland had moved with the times in order to experience some of the culture changes that Elvis set. The song focused on an important era with rock stars like Elvis, bringing, not only the musicians, but everybody else who experienced this time, to look back with fond memories.

By the mid-1960s, modern music kept progressing in Ireland and new musicians broke free to fulfil their passions in an ever changing country. Ireland had developed an incredibly fresh and extensive Beat scene between the mid to late '60s. Bands such as the Kingbees, the Strangers, the Creatures and the Chessmen brought the country further into the realms of modern popular music. 1965 also saw a British born student of Trinity College, Dublin, named Ian Whitcomb, along with Irish beatgroup Bluesville, go to number eight in the American charts with the song, "You Turn Me On". It was also around this time a musician named Rory Gallagher began a professional music career with a showband.

Gallagher was born in County Donegal on 2 March 1948 and was raised in Cork. He first began playing, at the age of sixteen, with the Fontana Showband, which later became known as the Impact Showband. This stint in a showband came about as there was no other type of groups being formed at the time. There was nowhere else for musicians to perform and unfortunately for serious blues and rock fans, a showband was the only place to go.

Rory first discovered a passion for rock music after seeing Elvis Presley on TV and hearing him on Radio Luxembourg. When he was eleven, he became very enthusiastic about all kinds of music and it was Presley among others which inspired him. Rory once said in an interview, "When I was growing up and I heard Elvis Presley . . . I was gone". Rory had a large collection of Elvis records and he was another person Presley helped introduce to the blues. "How could anyone not relate to 'Jailhouse Rock' and 'Heartbreak Hotel'?", he asked.

After seeing Elvis perform on television Rory purchased his first guitar and his desire for making music began. Once he started performing he added to other songs and conveyed a very liberal feel in his music with overtly sexual connotations. Since he was still at school once he started in the popular music field, the Christian Brothers were outraged that a pupil of theirs would have any association with rock 'n' roll and reacted with hostility. At the age of eleven, after Rory had received and learned how to play his first guitar, he began looking for audiences to entertain so he entered talent contests. Sharing a similarity with Presley, Rory was just as devoted to his music as he was a sensitive young boy.

In 1967, with the expansion of the international rock scene, Rory progressed as a musician when he formed the group Taste. However it was 1965 which set the foundations for his future success. He would escape the showband phase in order to establish himself as a serious blues artist. From there he became Ireland's first rock star who blazed a trail for many more who were yet to come. Some of his best tracks included "Shadow Play" and "Bullfrog Blues". Through his thirty year career he sold fourteen million records and became internationally respected, not only for his talent, but for being a gentle and dignified man. He was a musician whose soul was deeply involved in his perspicacious passion for performing the incisively fervent sounds of the blues.

After Elvis Presley had proven to the world that a white man could perform the blues, Rory proved that an Irishman could do it too. Presley was one of Rory's most favourite musicians for whom he held great admiration. He later owned two lithographs of "The King" which he hung on his wall, one which included an old Presley concert ticket. Not only did he admire Elvis for his music but for his character, personality, artistic merit and professional attributes. Rory maintained that the biggest regret of his life was missing Elvis live in concert by just one night during a tour of New York. Sadly, after years of securing his name as a talented blues musician, Rory tragically died from alcohol poisoning in 1995.

With the introduction of new successful performers in 1965, many claimed Elvis's time had passed. He was not drawing the same sales as before. The music had really gone downhill and he wasn't delivering his own music through concert appearances. He knew something had to be done, but what? In February, MGM began preparation for *Harum Scarum*. The title song, "Harem Holiday" would be used as the film title in Ireland. Elvis detested the film and it was at the bottom of a barrel full of bad movies, with another insipid soundtrack. With *Harum Scarum* in production, *Girl Happy* opened. The line had now been crossed. There were too many predictable, pointless and appalling films. Parker's tactics of keeping Elvis a respected star were crumbling. The criticisms and the exhaustion of wasting Elvis's time doing unproductive work in Hollywood enraged him.

Nobody could understand why Elvis didn't just leave. However, there was an honest loyalty that he sustained for his manager. What has to be put into perspective is Elvis's background. From the way he was raised, he would not have comprehended expressing disrespect by contradicting his manager's decisions. Parker had made Elvis - "ELVIS!" - the greatest phenomenon in entertainment history. Parker did have a great sense of humour and many found him an interesting person but there was no doubt about his shrewdness.

While Elvis enjoyed the immense earnings from his films he

wanted to make movies which were far more challenging, creative and compelling. As the great Irish writer Jonathan Swift once said, "A wise man should have money in his head but not in his heart". Elvis wanted to make movies but not the ones that lacked meaning. His management was failing to tend to his artistic potential. The star was falling and nobody could hide the fact that bands such as the Beach Boys, the Rolling Stones and the sounds of Motown were flying right passed the one time dominator of the music industry.

Elvis was mocked for his films and critics easily forgot his original importance in the business. A new stereotype of being the product of sheer commercialism began to cling to his reputation. Regarding this commercialism, Parker could only see a product. Presley, on the other hand, was an artist, a genuine creator of sounds, not conforming to anything with category but rather instinctive emotions, longing to express all his feelings in an original and wondrous style.

These attributes were what *The Irish Times* literary correspondent Eileen Battersby discovered. Having spent much time an admirer of the all time classical greats, such as Beethoven and Mozart, Battersby found herself hearing the beauty of Elvis's voice as he sang one of his deep love songs. She remarked, "this guy's a really good singer, he had vulnerability, an emotional intelligence, a multiplicity of voices, of styles, genuine musicality. Most of all, you can understand every word".

With anything as immensely popular as Elvis Presley, there will always be quibblers and with Elvis a divide has emerged from critics who enjoy launching scathing attacks on him. One cheap shot is usually his movie career. Nonetheless the endeavours of some critics to ridicule him for his movies is nonsensical in the twenty-first century as it has been well highlighted how he detested these himself. Then there is the lack of writing songs which is another weak attack and rush to judgement, emphasising the inability to look deeper. Because of an increasing rush to judgement, Elvis is a largely misunderstood artist. Nothing about Elvis was black and white. Nothing was simple enough to conger up in one line.

Presley's cultural impact is immense and sometimes this can make him seem too perfect for the critics who attack him. For his initial reputation he did get lucky but that fame and fortune came from the workings and formation of the most radical culture change seen in a long time. His impact helped lead to the formation of every great rock act to follow in America but equally as much in a country such as Ireland.

What must be realised is how the roots of Elvis were as far down-to-earth as one could imagine. This is the story of a poverty stricken boy who strove for success and adapted his inner spiritual emotions to bring out all meaning in what became an inspirational interpretation of songs. Throughout his entire life, he appeared to be a combination of everything. There will never be one stereotype for who and what Elvis was. He sang with a drawl, he sang clearly and his diction was perfectly precise when a song required that style. He was gospel, he was rock. He was country, he was blues. He did good music, he did bad music. He was a good actor, he was a bad actor. He did good movies, he did bad movies. He was rich, he was poor. He could easily curse but could also express some of his own profound philosophical theories. He was cool, he was uncool. He was liberal, he was conservative. He was black, he was white. He was multicoloured. The list goes on with the vast mixture of characters he was.

Elvis Presley was a spiritual performer first and a rock 'n' roller second. Music was his life. It became the meaning of his life and he gracefully exhibited it. He continued his search for meaning and this became an important element of his life as he interlinked it with his music. There was a higher spirit which he desperately sought to discover but he knew that his place was to be a performer and bring enjoyment. If anybody ever wanted to fulfill a goal, Elvis did it to the very optimum.

Some critics argue he only used his sex symbolism to succeed. However, the sexual implications in his performance were simply a reflection of the music. It was the animalistic sexual nature rooted in the music. When covering a song with meaning, he did it with meaning, singing tears and yearning efficaciously. Passion was essential with Presley because that was what he found fundamental in music. Elvis's genius came from being able to vocally explain the consciousness in songs, in his own unique way.

* * *

In April 1965, Elvis's gospel gem "Crying In The Chapel" hit the charts. It reached the top spot in America and in June 1965, it also got to number one in the Irish charts. For the week ending 24 July 1965, Ian Whitcomb's song "You Turn Me On" would share America's Billboard Hot 100, while at number ten, with Elvis's releases of "Crying In The Chapel", "Such An Easy Question", "It Feels So Right" and the *Tickle Me* EP. Also in the same official chart for that week, at twenty-four was "Here Comes The Night" by Northern Irish group Them. A re-issue of "Crying In The Chapel" gave the song another chance in the Irish charts, reaching number twenty-six on 21 April 2005.

Just three weeks after walking from *Harum Scarum*, MGM's new movie, *Frankie and Johnny*, a period drama with unpalatable music, went into production. The film was to be directed by Frederick DeCordova, who had previously directed Ireland's Maureen O'Sullivan in *Bonzo Goes to College* (1952). Not too long after, production was set up for the new Paramount movie, *Paradise: Hawaiian Style*. While staying at Illikani Hotel in Hawaii, the group met the famous Irish actor, Richard Harris, who was also a guest there while making his film, *Hawaii*. Richard, originally from Co. Limerick, used to regale Presley's group with many amusing stories on the hotel patio and Elvis enjoyed his company.

Soundtrack recording commenced and again, nothing new, nothing offered, nothing gained. Elvis had to put up with cutting "A Dogs Life" and "Datin' ". At some point during each soundtrack session there would be a stage when Elvis got suddenly angered. Going from song to song, he became embarrassed with certain tunes. Then other times he just laughed through each take, knowing the stuff was complete nonsense. Usually he just suffered an anomalous rate of boredom recording them. It was obvious Elvis was overwrought because none of it was meritorious.

While in Hollywood, the Beatles met Elvis at his home and plans for a meditation garden at Graceland went underway. This section of the grounds became a tranquil place at his home for Elvis to relax and meditate. A new radical form of popular culture was on the horizon and an open-minded approach to spirituality was being discovered. While others got public attention for their interest into Eastern philosophy, Elvis was seen to be out of touch. Little did people know that he had already privately researched Eastern philosophy himself and had become involved in the Self-Realisation Fellowship, spending time at the Lake Shrine retreat. Presley found this one of the most important factors of his life.

While Elvis was making those silly movies and had faded from the rebel spotlight, the new liberals of America and around the world were forming a new revolution. The late '60s saw the birth of the "hippie" in the wake of war protesting. This was combined with the civil and human rights movements, which became a defining factor of the 1960s and early '70s. Most of the young popular singers reflected these changes and it lead to new fashions, new styles of music and new ways of life.

Although these new artists had grown up with admiration for Elvis, his popular image was declining. However, what now dominated music didn't concern Elvis a great deal. He had become more interested in entertaining a maturer audience. The "hippies" were an extension of the social rebellion created by the 1950s rock musicians. They followed the trend Elvis had set of long hair and side burns, which he had been mocked for in the '50s.

In Ireland, a country which was gradually coming closer to adapting with modern times throughout the rest of the Western world, civil rights movements also took effect. Not as much to the vast extent as in Britain or America but these countries' influences made an impact on many Irish youths. Throughout Europe and including Ireland, the late '60s brought about many student protests. The aim was to stand up against a one dimensional society and system. Something Elvis did through his music and actions in the '50s.

The composer Leonard Bernstein was one to realise Presley's

'50s impact taking effect on the '60s. He explained, "Elvis is the greatest cultural force in the twentieth century. He introduced the beat to everything, music, language, clothes. It's a whole new social revolution - the '60s comes from it". Elvis helped set a trend of powerful and determined rebelliousness for young people to pursue what they desired.

While Presley was one of the first voices for the teenage generation, he never comprehended making any formal statements or expressing opinions. His mind was implanted in his music. Whatever way his music would be interpreted he was only doing things the way he emotionally felt. After Elvis a chain reaction of occurrences transpired and anybody, no matter what their background was, could have a say on something. It was realised that if rock artists could change society with music, anybody could change society with more focused issues.

A special moment of change in Ireland occurred in February 1966, when the Bishop of Clonfert, Dr. Thomas Ryan protested at the content of RTÉ's *The Late Late Show* the previous Saturday. During the programme, host Gay Byrne asked a married man what colour his wife's honeymoon night dress had been. The man replied that it was transparent, but his wife said she hadn't worn one at all. RTÉ bowed to the complaint and apologised. However, such an issue proved the powerful liberation TV could provide in Ireland. Exactly ten years after Elvis had used television to ignite a firestorm of controversy, the likes of which America had never seen before, Ireland now also used that powerful instrument to shake up a nation. Both issues fused anger from authorities and both had also centred on sexual suggestiveness.

In March 1966 when a Trinity College student named Brian Trevaskis was on *The Late Late Show*, a heated debate on the role of the Catholic Church in Ireland became a major topic. Brian criticised the Dublin Archbishop John Charles McQuaid in relation to the treatment of a novelist named John McGahern who had been dismissed from his job, simply because a book of his was banned. This discussion lead to Trevaskis calling the Bishop of Galway, Michael Browne, a "moron" in front of the entire country and later questioning the same Bishop if he knew the meaning of the word "Christianity".

These events were a sign of the direction Ireland was taking. At last, some citizens of the country were challenging highly questionable authority. Just like Elvis, some of it was unintentionally controversial, but just like Elvis it all reflected a radical attitude. Western culture had progressed a lot more from the 1950s and Elvis was no longer seen as culturally significant but nothing could deny his everlasting impact. The revolution of the time provided encouragement to rebel against the system. Rock 'n' roll had helped pave this path, Elvis Presley's daring nature on television influenced new attitudes and the rebel spirit of American popular culture assisted a shake up to soporific societies.

The Irish showbands, who still enjoyed success mostly in rural locales, were put aside by most modern young people in favour of the popular British and American artists of the times. The Beatles and the Rolling Stones performed concerts in Ireland and introduced themselves to new people while attempts had been made to keep Elvis and 1950s rock from the ears of the Irish youth. The time of Elvis's appeal to young people on a mass level seemed over. He was not the hyped and continuously talked about entertainer anymore. His movies had little attraction among popular culture. Then what he recorded himself seemed too prosaic for young people who made up the charts with their purchase of rock 'n' roll records. Elvis still attracted a broad following but the days of his domination had sunk to an all time low.

Chapter Fourteen

In early February 1966 Elvis began work on the next movie, *Spinout*. One afternoon on the set of the film, which would be released as *California Holiday* in Ireland, Elvis met Irish showband star Brendan Bowyer. Bowyer who had spent the early '60s as Ireland's most popular and successful showband performer, moved out to Las Vegas in 1966. While the showband phase had reached its height in Ireland, Bowyer realised a move was in order, to reach bigger and better things.

Through his contacts in America Brendan got a call one morning that he could have an opportunity to meet Presley that day. A tired and unshaven Bowyer jumped up right away not to miss the opportunity. That afternoon Elvis came walking towards the Irish group, singing a few bars of the Irish classic "Galway Bay", greeted his fans and posed for a photograph with Bowyer. Nonetheless, this would not be their only time to meet as they would be reunited and become closer friends a few years later.

By 25 May 1966 Elvis had not recorded any non-soundtrack songs in three years. In that time there had been many new producers of the sessions working for RCA but his most recent recording session in 1963 was the last time Steve Sholes worked with him. Steve was the man who along with Parker had helped Elvis to the top of show business. He played a major part in the rising career of Elvis Presley. The new producer was Felton Jarvis, who was more suited to the nocturnal lifestyle of Presley.

With the last few years of Elvis's personal interests mainly centred around spirituality, there was no better choice of music for him than gospel. At home he would sit around with his entourage and family and pass the time singing favourite songs, sometimes recording them with his own recording equipment. Many of these included his favourite gospel songs and one such track was "Oh How I Love Jesus". It was written by the English-born Frederick Whitfield who attended Trinity College in Dublin and had this hymn printed while at Trinity in 1855.

A new spiritual album was in mind for Elvis including such songs as "Run On", "Without Him" and "How Great Thou Art". One of the many performers who have recorded "How Great Thou Art" since, include "International Irish tenor", Mark Forrest. Born in Dublin, Mark began to gain notoriety as a tenor after studying at the Royal College of music. Basing himself mainly in America, Mark has become a respected tenor. Forrest has also coincidentally recorded up to fifteen songs which Elvis also did and this fully confirms Elvis's broad range of music as this is all music distant from rock or pop.

The recordings which both Mark and Elvis share the common interest in have included the traditional and commonly recorded spiritual gems, "I Believe", "You'll Never Walk Alone", "I'll Be Home For Christmas", "Winter Wonderland" and a selection of other Christmas classics. "How Great Thou Art" would also become a number five hit for the Irish showband Kelly and The Nevada in 1972.

Presley's versions of his latest gospel songs were beautifully articulated and completed with a subtle and deep felt conviction. His vocal range expanded, but more importantly the affection was so easily and convincingly triggered. Like all the music he so deeply cared about, he sustained a dedication and effort. Usually he would close his eyes to shut out all distractions and used his mental vision to glide him through the performances. His heart lay amply in gospel music and "How Great Thou Art" was the total proof of the fantastic quality he sustained. In his lifetime, he won only three Grammy awards and these were all for his gospel work.

Despite the gospel recordings Elvis again kept the music taste diverse at this session. "Down In The Alley" brought him back to his earlier encounters in the studio, oozing a raunchy sexual rhythm. Admiring Bob Dylan's writing he chose "Tomorrow Is A Long Time". One other song done throughout the session was "Love Letters". Even though Presley had recorded much easy listening material from 1960 to 1963 this song outdid many of those. By July of '66 it had come in at number seven on Ireland's charts.

As the main concentration for the session was gospel, Elvis hired the Imperials for additional harmony. They brought a new energy to the session and worked with Elvis for many more years. After a brief break, several weeks later they finished off the remaining tracks which were "Indescribably Blue", "I'll Remember You" and "If Every Day Was Like Christmas". Each one of the songs had feeling and compassion. Elvis was back on track now and everything began to look bright once again. "If Every Day Was Like Christmas" reached the Irish Top 10 just in time for Christmas of 1966.

The session indicated how Elvis was beginning to experiment again, to re-discover himself and break away from the films. "Down In The Alley" and "Tomorrow Is A Long Time" set a great change of pace for Presley but became underrated classics. Most of the songs from this session became soundtrack fillers and it was another wasted opportunity for Elvis to show signs of self-liberation from Hollywood.

At the time when all hopes were on a high, MGM called Elvis out for his new movie *Double Trouble*. Following this film Elvis began work on *Easy Come, Easy Go*, co-starring actor Frank McHugh. This was Frank's last movie after appearing in over one hundred pictures including *The Irish In Us* (1935) and another movie titled *Easy Come, Easy Go* (1947), whose lead star that time was Irish actor Barry Fitzgerald.

On his latest break away from any music or movie production Elvis began to take a keen interest in horses. He began purchasing many and used the field behind Graceland as a place for the horses to graze. Then he started giving horses to friends and family. He built stables and often went trekking in the grounds of Graceland. To this day Graceland is a home for horses, including many that have been put out to stud.

His love for Priscilla remained the same and this lead to a more loving relationship as they became more than good friends. She seemed the right woman for him, despite his regular affairs with other women. However, many of these women didn't appeal to him in the same way. Priscilla Beaulieu was the most important of them all. This lead to the event which took place, when on Christmas Eve Elvis proposed to Priscilla. The big question had been popped and Priscilla accepted.

In early 1967, travelling to Mississippi, Elvis purchased a one hundred and sixty-three acre ranch as it provided space for his increasing stables. Caught up in all this activity, he began to forget about work. Parker had been settling new deals and further plans from movie companies went into production. His upcoming film was titled *Clambake*. It took time to get Elvis into the recording studio to begin work as his enthusiasm for his new ranch had completely turned him in the opposite direction of Hollywood. It came to a stage that he didn't even think about the drudgery of film making. Back at the ranch Elvis called on a doctor, apparently suffering from saddle soars. A recommendation of Doctor George Nichopoulos (also known as Dr. Nick) was given to Elvis. Calling the doctor was only an excuse to keep away from work.

Despite the mediocrity of his movies some people managed to gain great enjoyment from them, if only for their good cheer or vague story. In the group's 1988 documentary *Rattle and Hum*, Dublin drummer Larry Mullen of the legendary Irish rock group U2 recollected watching Presley's films and commented, "I love the Elvis movies" and he described how that in his movies Elvis "wasn't acting as a car salesman - he was acting as a car salesman who loved to play the guitar. I could relate to that". If only in an extremely mediocre way, the movies often represented what Elvis had been about; a regular guy with a regular job, who loves to play music in his spare time.

During production, Elvis fell and hit his head while in the bathroom. Although nothing serious occurred from the accident, he still had to rest for several days. Soon after recovering, *Clambake* filming came to an end and his marriage to Priscilla was just around the corner, set for 1 May. Around this time, *Easy Come, Easy Go* and *Double Trouble* were released to cinemas within weeks of each other. After years of these senseless pictures succeeding exceptionally well at the box office, now the senseless pictures were failing. Reaching the fiftieth and fifty-eighth position for the year, each film did miserably. Rather than giving the standard scathing review of Elvis movies, *The Irish Times* film correspondent Fergus Linehan, reviewing *Double Trouble,* wrote "one thing that can be said for Elvis Presley: he's hard-working. Hardly a month seems to go past but there he is popping up again in the Adelphi". However, Elvis was slipping and it was time to start setting his sights on something more constructive.

The wedding day arrived with the ceremony taking place at the Aladdin Hotel in Las Vegas. The news of the marriage was printed by the press internationally. Ireland's *Evening Press* printed two separate photographs of Priscilla and Elvis on their front page. At the time, the Adelphi Cinema in Dublin cashed in on the hype and repeated a screening of the ten year old movie *Jailhouse Rock*. Although the couple's love for each other was genuine, the marriage was one way of getting some well needed publicity. Parker had been pushing the idea as it would guarantee newspaper headlines.

Elvis was not the marrying kind and did not want to get married but it was the only logical way of keeping Priscilla by his side. After the wedding in Vegas, the two travelled out to Palm Springs for a two day honeymoon. They were accompanied by all the entourage which was a visible sign of his everlasting insecurity. It was not the typical marriage and Elvis was not the makings of a normal husband but rather a fellow who wanted to hang out with the lads. Afterwards, things were back to normal. Priscilla and Elvis who had already lived together for years, still lived together. It was just that now they were legally bound to one another.

On 17 May 1967 Presley's film *Spinout* premiered for Irish moviegoers at the Ritz Cinema in Ballsbridge, Dublin, under the title *California Holiday*. A month later, on 19 June, Elvis reported into MGM for the beginning of his new picture, *Speedway*, which based Elvis again as a singer and racing car driver. For the first time since Ann-Margret, another big star played the part of the leading lady and this would be singer/actress Nancy Sinatra.

Soon after the wedding it was announced that Priscilla was pregnant. With a baby on the way and a marriage in its early stages, it was time to start living a more settled life. However, after Priscilla gave birth, Elvis rarely, if ever, slept with her again. She had been a friend, a companion. He had, in a certain way, found her the replacement to his mother. Once a woman had become a mother he believed they were to be treated like one. Despite this, he was undoubtedly delighted about the pregnancy. Bursting with testosterone and ferocious sexual drive, it appeared their marriage was not meant to be as Elvis had many other women. It was not long until Priscilla sensed something, but she carried on with the idea of making things work.

After taking up a new interest at his ranch which involved gun target practice, Elvis purchased rifles and other shooting equipment. This remained a hobby for a short while until the decision came about to sell the ranch.

In early September in Nashville, work began on a new non-soundtrack album and he kicked off the session with a great country rock tune titled "Guitar Man". Following this number came the energetic blues song "Big Boss Man". Although the session had struck off to a great start, most of the following songs did not carry the same glory. Some were quite prosaic such as "Singing Tree" and "Just Call Me Lonesome". However, it was all brightened up again with the inspired gems, "We Call On Him" and "You'll Never Walk Alone".

On meeting Elvis, Jerry Reed, who wrote several of the songs and played guitar on this session, was stunned by his incredible beauty. Elvis has proven to be one of the only men who can be admired for his looks by all sexes and sexualities. Irish journalist and presenter Brendan O'Connor humorously remarked, "It's a known fact that if you ask any heterosexual man which other man he would sleep with, if he had to sleep with another man, he would probably be Elvis".

Soon again Elvis was back on a film set, this time titled *Stay Away Joe*. Elvis's co-star was actor Burgess Meredith, whose other works have included acting in Broadway productions of the Irish plays *Playboy Of The Western World* and *Major Barbara* and a TV production of Samuel Beckett's *Waiting For Godot*. He also directed a broadway adaptation of part of Irish writer James Joyce's *Ulysses* and narrated a track on an album for the Irish traditional group the Chieftans.

As *Stay Away Joe* began filming *Clambake* got its cinema release and went to fifteen in the movie polls for a week. The movie's Irish premiere took place at the Royal cinema, Bray, Co. Wicklow on Thursday 12 December the following year.

1967 offered very little to Elvis's career and it appeared he was drifting away from the entertainment business. Then suddenly, Parker began arrangements for a TV show for the following Christmas. The Colonel had arranged many TV appearances for Elvis to be part of, ever since 1960 and the Sinatra show, but nothing ever went ahead. Parker demanded his selected charges but never got them and with nothing happening outside Hollywood, it was time to make a deal and go with it for once. This new project was only in the early stages and Parker pictured Elvis performing an hour of Christmas songs. However, Elvis had other ideas. He saw this as a chance to do something else as the movie contracts began to run out.

Nobody in Ireland had ever seen Elvis perform and this was not just because he hadn't come here but because he wasn't doing shows, in person or on TV. The only way Irish people knew he existed came from the record releases or fluffy movies, which had been his only introduction to the Irish people. There was no insight into who this man was, which was highly irregular with any other performing star. Everybody got to know the Rolling Stones and the Beatles but Elvis became a mythical figure. There were no guest appearances or TV interviews, not just in Ireland but even in America.

Within twelve years of a popular career Elvis had only appeared on TV thirteen times and other than the Sinatra special, these appearances had been made eleven years previously. He needed to do something new that could bring him back in contact with an audience, even if it was a TV audience at first. It was definitely time to get down to business.

Chapter Fifteen

The year 1968 began with negotiations, deals and agreements for a TV project concerning Elvis at NBC TV studios. For the first time in nearly eight years he was going to make a return to television. The public had rarely seen the real Elvis over the years and this low exposure was making him forgettable.

On 16 January Elvis was back in Nashville for a brief session which formed his cover of the Chuck Berry tune, "Too Much Monkey Business". An outtake of this track includes another sudden burst by Presley into the song, "When Irish Eyes Are Smiling". Elvis then covered Jerry Reed's "U.S. Male", which eventually only got to twenty-eight in America, but gave Elvis an Irish number twelve hit the following June. This would prove to be the final recording session with Scotty Moore and D. J. Fontana.

Despite plans going into operation for the show, nothing got in the way of the event that was about to take place. On 1 February 1968, exactly nine months to the day of their wedding, Priscilla Beaulieu Presley gave birth to a baby girl, which they named Lisa Marie. Elvis was elevated with delight and "The Memphis Mafia" recalled that it was possibly the greatest moment of his life. It was a feeling that transformed Elvis and built the best motivation for his forthcoming projects.

Soon after, MGM had him booked for *Live a Little, Love a Little*, a lighthearted tale of sex and obsession with a short soundtrack including the song "A Little Less Conversation". Meanwhile the Colonel was currently sorting out all deals for the upcoming TV show. What Elvis wanted was to go into new areas completely different to anything he had done before and he worked closely with director Steve Binder. Elvis loved Binder's frame of mind and was delighted to be working with him. The suggestion was to create a show that was different but captivating, new and exciting and present Elvis Presley in a fantastic new format. It was his return to the stage and an important moment to see where he stood in the music business.

Elvis took his family to Hawaii and during this time he lost weight and got into the best shape of his life. He grew back his sideburns which he had cut off for the last eight years. Eight years which kept him clean cut and conservative. This time the sideburns, which were one of his own fashion trend trademarks, were longer. Elvis was again a symbol which appealed to both sexes. His music incarnated testosterone and with the self-mocking, he remained a perfect idol for men too. Northern Ireland-born broadcaster, Eamonn Holmes said, "I like Elvis because he's a man's man and yet a woman's man as well. So many stars are exclusive to either women liking them or men liking them, but I think that it's not unmanly to say you like Elvis".

While the golden era of rock 'n' roll had diminished along with greasers, Elvis saw the chance to show how he kept modern and went over ideas on how to approach the show. A set was constructed at NBC TV in Burbank, California and Elvis met with costume designer Bill Belew to arrange something special to wear. For the main part of the show Elvis was set to wear a black leather outfit. Elvis grew excited as a definitive plan lay out went into production. The opening segment had Elvis with a guitar performing the song "Guitar Man" in front of a gigantic hoarding stating E-L-V-I-S, all done out with red light bulbs.

Joining him on stage in front of a small audience were his original band members Scotty Moore and D. J. Fontana with Charlie Hodge on guitar and adding vocals. By suggestion of Steve Binder, the attitude in rehearsals would be kept similar while cameras were rolling. In one segment the group just sat back in a small square stage, had informal interactions and made sure to get in a certain amount of songs. It didn't matter if they made mistakes, forgot lines, lyrics or miss a note. Throughout these performances Elvis seemed to be distant from all his entourage and more in touch with Scotty and D. J. A sheer sign of how great it would have been for his personal life, health and well being to return to his original group.

The concept of a seated informal show in a small space later became the most important influence for MTV's "Unplugged" sessions. It was the beginning of something that added a great deal to how music was presented. It helped audiences get closer and more in touch with their favourite musicians who played raw without studio mixing. MTV "Unplugged" lead to the creation of some critically acclaimed albums for groups such as Nirvana. It has also been an advantage to groups such as Ireland's the Corrs, a 1990s family music group who mixed Irish traditional music with an international pop sound.

Between 20 and 23 June, the musicians began recording "Trouble", "Guitar Man", "It Hurts Me" and "Big Boss Man" for a dramatic section of the show. The next piece covered was for a gospel segment, which showed the vast range of musical interest Elvis had adopted. Another tune recorded but never used for the final edit of the show was a new version of "A Little Less Conversation". This version was a rawer cut making it more exciting than the original. Although it never made it into the TV special, it was resurrected by Northern Ireland composer, David Holmes who used the song as the soundtrack composer for the 2001 movie, *Ocean's Eleven*.

Holmes was a fan of Elvis and said that Presley had always been a central influence on his family. With Holmes's vision and position, the song entered the popular mainstream conscience. A remix was used for a TV commercial and then released by Presley's record company in 2002. In June, 2002 the remix of "A Little Less Conversation" was an Irish number one for three weeks. It also became the eleventh most successful single of that year in Ireland. With a further rerelease the song became a number nineteen Irish hit on 12 May 2005.

One other song for the dramatic section was *Speedway*'s "Let Yourself Go". This track, like "A Little Less Conversation", today sustains a contemporary feel to it. The scene filmed for the song showed Elvis being backed into a brothel by what appeared to be a couple of prostitutes. Here they caressed him and themselves, played with each other and presented sexy looks and poses. The sexual innuendo was extremely high-pitched and it was considered too racy for the times, despite it being perfect at portraying the liberalism of Elvis Presley's rock 'n' roll. With America remaining sensitive on such issues, the whole scene was cut out and banned from the show. It was a sign that the actions of his beginning days were being repeated with more censoring. After being censored for sexually charged dancing on TV back in 1956, now in 1968 his sexually charged music video was also being stopped.

On 29 June two more performances in front of a live audience took place. These shows had Elvis standing on his own on the small square stage performing his classic rock hits. This portion of the entire project generated much electricity and magnitude. He belted out such hits as "All Shook Up", "Jailhouse Rock" and "Hound Dog". Faster than ever, rougher and rawer than before, the songs he had become famous for in the 1950s now seemed new and Elvis appeared fresh. He got deeply and emotionally involved in his work again and injected an irrepressible feeling into every song.

To the world Presley was commonly known as a movie star but now he was the ultimate rock star. His personal and professional life was at an all time high. Despite some repugnance from Parker towards Steve Binder, everything was pulled off magnificently. The TV special simply called *Elvis*, later known as *The '68 Comeback*, was a new presentation for a music star and did everything Elvis wanted it to. It also proved that the undisputed "King of rock 'n' roll" still retained that title.

During the making of the TV special it was decided by Elvis that he should do a tribute to the recently murdered Martin Luther King Jr. The civil rights activist had been gunned down earlier in the year and it had deeply upset Elvis who broke down in tears at the news. Parker had always demanded Elvis never make political statements and although Elvis always chose not to drift anywhere from music, he felt so strongly in himself to pay some sort of respect to those he deeply admired. He rebelled from his mentor and stayed true to yet another passionate belief. The song "If I Can Dream", written by W. Earl Brown, was chosen and was the perfect way to honour King. This was Presley's anti-prejudice and anti-war performance. "If I Can Dream" was a liberal song of peace and brotherhood. A song Presley attacked with conviction and emotion which concluded the show.

His 1968 TV special and first return to performances had come to an end. However, would the world respond to Elvis's return? At this stage he had very little to lose. His career was at a serious low point with the release of his last album *Speedway* only reaching number eighty-two in the American charts. The movie itself only gained moderate success when released in June in America and the following August, when it had its Irish premiere at the Adelphi Cinema in Dublin city.

After his NBC show, Elvis took a break with his family but his upcoming film was soon to begin. Elvis began work on the western *Charro!* The film had moments of being a rather dark and compelling drama which could have made a decisive change in his acting career. This marked the only movie where Elvis didn't perform a single song while in character. *Charro!* was the first serious role Elvis was given since *Flaming Star*.

Elvis had been offered other parts in big movies but Parker had always turned these down. Nobody knows how different Presley's acting career could have been, had he been allowed to star in the movies offered to him such as *Thunder Road* (1957), *West Side Story* (1963) or *Midnight Cowboy* (1969). Unfortunately this money conscious manager did not have any understanding of the arts. In October preparations commenced for yet another movie titled *The Trouble with Girls*. It was Parker's idea to drain out the last drop of Elvis's ability to receive any box office profit.

Christmas drew closer and the TV special *Elvis* was set to air on 3 December 1968. On its premiere, fans went wild. Gaining forty-two percent of the American viewing audience, the show was a smash hit and many critics were enthralled by the power of Presley. He was back on top and music fans had fallen in love with Elvis Presley once again. The world had only seen Elvis as a movie star up on the silver screen playing somebody else. Now this was him, the man himself, doing what he did best. Elvis was at the highest point in his career since 1960.

Ireland's sole television broadcaster RTÉ was the first channel in Europe to purchase the rights to broadcast *Elvis*. In a change of attitude from the channels decision not to broadcast Elvis songs on radio during the 1950s, the Irish broadcasting service decided to be ahead of the game and be a little more innovative this time. Nonetheless, the decision was not met without some adverse reaction.

On 22 December 1969, *The Irish Times* republished an article from a little rural paper called *The Longford Leader* which criticised RTÉ for spending money on the programme. The article informed readers how RTÉ had boasted of paying a record sum for the show. However, the writer continued, "is the Irish nation slowly going mad?" and asked if public money must be spent on "the antics of America's oldest teenager?". The ramblings questioned, "Has a kind of masochism gripped this nation whereby we deliberately under-rate anything of the phoney entertainment featuring a sloppy mouthed pop singer knee jerking in neurotic rhythm to inane outpourings?".

Despite these criticisms, the show was broadcast on Christmas Day 1969 on RTÉ at 6.45 P.M. under the name *Elvis: A Presley Spectacular*. Nevertheless, the establishment in Ireland couldn't hold back their detractions when it came to a follow up review in *The Irish Times* with TV reviewer Ken Gray stating, "the performance with much shaking and swivelling and sweating confirmed one's worst fears. If I say that it was vulgar and humourless, possibly that is became I am neither female nor under twenty five".

After the show was broadcast originally in America in December 1968, the soundtrack album went on release and achieved higher sales compared to Elvis's movie albums, reaching number eight. It established Elvis in a new position and was like a new beginning for his career. This soundtrack defined Presley; raw, eager and energetic. Due to the success of the show and the evidence that Elvis was once again being seen as a popular entertainer, Parker went straight into negotiations to get him performing live concerts. It was what Elvis had always wanted and economically it seemed the best way for Parker to go. Therefore Colonel Tom decided he would put "his boy" in Las Vegas, which Sinatra and the Rat

Pack had been dominating for years. With the right promotion, persuasion and publicity Parker decided it was time for Elvis to take control of that city and make it his own.

Entering 1969, ambitions, ideas and beliefs were on a high. Elvis was more confident than ever. The first in a new string of recording sessions was set for January at American Studios in Memphis and it was something Elvis looked forward to with great aspiration. This was his first time recording in his home town in thirteen years. Set in a down market area, the studio gave Elvis the chance to express the sharpness of his youth yet again. He began the session with the dark ballad "Long Black Limousine" and recorded mostly softer and mellow tracks at first, including "This Is The Story" and "Gentle On My Mind". One other tune recorded in the first collection was Hank Snow's "I'm Movin' On", which was also covered by Irish rock star Rory Gallagher around the same time.

On the third day of recording one song elucidating his selection of music was "Don't Cry Daddy". The sensorial and emotional feel that came out in his performances of such songs was contained deeply in him. It was a reflection of the love he embodied and from the tragic events he had encountered throughout his life. "Inherit The Wind" was the next ballad in line, embodying a modern and philosophical message. This particular song was written by the first generation Irish-American songwriter Eddie Rabbitt. Eddie was born in Brooklyn, New York in 1941 to Irish parents who immigrated to America in and around 1924.

After a three day break, Elvis returned back to the studio to get going on what would become one of his all time greats. Based on a poverty stricken family suffering in dire circumstances, "In The Ghetto" was a statement about the difficulties between violence, loss and grief in poor neighbourhoods. Aware of this sort of lifestyle after growing up in poverty, between Tupelo and Memphis, "In The Ghetto" suited Presley. Since the song dealt with a controversial issue some people advised him not to do it but Elvis went ahead. As with "If I Can Dream", Elvis showed how he differed from other southern performers of his time. "If I Can

Dream" was soon to be released and would go to number thirteen in the Irish charts on 29 March 1969 and re-enter the Irish charts, as a rerelease, at number twenty-seven on 25 October 2007.

"In The Ghetto" became a cherished performance worldwide and although "If I Can Dream" reached number thirteen in Ireland, this latest track touched people even more, becoming a smash hit, exploding to the number one spot. It failed to reach the top in America but lasted for twelve weeks on the Irish charts, from July of '69 onwards. Nobody could deny the affection in Elvis, as he portrayed the purpose of this number. Accompanying Elvis in the American Billboard Hot 100 was Irish star Richard Harris, whose track "Didn't We" was then at number seventy-eight. He was the first Irish soloist to appear in an American singles chart at the same time as Presley.

An Irish group by the name of Bass Odyssey covered "In The Ghetto" and in their own original way they contributed to the song. Another Irish band to perform their own rendition of this Presley classic was Co. Limerick group the Cranberries. Lead by vocalist Dolores O'Riordan, with her distinctive and powerful voice, the Cranberries became a successful Irish group in the early 1990s with their combination of pop and celtic tones. The group also includes Noel Hogan, Mike Hogan and Fergal Lawler. Their first great success was the 1993 international hit, "Linger".

Up next for Presley's latest session was the rock track, "Rubberneckin' ". A remix of "Rubberneckin' " would hit the Irish Top 10 in 2003. However, one song which stood out in his 1969 sessions would become one of his most famous recordings. It was a song that would dominate these studio sessions and would soon show Elvis's splendid ability to return to the top of the music industry. That song was "Suspicious Minds". It has stood out as one of the most breathtaking songs Presley recorded throughout his later career.

"Suspicious Minds" was so popular that many artists decided they should cover it. Over the years the Irish performers have included the Hothouse Flowers. Formed in Dublin in 1984, The Hothouse Flowers made a name for themselves for their fusion of rock with Irish folk. The band includes musicians Liam Ó Maonlaí, Fiachna Ó Braonáin and Dave Clarke. Their music progressed and they glided to the top of the Irish charts, into the early 1990s. Also in the category of Irish bands covering Presley's 1969 masterpiece are Whipping Boy. This group formed in Co. Offaly around 1989 and some of their songs include "Twinkle" and "We Don't Need Nobody Else". The group is made up of Colm Hassett, Myles McDonnell, Fearghal McKee and Paul Page. They recorded a self titled album in 2000, including a song titled "Ghost Of Elvis".

Yet another Irish performer to do a rendition of "Suspicious Minds" is Mic Christopher. Mic was born in New York in 1969 to Irish parents but moved back to Dublin in 1972. He remembered that the first gift he received around the age of three was a toy guitar and he eventually decided that he wanted to be like Elvis. Mic had an all-Irish school upbringing and played traditional music with school groups until he started busking at the age of fifteen. In 1990 he formed the group the Mary Janes and had success abroad until they split in 1999. Mic Christopher tragically passed away on 29 November 2001 while performing in Holland.

Some of Mic's songs include "Looking For Jude", "The Loneliest Man In Town" and "Taking Care Of Business". He performed the Elvis classic "Suspicious Minds" with the Irish group the Frames, who also covered the song separately as a tribute to Mic. The Frames formed in Dublin in the late 1980s by Glen Hansard, who appeared in *The Commitments*. There is also Damien Rice who covered the song in his solo career. Damien was born in Dublin, raised in Cellbridge, Co. Kildare, was once part of the band Juniper and has had hit songs and concerts around the world.

"Suspicious Minds" ended the first part of Elvis's '69 sessions masterfully. Elvis was always professional about the work he encountered. He was extremely patient and indicated great signs of diplomacy during all setbacks, expressing good cheer and amusement with his co-workers. Presley may have expressed frustration occasionally in the privacy of his home, but there were no signs of a conceited nature when he was at work or in public. Elvis may have been an exploited and over-worked performer but he was committed to the ventures he faced.

Having clearly demonstrated his dedication to the music, he took his family on a break where they celebrated Lisa's first birthday. However, it had been decided that there was going to be an extension to the recordings at American Studios, to commence around the end of February. The same musicians returned and Presley, like usual, played some guitar and piano.

Beginning on 17 February 1969 the first song cut to record was "True Love Travels On A Gravel Road". This was a gracious adult contemporary ballad, followed up by several songs of the same calibre such as "And The Grass Won't Pay No Mind". "Stranger In My Own Home Town" held a funky R&B beat and "Power Of My Love" blared out a voluptuous rock style. Another song that would add to those extra special tunes from the first session was "Kentucky Rain". It was again another resplendent adult song written by the Irish-American songwriter Eddie Rabbitt.

This would become his most imperative recording session since 1960 but for a journey into self-discovery, this marked his greatest session since his "Sun" days. A selection of the songs were to be released on an upcoming album that would see if Elvis still had the power to take hold of a large percentage of the music buying public. He had returned to Memphis for the first time since 1955 when the Sun recordings catapulted him into the big time. Ambitions were now being realised and no matter how much or how little he achieved in sales, he was doing something new and exciting.

The return to live performances drew closer but the nervous tension could not cease to exist. Everything had to be given a shot and without being full of himself, he could be sure of himself and marched straight ahead to take the chances. Just one unfortunate but unavoidable task was to appear in another movie. *Change of Habit* went into production shortly after Elvis finished his American Studio sessions and was going to be Presley's final drama. Now, like the movie's title, it was time for a change of habit!

Elvis played Dr. John Carpenter, a friendly ghetto doctor who is greeted by three Catholic nuns in disguise as ordinary nurses, with Mary Tyler Moore playing Sister Michelle Gallagher. While the women adapt with the dangers confronting the ghetto, the doctor begins to discover his attraction for Michelle. The story was risqué as it involved a nun questioning her celibacy. The story also included a conservative "Irish" Catholic priest, Fr. Gibbons, played by Regis Toomey.

The film was certainly a change of pace for Presley as it dealt with social and psychological issues such as drug abuse and loan sharks, neighbourhood violence and the recently discovered condition of autism. Work on *Change of Habit* came to an end in late April and Elvis walked off the set of a fictitious movie for the very last time on 2 May 1969. The movie business that had taken his image down the slopes and almost destroyed a fantastic career was finally over.

Chapter Sixteen

The late 1960s and early 1970s were the peak years when the sexual revolution got into full swing. It was a revolution for which liberals expressed their sexuality without fear. It was daring and controversial and was a lingering effect from the first sexually suggestive stars such as Elvis Presley.

Back in 1956 Elvis had broken the ice for helping controversial incidents gain extra popularity but he had done this unwittingly for he never set out to be anything other than what he was. And what he was, proved to be sexual dynamite and a young man who didn't fear to express himself. While this became his legacy, it was not what he desired or rejected. His music was special to him and he kept focused on this, while any controversy surrounding his sexual expression could be argued to be a reflection of a sexually frustrated society. His actions were a political statement of which he was initially unaware. Writing of Presley opening up to rock music and sex, Irish rock star Bono found in Elvis the outline of rock 'n' roll, which among various things included sexual liberation and controversy.

By 1969, Presley had been successful for such a long time now that he was no longer considered a hazard to young people. Ireland was changing and views towards sex and sexuality also changed with Western culture. Strict Catholic moral thinking within Irish life declined at snail pace. Especially around sex as liberals dared a trip to Northern Ireland where they could purchase the "evil" contraception, still forbidden in the Republic.

Away from the stage, Elvis gained a reputation as a major sex symbol, from his appearance, his stance and his many relationships. Elvis helped bring the innuendo, suggestiveness and the entire concept of it being a free pleasure into conservative societies. The sexual liberation made it clear world-wide that sex can be a wholesome, virtuous, healthy activity. It was something to open up to and enjoy and to disregard what the "neighbours" thought. Because of sexual expression, sexuality became an openly discussed subject. This encouraged its pleasures among consenting adults and brought its atrocious dangers to society's attention. The stimulation Presley discharged in his presence and performance encouraged people to become more excited about discovering their sexuality. Never before had a music or personality implied sex to such a capacity.

As tradition would have it, religiously-lead societies instructed lay people that sex and sexuality were something disgusting and dirty which was not to be thought about, at least not until the wedding night. However, upon the arrival of what would be the twentieth century's two most potent sex symbols, Marilyn Monroe and Elvis Presley, society decided to question sexuality further. American models directly brought sexuality out in the open but Presley's indirect approach of suggestiveness could not be kept back from all eyes and minds. His subtle methods of expressing sexuality grew as society duplicated it over and over.

The progression of the sexual revolution brought a change in Ireland in the 1970s when the Irish tabloid *The Sunday World* became Ireland's first publication of risqué but tastefully photographed images of female models. Sexuality, which many Irish writers had written about in books which became banned, had broken free. It didn't have to be written about to be released. It just had to be expressed visually, first suggestively, through stars like Elvis, then a little more explicitly. In result, this created a growing sense of freedom all round.

One of the pioneers of photographic modelling to appear out of the depths of rural Ireland was Nuala Holloway. Nuala who also became a Miss Ireland and actress and later an artist found in Elvis, "He was not afraid to stand up and be counted, he was himself. He lifted people's spirits and combined everything a woman would admire in a man. He was gifted and sexy but had a special kind of sexiness which made you stop and look and admire. His appearance was perfection. Elvis made the whole business of singing and performing look effortless which highlights a very special talent".

By 1969 Ireland's economy had grown a lot stronger, rising out of the burdensome 1950s. Music and entertainment had become an important aspect of youth culture and young people now found better chances to fulfil their ambitions as musicians. 1969 was a major year for progressing Irish musicians. The showbands had been on the go for almost ten years and imported music was taking a stronger hold on the country's social culture. A mixed variety of musical styles was available in Ireland, each one as popular as the other. Groups such as Granny's Intentions, the Movement, Eire Apparent, the Orange Machine and the Bye Laws catered for the rock 'n' roll craving Irish youth.

Elvis's influence still spread worldwide and he was continuously admired by many different types of musicians. One of these musicians was Christy Moore. Born in 1945 in Co. Kildare, Christy was inspired by Elvis Presley as a teenager in the '50s. The first record Christy owned was the archetypal rock hit "Hound Dog" and he enjoyed growing up listening to Radio Luxembourg and buying the latest Elvis records.

As Christy discovered further sounds, he became more enthusiastic about Irish folk music. It was especially after he moved to England as a young man and heard the original music of his homeland that he was transformed to it. Acquiring an acoustic guitar and bodhrán, Moore began busking on streets. He began to attract attention with his original folk songs and Irish ballads as he became part of the folk club circuit in 1967. But it was in 1969 that Christy Moore's very first solo album was released, giving him a chance to spread his sound to further areas. Passing through groups such as Planxty and Lonely Hearts, he became one of Ireland's most loved Irish folk soloists with his energetic and comic performances mixed with deeply passionate performances.

1969 also saw another Irish artist emerge to the international scene, who would retain his popularity decades later. Dancing out of Mullingar, County Westmeath, came Joe Dolan. Up to this point Joe had been the lead singer in a showband named the Drifters singing ballads and pop tunes. In 1964 he cut his first song, "The Answer To Everything" and instantly became successful achieving a string of hits year after year with songs such as "I Love You

More And More Everyday" and "The Westmeath Bachelor".

It was after the showband period that Dolan cut a song that would drift further than the corners of Ireland. "Make Me An Island" went to number one in fourteen countries and was the turning point in his career. It was after this hit that his career took off. Becoming popular in America and Britain, he had the opportunity to appeal to a mass audience. Joe Dolan admired Elvis and during his career paid tribute to him by covering "Can't Help Fallin' In Love" and "Suspicious Minds". Joe's music continued in the pop tradition and he often performed popular ballads with energetic and exciting stage performances. Dolan became one of the most charismatic Irish performers to come out of the showband era performing until his untimely death in 2007.

Making 1969 - 1970 extra special for the music business in Ireland was the formation of the rock band Thin Lizzy, lead by Phil Lynott and including Eric Bell and Brian Downey. This rock band, with the soon to be formed rock group Horslips, popularised a new sound for Ireland. They combined acid rock and Irish folk songs and blended them into a modern style, gaining admiration with hard rock fans. Other musicians who worked with the group included Brian Robertson, Scott Gorham, Gary Moore, Snowy White, John Sykes and Darren Wharton.

Phil Lynott was born on 20 August 1949 in West Bromich, England to an Irish mother and a Brazilian father. Phil's mother became a lone parent and raised Phil in Dublin. At a young age he expressed an interest and fondness for music and Elvis Presley became a substantial influence. Lynott's main introduction to performing music was when he sang with the Black Eagles and played bass for a short time with the band Skid Row which then lead him onto forming Thin Lizzy.

Phil has been compared to Presley because of their shy personalities and common insecurity behind the show business curtain. Phil always showed a soft, mystical side, which was an equal characteristic to Elvis. They both often worried about the quality of their recordings and were seriously devoted to the artistic aspects of their work. These two also became self-mockers, often joking about their ridiculous poses from the past. "Early Elvis Presley, I just go crazy over" Phil once explained as he spoke about his influences. Lynott became a major influence, not only on Irish musicians but on many current rock stars across the world for his unique style and tremendous talent. Over the years the band had several successful hits with songs such as "The Boys Are Back In Town" and "Jailbreak".

Phil exuded the same charisma, sexuality and masculinity that his hero Elvis had displayed. He was Ireland's first true rock giant, an Elvis of Ireland. As much as Elvis remained attached to Memphis, Phil was as true to Dublin. Nothing put them off their roots and they wore this fact proudly. They now both have honouree statues erected to them in their respective home cities. Years later Phil paid tribute to Elvis Presley with the song "King's Call", which cracked the Irish Top 20. It was written and recorded as a mark of respect to Presley and expressed Lynott's devotion as a fan who grew up in Dublin listening to his captivating records.

After concerts at different spots around the world, including Memphis, Tennessee, Thin Lizzy split up after they performed for the last time in 1983. Phil continued a solo career with songs that examined class and race and he also published his own poetry. Throughout the years Phil had been a heavy drug user and while friends attempted to help, he indicated how he wanted to burn out like Jimi Hendrix and Elvis Presley, who he cited as musical heroes. Phil succumbed to the virulent effects of drugs and alcohol with heart failure on 4 January 1986. Lynott was a fantastic performer who shone bright as one of Ireland's greatest artists and still remains an essential asset to Irish rock music history.

From the end of the 1960s to the birth of the 1970s, groups of young Irish teenagers attempted to create their own original rock bands in the hopes of making it big one day. While international success would come for some, Ireland is a country that today still sees the formation of hundreds of young groups each year. It is an event that stemmed from those times when the ball was set rolling by some daring Irish music lovers who were deeply struck by American rock 'n' roll singers. However it was the original rock bands in Ireland such as Thin Lizzy which brought something innovative to Irish culture. Irish people could take on rock 'n' roll themselves without having to listen to foreign records alone. They were an example of Ireland proceeding to join in with the modern world.

It was the end of the '60s, a decade that had seen great changes in the country since the '50s. It could be seen how music played an important part on motivating people to discover an alternative Ireland. Rock music was a major starting point in this progression. It was controversial, extraordinary, rebellious and completely new. Previously, little notice was put towards how powerful music could be to society but Elvis was one person who helped change this perception. Elvis had captured the imagination of young people around the world and from there musicians made rock music matter in their own country.

* * *

Meanwhile, as Irish musicians were working on their hopes and dreams, Elvis Presley worked on his ongoing comeback as preparations for further projects went into operation. He worried about his upcoming concerts in Vegas as he had performed there unsuccessfully in 1956. Back then the city was more adult-orientated and not suited to the young greasy rocker. Nonetheless, times had changed and now he was the adult star who could potentially take the city by storm.

As time moved on and as opening night, set for 31 July 1969 came closer, Elvis grew more and more anxious. He needed it to be a spectacular event that would be remembered, praised and respected. This was Vegas, the ultimate town of glitz. It was a town about showing and presenting the best. What was needed for Elvis to make a strong impact and to appear new and different was a memorable event. Clothes were a main importance of the show business feel that Vegas provided to visitors. To Elvis the flamboyant style he had always displayed was essential. This lead him to get back in contact with designer Bill Belew and together they came up with a plan.

Because Elvis was extremely fit and slim and exceptionally energetic and active on stage, a costume was specially devised to suit this stage manner. All the moving about and never ending perspiration lead to the most suitable suit for him. The costume came from the design of a karate jumpsuit, a sport to which Elvis was devoted. He chose plain black with a selection of flamboyantly designed belts. This was substantial for what the performer required.

In July, Elvis put together ideas on what material should be used. Up next was the choosing of new musicians. Elvis's line-up of Scotty Moore, D. J. Fontana and the Jordanaires had been asked to take part but they declined. Back in Nashville they were able to stay at home and earn more money so there was little point for them to join Elvis once again. In his search for a multitude of fine talent Elvis interviewed many musicians and eventually got drummer Ronnie Tutt and guitarists John Wilkinson and Jerry Scheff as well as James Burton, who had worked with Dublin based rock 'n' roller Ian Whitcomb on a studio recording. The pianist Glen D. Hardin would arrive to the group at a later stage.

For backup vocals and harmony Elvis hired gospel quartet, the Imperials and soul group the Sweet Inspirations who had previously worked with singing sensation Aretha Franklin. To finish off the group he gave a place to Millie Kirkham as another backup singer. She would be replaced the following year by Kathy Westmoreland. Charlie Hodge was also given a position as vocalist and guitarist. Then to create an extra power and to ignite a strength of streaming electricity he hired conductor Bobby Moore and his orchestra to add dramatic flair. All was now complete and from 18 July nearly every day was taken up with rehearsals as they worked on over one hundred and fifty songs.

While Presley was working away at the music, Parker was working at his favourite aspect, the promotion. Enormous banners were set up around Vegas and the entering roads to the city and commercials were played continuously on radio and TV. Posters, calendars, balloons and photos were stacked in the hotel to present the opening of Presley's comeback to live performing. The Colonel brought back his carnival influence which eventually marked the beginning of large scale concert merchandising seen with every major performer today.

Eventually the day arrived. All fired up, excited and full of energy, the rocker was in his prime. Appearing his leanest and wearing extravagant stage gear, he blazed with ambition and looked more handsome than ever, defining his nickname of "The King". At 8.15 P.M. the Sweet Inspirations opened the show and an instrumental riff fused up the atmosphere in the audience. An audience which consisted of many stars of the performing arts, including Shirley Bassey, Henry Mancini and Fats Domino. Elvis began to panic and suffered from extreme stage fright, something he never seemed to get over throughout his whole career.

It was not until after 10 P.M. that he headed out on stage, still tormented from nerves. Elvis walked out to an ecstatic audience and pausing for a moment he then belted into "Blue Suede Shoes". The crowd went wild. It was like his days on the Louisiana Hayride. It didn't take long for Elvis to take full control of his audience. His spectacular image was displayed in full. This was his ultimate high point in his later career. Some critics ignore his Vegas years but his 1969 return was certainly something not to be overlooked. These were adrenaline pumped hard rock performances at their best.

Rolling on into "I Got A Woman" and "All Shook Up", he did hit after hit and got back in touch with his fans, with the songs for which they remembered him. Then when he knew anything would work he started performing his latest songs such as "Suspicious Minds" and "In The Ghetto". He even did a tribute to the Beatles by performing "Yesterday" and "Hey Jude".

The audience, packed mainly with celebrities, got off their seats and moved in harmony with Elvis, as the marvellous atmosphere spread across the showroom. Elvis was obviously the centre of the show but he never failed to give credit to each musician, making sure the audience gave them their attention. Presley got deep into his performance and making use of the space, began jumping and sliding about, falling on his knees and moved non-stop to the beat of the sounds. The place went crazy and there was little difference to his appeal thirteen years previously. Most of all, Presley enjoyed himself immensely. One thing was for certain, Elvis was back . . . *again*!

CHAPTER SEVENTEEN

On the night after Elvis's live comeback Parker decided there had to be a new contract negotiated. So much love and admiration had been directed from the crowd towards Presley. Parker knew he had to cash in on it some more. He made a deal with the hotel president to extend Elvis's performance schedule to two seasons each year for the next five years and wrote out the contract on the tablecloth in front of him.

In the meantime Elvis prepared again for the next performance, knowing there would be a new audience and they needed the same treatment. He also held a press conference where he answered questions. During the conference the topic of current music was brought up and the song "MacArthur Park", which had been a major hit for Ireland's Richard Harris, was mentioned. While the song has garnered much ridicule in the years since for its overly sentimental tone, Elvis expressed his admiration for the song and explained that if Richard Harris hadn't recorded it, he would have. However Elvis can be heard during outtakes on his 1968 special singing lines from the song in irreverent fashion.

News reports across the world announced Presley's return and highlighted the excitement of his stage act. People who didn't expect much were left entranced and others who were not fans were converted right away. The dreams had finally come true and Elvis was in a state of notable vivacity. To add to this, the single "Suspicious Minds" was released reaching the number one spot in America, remaining on the charts for fifteen weeks. The song also did well in Ireland, reaching the charts at number two. It also got to number twenty-one on its Irish rerelease on 16 August 2007.

The year ended with Elvis taking a holiday in the Bahamas where he attended a Christmas show by the Northern Irish showband, the Witnesses. This showband first emerged in Belfast in 1963 and gained singer Colm Wilkinson as a vocalist. Elvis met with the band after the show and bought them drinks while expressing his enjoyment of their performance.

Departing 1969, Elvis had achieved what he wanted. He loved the performance aspect of show business, creating the feel of unblemished excitement. He would later explain how all the electricity and energy generated by live shows made them his favourite part of the job. Despite the great success and accomplishments Elvis and Priscilla's marriage has not been looking good for some time now. Elvis could not remain a one-woman-man and he disappeared without her many times. It was unfair to his wife who expected her husband to be monogamous but this was Elvis Presley and he had some of the world's most beautiful women swarming around him.

In January of 1970 the second Vegas engagement was set to take place and some changes were made with a new and improved selection of songs. To his original hits Elvis added "Polk Salad Annie", an excellent funky rocker with its share of R&B. Another song executed with integral energy was the rock song "Proud Mary", a regular for charismatic concert performers including Wales's Tom Jones and Ireland's Joe Dolan who did their own special covers of it.

While Elvis continued to put music together, Bill Belew prepared a new costume. The colour changed from black to white and he added new designs to the cuffs, collars and belts. 26 January was the opening of the four week engagement and Elvis gave just as good a performance as before, leaving the audience enraptured. RCA again decided to get an account of this season. A collection of songs were recorded for the upcoming album, *Elvis: On Stage*.

Among the songs that made it to the original album were "See See Rider", the opening song that Elvis rushed on stage performing. As an exciting opening riff it became a trademark Elvis concert opener as he would use it for years to come. Northern Irish alternative metal group, Therapy? later recorded this song for a single release. Therapy? was formed in 1989 by Andy Cairns and Fyfe Ewing and some of their songs include "Teethgrinder", "Screamager" and "Evil Elvis".

During days off, Elvis got back into rehearsing and he didn't let a day go to waste as he searched for new material. He came up with "Walk A Mile In My Shoes" and the affectionate "The Wonder Of You" which once again demonstrated Elvis as a dramatic vocalist. This song had already been a number two hit for Brendan Bowyer in 1965 and was also covered by Irish trumpeter Johnny Carroll who gave his rendition among a medley of other Elvis songs including "Can't Help Fallin' In Love" and "Good Luck Charm". Johnny started his music career aged 13 in 1958 with the Pioneer Showband in Co. Roscommon and subsequently worked with different bands until eventually going solo as "The Man with the Golden Trumpet".

Elvis Presley's last performance of the season lasted for almost three hours and he went completely wild on stage as did the audience in reaction to him. Only two days later Elvis was back to business with his first concert outside Vegas since the beginning of his comeback. He flew to Houston, Texas, where Parker had arranged three appearances and attendance records were broken.

On the last day of his Texas engagement he received gold record awards for his singles "In The Ghetto", "Don't Cry Daddy", "Suspicious Minds" and his last two albums. It was far from his first award for sales but it was a terrific moment in his life because it was a sign that he was back making quality records again and back in the top group of artists. Since the beginning of his career Elvis Presley has racked up over one hundred and fifty platinum, gold and silver disc awards for sales, more than any other performing artist in history.

Elvis gave a press conference where he talked about his roots and how his style of music originated from country, gospel and R&B. He also joked about his Sun Records and how strange he found the sound now and how high his voice was back then. No matter what, they would always be considered his very best work. Although, what he did now went beyond satisfying his audience, the early days were when he was experimenting and creating new and bizarre music which lead onto something mammoth. Vegas was about glitz, something that was not expected from the rough, tough rock artist who made parents lock up their daughters back in the 1950s.

On 4 June 1970 Elvis began cutting new songs and began the session with the radiant ballad, "Twenty Days And Twenty Nights". This sort of song was typical of what Presley was now choosing. Rock fans could pass this material off as insipid love songs but for others this sort of choice was exquisite. They were beautiful songs that depicted Elvis in fine voice, basing his selection on adult themes. He was extremely enthusiastic about the music and was dedicated to getting the job done. The following day he began with "Bridge Over Troubled Water" and the evening went on with a varied choice of musical taste.

Issuing bluegrass, ballads and blues, he chose songs such as "Got My Mojo Working", the fantastically funky "Stranger In The Crowd" and the mellifluous "Mary In The Morning". Day three included his version of Irish-English singer Dusty Springfield's "You Don't Have To Say You Love Me" and the fourth day was full of country songs such as "Faded Love", "Tomorrow Never Comes" and "Make The World Go Away".

Eventually by the fifth day Elvis had recorded more than enough music to fill many albums to come. "There Goes My Everything", "Only Believe" and "Sylvia" filled up the session before he ended it all off with a blazing rock 'n' roll piece titled "Patch It Up", written by the Irish-American songwriter Eddie Rabbitt. The group packed up and left behind them an incredible recording session that consisted of thirty-five master takes. The five day period represented one of the most productive sessions that Elvis ever encountered. This session did not have the same merit as his 1969 American Studio recordings but the effort, eagerness and sheer determination now overtook all and set Elvis out on a lucid path to accomplish a lot more.

With Presley's third Las Vegas engagement set for August, production on a new MGM documentary, titled *Elvis: That's The Way It Is*, began in July. This time Elvis was not handed any script, he was not given any directions and all the music was of his own choice. All he had to do was to be his natural self and let the cameras roll. The objective of the movie was to give a candid view of Elvis's life in the studio and on stage. While cameras rolled, the band jammed away on old and new songs and experimented on tunes they felt could be added to the show such as "Something" and "You've Lost That Lovin' Feelin' ".

Elvis then rehearsed an original track, the contemporary love song "I Just Can't Help Believin' ". Elvis gave it a great sense of feeling and it surpassed most of his recent work. In tribute to him and the song, Irish rock group Aslan covered it on an Elvis tribute show for Irish TV. Aslan formed in Dublin in the mid-1980s, with the musicians Christy Dignam, Joe Jewell, Tony McGuinness, Billy McGuinness and Alan Downey. Some of their well noted performances include "This Is" and "Feel No Shame". On Elvis, lead singer Christy Dignam confirmed, "He had a great voice, technically a brilliant voice".

Irish band Juniper also recorded the track "I Just Can't Help Believin' ", this time for an Elvis tribute album. Juniper was formed in 1991 in Cellbridge, Co. Kildare by school friends Damien Rice, Brian Crosby, Paul Noonan and Dominic Philips. They had reasonable success with the single "Weatherman" but the group known as Juniper ended in 1999 when Damien Rice left to pursue a solo career. The remaining musicians then formed the band known as Bell X1 which have been a great success since.

On 7 August 1970, Elvis and his group moved out onto the stage to continue rehearsals. With a new addition of Joe Guercio leading the orchestra, the opening night commenced on 10 August. Again Presley was as nervous as ever and it was caught on film this time. Elvis never got over the stage fright, but felt that his nervous tension could help him give a fantastic performance. His entrance was met with sheer delectation as the screaming crowds got up to greet him.

The concert was a rip-roaring success with Elvis going from rock to ballads and from blues to country. He was an unpredictable singer and each performance differed from the next. Just like his single releases, each song that came next was usually different from the last. He had something to suit everybody. As Shane MacGowan maintained about Elvis, "Pop, rock, white soul, country, whatever. A giant of a man".

For the next six consecutive shows, the MGM cameras got Elvis at his best on film. His hair and sideburns had also grown a lot longer and wilder again. He remained as slim as ever and was able to give yet more undoubtedly energetic and sparkling performances. It was unfortunate to later learn that these times would be some of his last incredibly powerful shows. His voice would always remain good but physically it was following these shows that he started to slow down as the fire in him waned.

Elvis glided through the songs like a free spirit and when he came to "Love Me Tender" he felt the urge to climb down into the audience where he came in contact with his wild, roaring and adoring fans. Although MGM packed up after his sixth night, the shows continued. The cameras were gone but the performances remained heart-pounding, pulse-racing, exciting experiences. The documentary represented the highlights of Elvis's phenomenal performance capabilities. Covering his life, not many documentaries have captured the truth of Elvis's performance talents but *That's The Way It Is* caught on film the essence of it all.

Many other movie documentaries based on the man have either not portrayed Elvis clearly or have been just totally inaccurate. From Kurt Russell's average performance in a badly researched dramatisation to Don Johnson's lacklustre attempt to portray "The King" in *Elvis and The Beauty Queen* (1981), from Irish producer Charles B. Fitzsimons. There is also the 2005 television mini-series *Elvis* where "The King" was played by Irish actor Jonathan-Rhys Meyers. Meyers was born in Dublin in July 1977, raised in Cork and began acting at a young age. He went on to win the Golden Globe award for best actor in a TV mini-series at the prestigious awards ceremony in 2006 for his portrayal of Elvis.

The movie *This Is Elvis* (1981) gave a good portrait of Elvis but what remains to be seen as the greatest film came in 2000 with a remake of 1970s *That's The Way It Is*. The picture was a newly edited project featuring unreleased footage, but unfortunately got a limited showing in selected cinemas in few countries. Fortunately for the Irish, the movie was screened exclusively at a cinema in Dublin. However the DVD release became a major hit reaching the Irish Top 10 charts, setting a longevity record for a music release in Ireland, having spent eighty weeks in the charts by the beginning of 2004.

The original version was released in Ireland in June 1971 with *The Irish Times* reviewing that the film "makes Elvis Presley look somewhat better than the rather gormless films in which he usually stars" and that it reveals him "as having that complete professionalism which is the mark of all top American pop singers and which is so often absent in their counter parts on this side of the Atlantic".

Shortly thereafter, while continuing to thrill crowds, a mysterious phone call to the hotel explained that Elvis would be kidnapped and another mysterious call suggested he would be killed. All that could be done was done, and Elvis's own private security, as well as extra hotel security and the FBI were on guard. Everybody was packing a gun and even Elvis carried two on stage which he kept concealed in his boots. Over the next few days it turned out that the whole incident was a hoax but it still remained a fact that somebody went so far as to make dangerous threats.

7 September 1970 saw the end of Elvis's summer Vegas season. Attendances again had been enormous with each night sold out in a flash. For this achievement the hotel presented Elvis with a gold championship belt for the greatest attendance records. Each night had left him tired and exhausted but his ambition gave him the ability to keep going.

The end of the Vegas season did not mean a long rest as Parker now had him booked for eight concerts beginning in two days. After that tour the band went their separate way but Elvis headed for Nashville for some brief studio work. Arriving in Nashville on 22 September he worked on the songs "Snowbird", "Where Did They Go Lord?" and finally "Rags To Riches" which became a number twelve hit in Ireland the following year.

His recording of "You Don't Have To Say You Love Me" became an American number eleven in November. For the Billboard Hot 100, week ending 28 November 1970, Irish blues musician Van Morrison shared the chart with Elvis, appearing, at that time, at number forty-seven with his song "Domino".

After the death threats in Vegas, Elvis's interest in law enforcement and weaponry took a great leap forward. This encouraged his enthusiasm for guns, although he did own some already. In September, 1964 Elvis was given the first of what would later become a long line of honorary police badges. He had been appointed Special Deputy Sheriff, receiving the regular police force credentials.

The death threats seemed to intensify any conservatism within him, as he appeared to be against the drug culture and anything that challenged America's mainstream society. This would be made clear as he made a spontaneous trip to Washington DC and wrote a letter to U.S. President Richard Nixon. Nixon was just back two months after a trip to Ireland where a mix of Irish people came out to greet him and many war protesters came out in anger at him.

In his letter to Nixon, Elvis scribbled a note claiming he was concerned for the country and the issues with the drug culture, hippies and other factors. He then explained how he wished to help the country in any way he could and that he would do a better job if he was made a federal agent. Early that morning Elvis travelled to the White House, handed the letter to the guard out front and headed back to his hotel. The President's staff took note of the singer's patriotic view and later that day a meeting was arranged between Elvis and the President. On 21 December 1970 Elvis Presley arrived at the White House. As a gift for Nixon, Presley brought a special World War II pistol. Then what became one of the most extraordinary meetings in The White House took place as the rock star stepped into the Oval Office.

Elvis walked in and shook hands with Richard Nixon. The meeting soon became informal as Elvis showed photographs of his family and the badges with which he had been presented. Elvis was calm and comfortable and connected exceptionally well with the President. He proceeded to talk about the issue of anti-Americanism and the dangerous effects of illegal drugs and giving what Nixon wanted to hear, he explained that the Beatles were an example of this influence. The meeting lead to Elvis's request for the credentials of a narcotics agent as he emphasised how he could help the drug problem faced by the country as long as he had these. Nixon agreed to provide him with an honorary narcotics badge.

Elvis left the mansion pleased, having come along to get something and having received it. However the meeting is still a mystery to some. Despite what he had said about the Beatles he admired their music and paid tribute to them with covers of their songs. What he said to Nixon was most likely a method of persuasion to get what he wanted. It is clear that Elvis didn't lean specifically towards either the Democrats nor Republicans, expressing admiration for politicians of both parties on different occasions.

Views vary on his motives, but the main thing Elvis clearly emphasised was his problem with those influencing dangerous narcotics amongst young people who didn't know better. What may also be seen from this escapade is one of the greatest "rock 'n' roll moments". A phrase often used to pinpoint the wild and extraordinary actions undertaken by rock stars. Here was a rock 'n' roll star, wearing an extraordinary outfit, showing up at the White House, heavy on medication and with a gun, persuading the most powerful man in the world to make him a narcotics agent. Looked at from this perspective makes it quite amusing and puts Elvis back on his ultimate rock 'n' roll pedestal. Few rock stars dare to do anything as daring. Elvis could get bored easily and this latest adventure was most likely a bit of fun for him.

Away from the personal hobbies, the music was still a serious matter. By the end of 1970, Ireland had provided Elvis with another four Top 20 hits comprising of "The Wonder Of You" at number one, "Don't Cry Daddy" at four, "Kentucky Rain" at fourteen and "I've Lost You" at fifteen, which kept him for two thirds of the year on the Irish charts. "The Wonder Of You" reached number twenty on the Irish charts with a reissue on 28 April 2005. Elvis remained popular but the year 1970 faded out without a clear focus on what was to come next.

Chapter Eighteen

Irish writer Joseph O'Connor once wrote of Elvis, "He was born in a shack. He was the King of America. He was the most popular star ever in the history of pop music". As part of his book *Sweet Liberty: Travels in Irish America*, O'Connor paid respect to Elvis's memory through journeys from Nashville to Memphis where he visited some Elvis themed sites such as Graceland and RCA studios and discussed the possibility of Elvis's Irish roots with a local music shop owner.

Joseph writes how Elvis "was pilloried and condemned and widely banned for wanting to destroy American youth" and how "people said he was anti-authoritarian. People said he was a dangerous anarchist". He also adds, "He sold more records than anyone. He was and still is and always will be the definitive voice of the twentieth century". It is these sentiments which help describe Elvis Presley's career and legacy and ultimately, an American legend.

Through this we can see how Elvis was a hero to American democracy and American youth. All he wanted was to have a career and a voice that would be recognised and admired and he achieved his wish. The irony is that the establishment which he once rocked now embraced him, when in January 1971 the Junior Chamber of Commerce of America selected him as one of the nations "Ten Most Outstanding Young Men of the Year". Elvis was included with a medical researcher and a civil rights activist to be given this honourable accolade.

At the event Presley accepted the award which honoured him deeply. He was overwhelmed to be considered one of the nation's most outstanding men. It was a spectacular achievement in his life which he treasured. On acceptance of the award he read a poetic speech which emphasised the fact that he had lived the American dream. He had gone from rags to riches, a poor country boy to the world's greatest star. He was the genuine true working class hero and was a great inspiration to millions across the world.

He had become an entertainer and would always be committed to delivering songs to the hearts of people. He had gone from nothing to everything, motivating the dreams of people who had very little.

Music was in his blood and he delivered it in the most elusive fashion. He reached folk hero status and became a larger-than-life symbol. Naturally, as a man, he had his flaws but flaws that were of little danger to anybody but himself. He was a born icon, who happened to enter the world in a shack. Through the emotion so irrevocably exhibited in his work Elvis helped millions of people feel alive. That emotional intelligence, acumen and prudence was his ultimate dexterity. In the words of Bono, "Elvis had the wisdom that makes wise men look foolish".

On 26 January 1971 Presley was back preparing for his fourth season in Vegas. Joe Guercio and Elvis felt that there was a need for a more dramatic opening and they came up with the idea of having "Also Sprach Zarathustra" played by his orchestra before Presley appeared on stage. The huge crashing sounds, sense of mystery and grand suspense made the show more exciting for the audience. He later added the vocally challenging tune, "The Impossible Dream" which became a favourite for some time after.

Another accomplishment at that time was having another hit in Ireland. "You Don't Have To Say You Love", entered the Irish Top 20 at number seventeen on 13 February 1971. This recording also went on to become a Top 30 hit in Ireland through a rerelease on 15 November 2007. The same song would be a better hit for Irish star Red Hurley who achieved a number five hit with it in 1978. Red started off his music career singing as a front man for the Nevada Showband. Taking on a solo career Red tried out in Las Vegas with unsuccessful results. However, he still remains quite popular in Ireland and represented Ireland at *Eurovision* with the song "When" in 1976.

After another tiresome four weeks of shows, Presley and the group finished up on 23 February. Resting in Vegas, Elvis joined Priscilla as they enjoyed several nights out together catching various shows around the town. The day after Elvis had wrapped up his engagement they went to see Ann-Margret perform at the International. Then the following night they attended the Royal Irish Showband with Brendan Bowyer at the Stardust.

Brendan was one of the earliest Elvis tribute artists. On his arrival to Vegas in 1966 he went down very well with American audiences. When Elvis had returned to performing in 1969 both Bowyer and Presley attended each other's shows. One time when Bowyer was singing away at the Stardust he noticed a tremendous reaction to his show from his audience. The crowd seemed to be going wild, far more than usual. Brendan was delighted at the atmosphere but suddenly noticed a man standing towards the side of the stage. It was Elvis himself who happened to be in the hotel at the time. He had slipped in to see the show and his presence generated huge excitement as he gave a quick twist in rhythm to Bowyer's performance. Elvis enjoyed Bowyer's shows and kept a lower profile at other times. Presley once said, "Brendan Bowyer used to do an impression of me that was so cool, I just had to catch him at the Stardust after all my shows".

On one occasion Elvis invited Brendan and the band up to his suite. Brendan and Tom Dunphy began discussing Elvis's movie career and how he had made so many poor pictures. Elvis asked Tom if there was a film he liked him in and Tom replied with *Flaming Star*. Elvis was delighted by this and explained how he had hoped to progress as an actor but that the films became an assembly line due to all the millions which were offered for them.

Shortly after these times, the days of the Royal Irish Showband were numbered but Brendan set up his new band the Big 8, which lasted for just a few years. Eventually in his personal life Bowyer would drift into a long period of dangerous excesses at a time, which unknown to him, would parallel the life of his great hero.

Returning to work on 15 March 1971 Elvis made his way to Nashville to cut a few songs. In recent months Elvis had suffered occasionally with an eye infection and the problem was bothering him even more on the first day of recording. Nonetheless, Elvis was determined to get some new material recorded.

To begin the session, Elvis did "The First Time Ever I Saw

Your Face". This particular number was written by Ewan McColl who had written such classics as "Thirty Foot Trailer" and "Dirty Old Town" for legendary Irish folk group, the Dubliners. He also wrote "Go, Move, Shift", about the Irish travelling community, for Christy Moore, who also covered "The First Time Ever I Saw Your Face". Ewan McColl is also the father of singer Kirsty McColl, famous for the 1981 hit "There's A Guy Works Down The Chip Shop Swears He's Elvis".

For many years one of Presley's favourite gospel tracks was "Amazing Grace" and he felt that it was now about time he did his cover of it. "Amazing Grace" is one of the most famous gospel songs ever written. The song is a favourite of Irish tenors and has been covered by Frank Patterson, the Irish Tenors and Mark Forrest, who also covered "The Impossible Dream", which Elvis had begun to incorporate in his shows at this time. The Irish Tenors was a group of Ireland's greatest tenors throughout the 1990s and early 2000s. The original trio included Anthony Kearns, John McDermott and Ronan Tynan. Anthony Kearns who became one of Ireland's leading operatic voices, was born in Kiltealy, Co. Wexford on 17 August 1971. He expressed an interest in music at a young age and apparently this interest was expressed by his imitations of Elvis when he was a child.

On the first evening of Elvis Presley's March '71 session his eye problem grew worse and he felt as if it was burning. The following day he was diagnosed with iritis and secondary glaucoma and was hospitalised. This resulted in him receiving a shot of Demerol and then a shot of cortisone directly into the eyeball. After recuperating Elvis contacted karate instructor Master Kang Rhee to keep up his old hobby of studying karate. Elvis began attending his studio in Memphis and eventually received his fourth degree black belt.

The sudden urge to get back into the sport was due to the extra weight he put on while out of action with the eye infection and he wanted something new and energetic to add to his performances. He soon began losing weight and was back to his good old regular slender self. Priscilla also became interested in karate and she took lessons from Ed Parker. Presley's interest with spiritual discipline within the sport was renewed once again.

In May Presley was back in Nashville but not by his own initiative. RCA had begun pressurising him to return, as plans for new albums had been decided. Plans this time were for a new Christmas album. His albums now were not reaching the top spot anymore and his singles were rarely making the Top 10. RCA decided that rather than putting every effort into one release, they could profit off a string of lame compilations.

Elvis began the session with the religious number, "Miracle Of The Rosary" followed by the Christmas track, "It Won't Seem Like Christmas". This session which mainly consisted of spiritual and Christmas songs, became another marathon because in just a few days Elvis recorded over thirty new tracks. The first day was made up with "I'll Get Home On Christmas Day", "Holly Leaves And Christmas Trees" and the blues track "Merry Christmas Baby" which was the only performance Elvis really got into.

This Christmas track was flat out R&B and with Presley's sultry and sensual performance the song blazed out testosterone next to its lustful and lascivious feel. This track proved how Elvis was a spectacular and genuinely rhythmic blues performer. When it came to natural instinct of a performer who loved music and let his soul echo through the core of it, Elvis Presley came out on top.

On his singing, Northern Irish presenter Eamonn Holmes remarked, "He had it all. There are so few true world superstars. You really respect someone who has got a true talent and there is nobody who could doubt that Elvis Presley could sing. Nobody could say his voice was not up to much. His voice was totally different, his renditions were really quite unique".

The following day Elvis covered "The Lord's Prayer", "On A Snowy Christmas Night", and "The First Noel" among others. Elvis also found reason to record some other material of another style at this session. It gave him the chance to get away from the Christmas sounds and try something else for a short while. Presley followed with Bob Dylan's "Don't Think Twice, It's All Right" and the next day gave a splendid cover of Kris Kristofferson's, "Help

Me Make It Through The Night".

Elvis also recorded the sorrowful ballad, "Until It's Time For You To Go", which may easily have expressed the problems he was having with Priscilla, as it told the story of a troubled marriage. While Elvis had spent more time after his Vegas shows with Priscilla there remained a distance. Elvis knew deep down how meaningful she was to his life. However it was Elvis's absence, away for weeks performing on stage, which became difficult for Priscilla as she was at home taking care of their child.

The next few days of recordings included "He Touched Me", the title of his upcoming gospel album as well as "I'll Take You Home Again, Kathleen". The last two days of these long May '71 sessions came up with plaintive numbers such as "I'm Leavin' " and "We Can Make The Morning". Also added in was "It's Only Love", a great change of pace that lifted Elvis's spirits and added a more youthful feel. A week of recording eventually came to an end, a week which had formed a few magnificent numbers.

Around the time of Elvis's return to live performing in Las Vegas, he made his way to see a performance by Irish singer Colm Wilkinson. According to Wilkinson, who met Presley after the show, Elvis spoke of his admiration for Colm's rendition of the song "I'll Take You Home Again, Kathleen". Elvis admired the song and had been aware of it for some time at this point. Home recordings exist from 1959 of Elvis singing it in private. "I'll Take You Home Again, Kathleen" was a popular Irish folk song made famous by Irish tenors and folk artists. This confirmed the admiration Elvis held for Irish tenors which he spoke about during an army interview in Germany. It was written in 1875 by Thomas P. Westendorf, a music teacher from Illinois. It is not a tune of Irish origin but is very much about Ireland and has become an Irish standard.

Established Irish tenors to cover this old ballad about "Kathleen" have included John McCormack, Louis Brown, Frank Patterson, Mark Forrest, the Irish Tenors and John Feeney. Feeney was born in 1903 in Co. Mayo and gained a name as a noted Irish tenor in America, which he emigrated to in 1928. Popular folk singers who have also covered "I'll Take You Home Again, Kathleen" include Red Hurley, Chris Ball, Foster And Allen, and Johnny Carroll.

Next to John McCormack and John Feeney, one of the most popular Irish tenors is Josef Locke, who made "I'll Take You Home Again, Kathleen" one of his most popular numbers. Locke's performances were in the radio airwaves of Ireland and America during Elvis's youth. It is possible that he was one of the several Irish tenors Presley would have heard on the radio when growing up.

Locke was born Joseph McLaughlin in 1917 in Co. Derry and after pursuing his ambition to be a singer, the first song he recorded was "Santa Lucia". This is an old popular and traditional Italian classic, which Elvis Presley also recorded back in 1963 for the movie *Viva Las Vegas*.

Josef enjoyed much stage success in Britain from 1944 to 1958 and broke concert records. His most memorable songs have included, "Hear My Song" and "Galway Bay". He also recorded the Neapolitan standard "O Solo Mio", the inspiration for "It's Now Or Never" and "Come Back To Sorrento" which Elvis's smash hit "Surrender" was based. Locke died in 1999. "I'll Take You Home Again, Kathleen", with its Irish folk theme, has been a perfect number for Irish tenors but it was also an illustrious choice for Presley to broaden his voice and variety of music to further afield.

* * *

Early June 1971 saw Presley's brief return to RCA's Nashville studios. In a couple of days he did several more gospel tracks, including "Reach Out To Jesus" and "There Is No God But God". He also did his version of the Frank Sinatra classic "My Way". In late July Elvis was back in concert and was now at the beginning of a new engagement at Sahara Tahoe in Nevada. The concerts opened on 20 July to more screaming and adoring fans who quickly helped sell out all the shows.

The new season of shows by Presley broke attendance records

again after it came to a close on 2 August. Then exactly one week later Elvis opened his second Vegas engagement of the year. At this stage, the International Hotel had been replaced by Hilton Hotels. Although this move allowed Elvis's contract to be terminated if desired, Parker saw no need to quit and kept the contract with the new company.

The performances lasted four weeks again. His costume this time was black with more elaborate designs and for the first time Elvis introduced a cape for extra effect. This was the 1970s and "gaudy" defined the style of the times. As an individual, Elvis always had chosen whatever he wanted to wear. It was flamboyant, original, unusual and subsequently imitated. There was hardly any performer during the '70s who didn't wear similar attire after him. These were the years when flash went to extravagant levels. Every astronomical legend throughout these years wore flamboyant stage wear from Isaac Hayes to the Commodores. In Ireland the rock stars of Thin Lizzy and Horslips also wore the most unusual and extravagant of stage costumes. It was all part of the visual showbiz appeal.

Over the weeks leading up to the tour Elvis got to stay away from the business for a while. Parker had now started to push Elvis too hard with the long string of tour dates. Parker received a high financial cut but neither Elvis nor Vernon were financially aware to realise that they could have stopped him from gaining such absurd amounts. Presley even became America's highest income tax payer but he is known to have rejected having tax deductions for his charity donations. He believed that the charity would have no meaning if he were to get money back. Despite receiving a lot less money than he was worth, Elvis never knew exactly what he had. This showed how successful he really was as his purchasing power was high and even went as far as purchasing property for other people.

5 November 1971 brought Elvis to Minnesota where he started off his ten state tour and replaced gospel group the Imperials with J. D. Sumner and the Stamps Quartet. The concerts began to get more dramatic and while Elvis's performance reminded the world

of his supreme showmanship, Presley seemed, for some, to be more about show as he kneeled down, holding his cape open wide. Yet, Elvis, as an original of this style, could do these things in such a unique and charismatic way. He was giving all he could but for some the style of the concert presentation often displaced the importance of the music. Nevertheless, how the audience reacted was important to him and they loved every bit of his performance.

One thing Presley strictly did not do was wear sunglasses during his performances. He believed that eye contact was imperative for the atmosphere of the show and although he had his own trademark shades he didn't wear them on stage as that eye contact brought him closer to his fans and his fans closer to him.

1971 saw the beginnings of an Elvis beginning to feel low. Priscilla and Elvis were no longer close and they kept growing apart. It just could not work while Elvis cavorted with other women. He didn't work hard enough to keep her by his side. Their marriage was slowly crumbling apart. However, with regard to his legacy the year had its good sides including the tremendous and highly honourable awards.

His Tupelo birthplace was opened to the public in June 1971 for the first time. This confirmed Presley's status as a living legend. Another accolade transpired in June when the street outside Graceland was renamed after the most famous person in the area. Originally known as 3764 Highway South, it was changed to 3764 Elvis Presley Boulevard. To be given these honours while still living highlighted his prodigious popularity. Elvis's legacy was one that was becoming more special than an ordinary singer.

Irish musician P. J. Curtis construed, "For me Elvis is one of these music and human forces that arrives once in every generation. He gave a voice to youth and lit a fire that still burns . . . and they said it wouldn't last".

CHAPTER NINETEEN

Irish showbands did not dominate the spotlight in the 1970s as music enthusiasts were captured by more original talent, no matter what genre in which it lay. From the traditional Irish sounds of Christy Moore and Planxty to the Elvis-influenced sounds of rock and blues, among the likes of Rory Gallagher and Thin Lizzy, whose careers progressed further in the early '70s.

One of the musicians of the traditional group Planxty to aspire to even greater popularity was Paul Brady who was born in Strabane, Co. Tyrone in 1947. In 1991 Paul wrote and performed a song titled "Nobody Knows", part of which made a point about Presley's fate. Speaking of Elvis in the Irish book, *My Generation, Rock 'n' Roll Remembered: An Imperfect History*, Paul stated, "Elvis was simply an incredible singer. Instinct and talent shoot through every phrase of every line of every song, no matter what mood he was trying to convey".

Paul began performing as a hotel piano player at sixteen and played guitar during the 1960s for the R&B bands Rockhouse and the Cult. Brady enjoyed a career that saw him pass through several bands including the Johnstons and Planxty. Some of his tunes have included "Homes Of Donegal" and "Lakes Of Pontchartrain". He also collaborated with such performers as Andy Irvine and Richard Thompson. Thompson, in his own career, wrote and recorded a song titled, "From Galway To Graceland", which told the story of a Galway woman's journey to Presley's home.

By 1972 in Ireland, the youth searched for something stronger for which they could identify. Another new Irish rock group starting to see the light of success by 1972 went by the name of Horslips. They were founded in Dublin during 1970 and drawing on their Irish roots, they incorporated a tremendous ability to perform straight folk music and hard rock numbers.

With Barry Devlin on bass, Sean Fean on lead guitar, Eamon Carr on drums, Charles O'Connor on violin and Jim Lockhart on flute, tin whistle and keyboard, Horslips provided a chance for each musician to express their own distinct talents. They spent three years gigging around Dublin but eventually signed a deal with RCA that brought their talents to the attention of people in Britain, various European cities and America. Remembering Elvis, Barry Devlin recalled, "When I was a kid I wowed 'em in my father's pub in Ardboe with 'Teddy Bear', the first of many records brought home by my elder sisters. He was a constant presence on the dansettes and though the Beatles absorbed much of my musical life in the '60s, I later picked up on the Sun sessions and his days as the Hillbilly Hepcat and got an overview of his importance to popular music as it exists today".

Although both Irish rock groups Horslips and Thin Lizzy formed around the same time, Horslips set a path of influence on Irish audiences, for which Thin Lizzy would follow. They infused a Celtic element into their music but like Thin Lizzy became better known for their hard rock. Years later drummer Eamon Carr wrote various articles about Elvis and noted that "Elvis created a unique and revolutionary sound".

While Elvis made an impact which would be remembered and taken note of indefinitely throughout historic recollections, there were many areas of lost opportunities. By 1972 it was imperative that Elvis be booked for a world tour. Elvis really needed this but it was all Parker's say on where he was going to go. There is a myth that Elvis could not be booked outside America because Parker, as an illegal alien, worried about the problem of getting back into the country but it was not essential that Parker accompany him.

The real reason could rest in the fact that Parker was happy to keep Elvis exclusive to America. Here he could remain a myth for the rest of the world, unless they came to see him, therefore increasing his iconic status. The group had gone around America and reaching new places would have been a positive element in curing the boredom that persisted. No matter what was good for him, there were no signs of any overseas travelling as of now and it was just time for another exhausting season in Las Vegas.

New songs such as "It's Impossible" were introduced to the live shows that commenced on 26 January. Presley also began performing "You Gave Me A Mountain" which had been a number six hit in Ireland for Brendan Bowyer the previous November. Having seen Bowyer play Vegas, Elvis was influenced to incorporate the song in his act and it became a regular. Also included was "It's Over" which told the story of break up and it seemed inevitable that his happy days with Priscilla were disappearing.

Towards the end of the engagement he added "An American Trilogy", a powerful and patriotic performance. All these songs were histrionic and forceful and it seemed the only challenge Elvis could give himself. It gave him a chance to extend his range as he reached three octaves. As another powerful singer, Ireland's Jack L., said about Elvis, "What amazes me is his voice. The diversity of his voice, how he can go from raw rock to big ballads and how he could stretch his voice is how good a singer he was".

At the end of this engagement, Priscilla arrived at the show to meet Elvis. She informed her husband that she was going out with the karate instructor Mike Stone and then moved out of their Californian home, taking Lisa Marie with her. The news came as a shocking blow to Elvis and he became very distressed but it could not be unexpected. Like most great performers, he became too attached to his music and career. It was due to being away that he became involved with other women and it was because she rarely saw her husband that she realised it was time to get on with her life.

Elvis loved Priscilla but he was incapable of looking after his marriage. She needed a life and Elvis appeared to be having all the fun. The time had finally come and she was now in love with someone else for the first time. He was cast aside and he just could not take that too easily. Fury, pain and total sorrow began to build in him. He raged with anger at times and would go like this continuously until he wore out. A bleak outlook on life and an undeniable sadness loomed over him. How had he destroyed something which had meant so much? Like the tragic hero of Greek drama, his fatal flaw had become his downfall. Priscilla had been the most essential woman in his life since his mother died. She became his best friend but now he felt unloved, facing the future alone for the first time in his life.

In January 1972, "I Just Can't Help Believin' " was released on single, gaining a number twelve Irish chart position. Then 12 February saw the release of the album *Elvis Now* with songs recorded at different sessions over the last three years. The album was poorly compiled with a lot of weak material and due to this, only made it to number forty-four in America.

With a new recording session, the theme would only be based mainly on one thing; sorrowful ballads about loss. Arriving at Hollywood's RCA Studios the first song was titled "Separate Ways". The song explained the situation with which he and Priscilla were faced. "For The Good Times", had Elvis regretting and sadly reminiscing on what was once a wonderful romance. The next day, persuasion from those around him got Presley to record the rocker, "Burning Love". Elvis was not convinced that it was such a great rock song but he was not really interested, regardless of its quality. He did record it, despite his feelings, because of everybody's request and positive opinion of it.

"Burning Love" was later transformed and performed as a ballad by Irish musician David Kitt for an Irish TV Elvis tribute entitled, *Elvis: Burning Love*. Irish group Kíla have also done their version of this classic rock hit. Kíla, which is predominantly an Irish language group, formed in 1987 in Dublin by school friends Eoin Dillon, Rossa Ó Snodaigh, Rónán Ó Snodaigh, Karl Odlum, Dave Odlum and Colm Mac Con Iomaire. Several of the original members would eventually leave to join other groups or pursue other careers but Kíla continues as new musicians pass through it. The group recorded their first album in 1990 and have performed worldwide, covering Europe, U.S.A., Japan and Australia.

After giving his all on that only rock song of the time, Elvis went back to what he felt more suited to; the emotional love songs that told the story of his life. The song "Fool" described how he felt angered with himself for not taking care of the woman he loved. The song had Elvis beating himself to pieces for his mistakes. The performance indicated the sadness, trouble and strife life brought, when it was not being carefully played.

On the third and final day of the session, Elvis went straight into "Always On My Mind". A deep sense of tragedy could be heard in his voice, a sense of tragedy which had been with him all his life but which was projected firmly at this time. The art of the music was imitating life as Elvis knew no better way other than to express his feelings through a song. He had lived and continued to live the words he sang in these songs.

"Always On My Mind" inspired many others to perform it, including the Irish stars, Joe Dolan, Jack L, Damien Rice with the band Juniper, Chris DeBurgh and Dublin born entertainer Tony Kenny, who had a Top 25 hit with it in 1985. Chris DeBurgh was born in Argentina in 1948, the son of British parents, but was raised in Ireland where he still lives today. He became famous in the 1980s with hits such as "Lady In Red" but began in the music business in 1974, gradually gaining massive international success from 1975 onwards.

One of the great artists to pay tribute to Elvis with a cover of this classic is Dublin born folk singer Damien Dempsey. Damien was born in Donaghmede in Dublin. In 1997 he recorded "Dublin Town" and in 1998 he left for New York where he sang in a pub for three months straight. Some of his many great songs include "Apple Of My Eye" and "It's All Good". Dempsey sustains his own unique sound, invoking a fearless and confrontational edge to his performance and injects the same emotional power into music that Elvis Presley did, who he considers one of his major musical heroes.

With an extra addition of tour dates arranged by Parker for the coming year, Elvis was kept occupied. The latest sessions, which brought about a good but short selection of decent music, turned out to be his last for that year. Instead, MGM and Parker decided that it was time to make another movie on Elvis's current concert success to be titled *Elvis On Tour*. Filming commenced at the end of March and the crew took in Presley and his group rehearsing for upcoming concerts.

Since his break up with Priscilla, Elvis had quickly put on weight. The problems he had been faced with put his mind on more than looking after his appearance. Everybody knew Elvis as a fit, slim, perfect-looking man, so sometimes it was a tough battle, but he attempted to keep the weight down, mainly around the time of performing. While the sideburns had become shaped like large lamb chops, his hairstyle had grown longer and wilder with the style of the time but didn't do his good looks any justice. He physically looked a lot different than just two years previously when MGM had last got him on film.

In April Elvis was out on his first tour of 1972. Every day was taken up with a concert throughout the twelve-state, nineteen-show tour, leaving little time for a proper rest. A total of four shows were filmed by MGM. Distant and morose, Presley went on for a break in Palm Springs. Life was made up of rest, performing and recording. Since the beginning of 1971 he began to feel fed up.

In a short time he had dominated the performing end of the business after such a long time away from it. Everything he touched turned to gold but this was no longer fun. He felt worn out and bored and with the death threats, loss of Priscilla, phenomenal accomplishments and undying devotion from fans, he began to feel caged more than ever before. This made him rueful and deserted and brought on depression and an extension to his unsure and insecure personality.

His fame was as consistent as before and fans flocked to see him from every part of the world. This was something he had already experienced and loved, it was nothing new and Elvis needed something original to keep going. He was missing something, missing a true friend. As Irish producer B. P. Fallon once stated, "Elvis was a deity who was crucified by his lack of friends".

One of the major problems was that Elvis Presley was the world's first living superstar. Nobody was as big and nobody was loved as much in life and this was draining him out. Elvis had nobody to whom he could look up and from whom he could take advice. A grave mistake for a performer such as Elvis was not having the regular company of like-minded musicians. There would have been a great chance such company could have further inspired his creativity.

Parker booked Elvis into another tour set to begin in June

1972. The first venue was Madison Square Garden in New York. Presley arrived in the city and held a press conference in front of an enormous swarm of journalists and TV reporters. This was his first time performing in New York City other than the TV appearances that had brought him to America's forefront in 1956. At the interview he was asked how he felt about his image. Elvis explained, "The image is one thing, the human being is another". Here Elvis emphasised the difference between the man and the mediated persona.

His concert at Madison Square Garden was a great example of his everlasting appeal as the first show and the three to follow had been sold out in a flash, with fans sleeping outside for days to get tickets. Presley's two shows at Madison Square Garden on 10 June the next day were recorded by RCA. On its release the album reached number eleven.

The concert began with a brilliant version of "That's All Right" and it was this version the Irish music group Picturehouse referred to when covering the song for the 2002 Irish TV special *Elvis: Burning Love*. Aonghus Ralston of Picturehouse explained on the show, "Elvis was the original star, the first and the best, nobody has been like him since". Picturehouse, lead by singer and songwriter Dave Browne, are a Dublin based band that first came to notice in the late 1990s after the release of their first album. The band have toured Ireland and Europe extensively and have had hits with the songs "Sunburst" and "Everybody Loves My Girl". Another Irish performer to cover the classic "That's All Right" is Mundy. The Co. Offaly-born singer began in music busking on Dublin's Grafton St. before getting signed in 1995. Songs of his include "To You I Bestow" and "Soulmate".

In July 1972 Elvis was introduced to a young woman named Linda Thompson, the reigning Miss Tennessee whom he soon began dating. Then, around this time Parker announced to the press that Presley would be doing a live concert via satellite around the world from Hawaii. This was Parker's best way of opting out of touring the world for real.

On 4 August Presley was back in Vegas, slimmer and getting

a few better concert reports than previously. What was still so incredible was that after about seventeen years of a career he was still a much loved artist selling out auditoriums and concert arenas. He had that rare ability to connect with his audience and many fans never lost their fascination. Elvis interacted with the fans. They handed him gifts and he always joked with the crowds between songs or handed out his own gifts to them.

Elvis gave his first press conference regarding the satellite show on 4 September at the Hilton and explained how amazed he was at the concept of this show. Then in early November MGM's *Elvis On Tour* premiered. The stylish editing and in depth view into Elvis's life, on and off stage, earned the award for best documentary at the Golden Globe Awards.

In November Presley and his group went on tour once again, making this their third tour outside of the two Vegas engagements for that year. Five shows over five consecutive nights in California were followed by dates in Hawaii. Giving three performances in Honolulu over two days, this was his first time performing in the fiftieth state since March of 1961 when he had been a principal contributor to getting the Pearl Harbor Memorial erected.

Around this time Elvis had new chart success when "Burning Love" hit the American charts at number two in October. Irish blues star Van Morrison had another brief moment sharing the Billboard Hot 100 with Presley as his song "Redwood Tree" was at number ninety-nine. "Burning Love" would also become a number six hit in Ireland on its release in 1972. This would be followed by a rerelease hitting the Irish Top 30 on 12 December 2007.

For the rest of 1972, Elvis spent time between Memphis, Vegas and L.A., often with Linda Thompson. The press were aware of a divorce action taken between Elvis and Priscilla. While the year saw an end to his marriage and an obvious sign that he was no longer taking care of his appearance, a new unique production was set for the new year, which would give hope to a man who was regressing in both his personal and professional life.

Chapter Twenty

At the beginning of 1973, Elvis's concert via satellite, which became known as *Aloha From Hawaii*, was scheduled for 14 January. In the days leading up to the event his spirits were on a high. The show was going to bring something new to his career and he was delighted to be taking on a new project that would make history. In the course of this new venture, Presley exercised through swimming and playing sport to get into the best of shape. He lost twenty-five pounds and appeared to have toned up, looking fitter.

On 9 January, Elvis arrived in Honolulu, Hawaii and was greeted by hundreds of cheering fans, many of whom stacked garlands of flowers around his neck. As a mark of respect to his homeland, his choice of jump-suit this time included the symbol of the country; the Bald Eagle. This began the idea of using images of different creatures to make the jumpsuits more elaborate. Over the years designs of peacocks and tigers appeared on his clothing which all had special symbolic significance to Elvis.

On 12 January, a rehearsal show was performed and spectators were only asked to donate money to the Kui Lee Cancer Fund on admittance, as the satellite show was benefiting this cause. Then, just after midnight on the morning of 14 January, Elvis Presley took the world by storm once again. Running out on stage under a massive flood of dazzling lights Presley burst straight into "See See Rider". Appearing nervous at start, he soon got into the show and connected with the audience, but he certainly seemed far more timid than when caught on camera previously.

The show went directly live to a few East Asian countries including, China, Japan and Korea. It was also transmitted but with delay to Europe via the Eurovision Network and went to the televisions of twenty-eight European countries. Neither a showing nor a mention of the televised event appeared on Ireland's only state broadcaster RTÉ, who chose not to purchase the broadcasting rights. Coincidentally on the day of the concert,

The Sunday Independent printed an article next to the TV guide about Brendan Bowyer's next visit to Las Vegas to visit Elvis and present him with a plague of his coat of arms.

Aloha From Hawaii premiered in America four months later, when an astonishing fifty-seven percent of the TV audience watched it. This concert offered people one of Elvis's most spectacular performances of his later career. Presley gave viewers magnificent versions of "What Now My Love", "Welcome To My World" and "Steamroller Blues". *Aloha From Hawaii* was the first of its kind and although several events had been transmitted worldwide via satellite before, this was the first time one performer gave an entire concert to the world. Once the show had been screened worldwide, an estimated one billion people had seen it.

The greatest project Elvis had taken part in for years came to an end and after a renewed victory of conquering the music business, Elvis was back to a lower point on 26 January when he began his next four weeks at the Hilton. A report during this time gave explanations of Presley's lack of energy and interest. Despite becoming an even greater victim of exploitation, Elvis remained loyal to his manager. Parker was the first manager of a rock star and even more than that, he was the first manager of a superstar.

The lack of interest, which reports suggested, would remain, unless it was for something extraordinary and that rarely looked promising. Unfortunately the audiences were not aware of his personal life or how tough his professional life had become. For them they were here for a show, to see a legend. While the devoted fans were delighted to be in his presence, many of the shows did not impress the audience who were just there to see a concert by a popular name.

On 25 March 1973, a report appeared in Ireland's *Sunday World* tabloid titled, "Elvis is a fraud". Written by Kevin Marron, the article criticised Presley for the rather dull performance he had recently given in Vegas. Marron stated that "The King has lost a fan", for giving such a disappointing show. While the reporter had been told that Elvis had pneumonia, he brushed this off at the end of his piece with "excuses, excuses". Understandably there had to be some excuse if the man who was renowned for being a great entertainer was not living up to expectations. Here was a man who should not have been performing so often.

Brendan Bowyer went to see Elvis in 1973 and while Elvis waved at Brendan and his wife, they were not permitted back stage because Elvis was not feeling well. It was the first time Brendan wasn't granted this privilege but he noticed something wasn't right. He saw that Elvis's eyes were swollen and he was out of shape. Bowyer, who was starting to go through his own difficult phase could clearly see the pressures on Presley as the pressures of show business fell upon him too. Wanting to be young again to give his best, Bowyer became depressed and turned to alcohol. The deaths in the mid-'70s of his mother and then Tom Dunphy drove him into further despondency.

On top of the stressful schedule, off stage Elvis was falling apart. He began to take more medication for various problems. The mixture of many problems and too much work was putting an awful burden on him. Elvis wanted to feel twenty years old again, without suffering from the constant overwork and enjoy every moment of his performance. Doctors began prescribing him medication for muscular pains as well as diet pills, flu medicine, sleeping pills and uppers that gave him some boost to take on the shows he knew he had to do.

Ever since he had been introduced by other recruits to Dexedrine he had taken on a moderate but steady use of medication throughout the '60s but now the mixture of pills were starting to alter his system. Doctors never made it clear to him the dangers of misusing prescription drugs. Understandably he assumed that if a doctor prescribed something it was safe. Although Presley read about advances in medicine, the use of such legal pills, which made him feel better, satisfied him that he was not taking part in anything morally sinister.

During a gig on 18 February 1973 four men leapt on stage and while bodyguards ran to protect Elvis, Elvis himself knocked one of the supposed attackers into the audience. While the men only turned out to be over excited fans, Elvis was clearly insecure and there seemed no exit from the fear he exhibited in such situations. Then, due to misguided assumptions he accused Mike Stone for sending those guys to attack him. As Elvis's anger against Mike Stone built up he blamed Stone for breaking up his marriage and this lead to further rage. At the height of his outburst Presley ordered his bodyguards to have Stone killed but as he gradually calmed down he cancelled the idea.

After Vegas, Elvis began spending more time with Linda Thompson who added some cheerfulness to his life. While he was trying to relax, Parker was working out new deals with RCA. In order to earn a large sum of money instantly, Parker sold Presley's back catalogue to RCA Records for $5million, losing his and Elvis's rights to the music. RCA now had complete control of Elvis's music recorded before 1973. A new deal was arranged for further music but all the previous material was out of their hands.

Around the same time as Parker made the infamous deal with RCA, the soundtrack to *Aloha From Hawaii* made it's chart debut and it became Presley's first number one hit album since 1964's *Roustabout*. The album remained on the charts for a total of fifty-two weeks. Other chart success for Elvis in 1973 included a number nine hit in Ireland with "Always On My Mind" in January. An album, titled with this song would later become another Irish Top 10 hit in August, 1997 and a further rerelease of the single put it at number twenty-seven on the Irish charts on 22 November 2007.

In early April, friend and karate expert, Ed Parker, presented Elvis with a sixth degree black belt at his International Kenpo Association. Then touring commenced again, with a new set of performances devised to keep Elvis going non-stop. Elvis began a nine-day, twelve-concert tour and then went straight into a seventeen day set at the Sahara Tahoe Hotel.

Continuously feeling stressed and tired, as well as often indulging in unhealthy foods and medications his body was taking a hit. His father started to express concern and became inquisitive as to where Elvis was accessing such vast amounts of medication. An investigation was opened to find the source of the problem and it was found that three physicians and a dentist were responsible for supplying Elvis with prescriptions. However, Elvis's dismissal of how hazardous such medication could be put a halt to any sustained help.

Almost one month to the date that Presley closed his Tahoe shows, he was back touring. When this sixteen show schedule ended, Elvis returned back to his quiet lifestyle of attending movies and resting at Graceland. While some time was devoted to Linda Thompson, the rest of his time showed how Presley was gradually becoming a recluse. He would rarely be seen outside his home other than in concert. He felt the world caving in on him and the fire in his eyes began to fade.

In late July, Elvis's new recording session was held at Stax Studios in Memphis. A little studio only a few minutes away from Graceland, which had been responsible for the creation of southern soul. It had also been home to the soundtrack recordings by Isaac Hayes for the 1971 film *Shaft*. Many of the musicians were surprised by Presley's appearance as they had never seen Elvis with much weight and they also took note that he was not in the best of moods.

For the next few days of recording it was obvious that Presley put little passion into the music. While the musicians and backing groups gave the usual spark, the main vocals were lacking energy. Over the next three days things slowed down and Elvis only finished up on four songs. "Raised On Rock" was followed by "For Ol' Times Sake" which was again another song about losing love, which became his common genre.

One of his better tracks from this session had been recorded on the first day. "Take Good Care Of Her" was based on a man losing a woman to another man and it was hardly a coincidence that Elvis did this song. That song was also recorded by the Irish country singer Daniel O'Donnell who covered many Presley songs and songs Elvis helped make famous. Besides this one and "From A Jack To A King", Daniel has done "A Fool Such As I", "Wooden Heart", "How Great Thou Art" and "Little Cabin On The Hill".

Co. Donegal born O'Donnell began his career in the early

1980s singing soft sleepy ballads. In his concerts he incorporated a tribute to Elvis covering "That's All Right", "Love Me Tender", "Are You Lonesome Tonight?", "Girl Of My Best Friend" and "Don't Be Cruel". In 1988 Daniel played Nashville at the Fan Fair show, with Presley's famous backing vocalists the Jordanaires. In 1997 O'Donnell accompanied a few of his fans from Co. Waterford to Memphis when they won a trip to see Graceland. O'Donnell found after his visit to Graceland that he made a connection with Elvis and as a result, any time he sings an Elvis song now it has a greater meaning for him.

Around the end of July 1973 the new album *Elvis*, including the song "Fool" entered the charts. After the success of *Aloha From Hawaii* this one failed to reach similar heights, reaching only number fifty-two in America. The previous June his R&B track "Polk Salad Annie" entered the Irish charts at number sixteen.

On 6 August Elvis was back at the Hilton. The opinions of reporters did not vary and they remained as sour as before but did explain how the shows had differed so much since 1969 and 1970. The overblown dramatic formats had pulled him far away from the young boy full of raw passion. He constantly wanted to make things bigger and better than before. He was almost reliving the dramatic stories he read about in comic books as a child. Vegas was destroying him because its mythology of larger than life was a disastrous influence on Elvis. He was well aware that he was the biggest star in the world. While he didn't have an ego that was smug, he knew if he pulled back from this huge star his ego would be bruised.

Shortly after his last performance on 3 September Presley and Parker had a row. Elvis, who had got to a stage where he had become more daring in his discussions with the audience, complained about the Hilton Hotel's intention to fire one of his favourite employees. Looking out for the working class, Elvis attacked what he called "the hierarchy of the Hilton Hotels". Parker wanted to keep the best of feelings with the Hotel and gave out to Elvis for making negative comments about the company that was paying him. The two burst out in dramatic rage in front of the entourage who could not believe what they were seeing.

For years Elvis had kept feelings under a tight wrap but this explosion just blasted everything right out. Suddenly, it came to an end when Elvis Presley fired Colonel Thomas Parker. In response, the Colonel stated that he quit as his manager and went back to his suite to write up his bill. Elvis's massive spending and charitable donations now put him in an awkward position. It turned out that he had no choice but to keep onto the services of Colonel Tom and Elvis rehired him although he demanded a wage increase. With business continuing like usual, all issues got back to normal.

* * *

August 1973 saw another Irish chart Elvis hit with "Fool" reaching number eight. Due to a shortage of recordings at his last studio sessions, RCA sent a mobile recording truck to Presley's Palm Springs home on 22 September 1973. There he cut the songs "I Miss You" and "Are You Sincere?".

Most of the time around now was spent in California and Linda Thompson had become a regular girlfriend. All his life he had suffered from a poignant loneliness. The surroundings of quite a number of men only sheltered him from the world which had negative effects. The healthier option of going out to take the risks of experiencing the real world never surfaced. He had never properly done this as an adult due to beginning and continuing a popular career from such a young age. He could never know what he would have had if he had not gained that fame and fortune.

On 9 October Elvis's divorce from Priscilla was finalised. At the Los Angeles Superior Courthouse both Elvis and Priscilla showed up to make the settlement that would officially part them on their separate ways. In the following few days after he knew for sure he had lost the love of his life, Elvis began to experience breathing problems which persisted for a number of days until he was hospitalised at Baptist Memorial Hospital.

It was discovered that a doctor in L.A. was prescribing drugs to Elvis. He had received acupuncture treatment with an injection of Demerol as well as a selection of other prescribed medications.

While he had almost instantly gained an addiction to Demerol, the reliance on medication left him biologically dependent on drugs. The effects came out in his appearance as he began to look sick and his behaviour was often irrational.

Elvis was released from hospital after several weeks. The awful physical state he had fallen into just after his divorce shook him and he realised he would have to try and get off the pills. While he was in the hospital, he got down to one sleeping pill a day. In order to get fit, he took up a sport and his personal physician Dr. Nick got him interested in racquetball.

During his attempt to clean up his health and career, Presley travelled back to Stax studios on 10 December to begin a new week long recording session. Elvis was in upright form and appeared to be quite enthusiastic about the music he was going to record. Kicking off at 9 P.M. the first song was the fast paced country track "I Got A Feeling In My Body". Elvis sang with eagerness and it was a change from his previous Stax recordings earlier in the year.

Moving away from the sad lonely ballads, he did the strong rhythmic soul tune "If You Talk In Your Sleep" which added excitement and a sexually charged energetic flow. The following days included sombre and downhearted performances such as "Loving Arms" and "Good Time Charlie's Got The Blues". The latter was a folk song about a man who sees all his friends leaving for better places and better lives, bringing about this one man's loneliness. Aware of the similarities through this song and his life he again sang with enthusiasm, melancholy and sensitivity.

Over the next few days the style would change in the music and the mood took a new root with more upbeat tunes including "Talk About The Good Times" and then Presley's superb version of Chuck Berry's "Promised Land". This was one of his last fantastic rock 'n' roll performances. Moving back into easy listening mode for his last recordings he went through "If That Isn't Love", "Spanish Eyes" and "She Wears My Ring". This brought 1973's projects and accomplishments to a close and it turned out to be a year of many ups and downs, starting and ending with positive aspects in Elvis's life and career, but also including some of the worst of problems. Luckily he seemed confident once again and was determined to take new steps in the appropriate direction.

One of the most memorable tracks throughout his latest session which would give Elvis another major hit, both in America and Ireland was "My Boy". Other singers who have covered this include Irish *Eurovision* star Johnny Logan, but it became a Top 20 U.S. hit and an Irish number four hit for Presley. "My Boy" was a French song written and recorded by Claude Francois in 1970. It was then rendered into the English language by Northern Ireland songwriter Phil Coulter and Scottish songwriter Bill Martin.

Phil Coulter was born in Co. Derry, Northern Ireland in 1942 and became a respected artist from the late 1960s onwards, writing and performing many popular numbers including *Eurovision* hits and songs for the Dubliners as well as the Irish rugby anthem "Ireland's Call". While Elvis did cover, and was victorious with "My Boy", it was Irish singer/actor Richard Harris who first had success with it in 1971 when it was entered into a Radio Luxembourg song contest. This introduced it to the world and Elvis.

Elvis had begun singing it at concerts and would for a long time, giving credit to Harris for popularising it. The song was never written for Elvis but he gave it an earnest and efficacious rendition, as its story about relationship and marital breakdown fitted his current repertoire. It was his last highlight of 1973 before a pattern of frequent tours and performances would dominate the following year.

CHAPTER TWENTY-ONE

Returning to Vegas on 26 January 1974 Elvis was advised by Dr. Nick to have the last two weeks of his regular four week engagement cancelled. His constant tours only lead to exhaustion, an increasing demand for medication and further hospitalisation. Nonetheless he was back on the road soon enough. Beginning on 1 March 1974 Parker booked Elvis for twenty consecutive days with twenty-five concerts. This brought a return to the gruelling tour schedules that lead to extreme exhaustion.

His concert on 16 March marked his first performance in Memphis since 1961. Everything was a sell out and this kept Elvis at the top of the box office. On 20 March, RCA recorded his performance at the Mid-South Coliseum in Memphis for his upcoming release, *Recorded Live On Stage In Memphis*. Then, after an additional five shows were carried out in California, Elvis returned to Nevada for his Sahara Tahoe engagement. The pressure was only on again afterwards as Elvis went into his third tour of the year. This would then lead into his second season of the year at the Hilton.

In July the soundtrack to the Memphis concert was released and went to number thirty-three. Fortunately it was a step up from his album *Good Times* released earlier in April, only to peak at ninety. Even though it contained some good work it became Elvis's least successful album of all, outside of the greatest hits and budget album releases. Yet, despite this low position, it is important to note that in his two decade long career, his singles or albums were never kept outside the Top 100.

When Elvis returned to Vegas he had again put on weight and was taking less care of himself. The plans to get back onto a careful, healthy, safe lifestyle crumbled and his addiction to medication did not seize. The big problem was that he pushed himself to the limits of concert performing. Elvis was only happiest when on stage. He would have lived every minute on that stage if he could have, because entertaining people became the driving force of his life.

Off stage Elvis still continued to enjoy a variety of women. However this did not drive Linda away as she sustained a love for the man, who in his own way returned that love too. Unfaithfulness was one of his greatest weaknesses. Every temptation was laid directly in front of him and the impulsive desire for new women and casual sex was a pleasure too difficult for him to resist. The main problem now was his inability to battle his vices. While Elvis occasionally smoked cigars, he never drank alcohol. Never drinking was a sign of how he had learned from his parents' mistakes. Sadly, what alcohol does for most is what the medicine was doing for Elvis.

Several weeks after his second season of shows at the Hilton, Elvis began his fourth tour of 1974. After a total of fourteen shows, which didn't include any rest days, the tour came to an end and Elvis then went straight into another Sahara Tahoe engagement. In the aftermath of the concert performances Elvis began detailing ideas to make a documentary about karate.

After years of studying the martial art and being involved in karate demonstrations at places such as the Tennessee Karate Institute, Elvis felt the urge to express his enthusiasm for the art. This documentary film was to be titled *The New Gladiators* and document the art's most talented contributors. In early November it began to take off with full devotion and a lot of Elvis's talents and techniques in the sport were filmed.

Suddenly, after a great deal of time was set on continuing the film, the whole idea vanished. The plans rapidly fell apart and were never completed. It was an unfortunate end as this project would have shown Elvis's passionate interest in something other than singing. He was also going to narrate the documentary film and explain the philosophical discipline involved in the sport. This part of Elvis's life, which he took very seriously, went very much unnoticed. Health problems were the explanation given to the sudden close down, and this was no joke. During the last several months of the year he had been having intestinal problems. Various problems persisted throughout the months and due to this, Elvis's January 1975 Vegas season had to be postponed.

By 1975 he had begun to slip back into the lifestyle which saw him failing to take care of his health. Concert performances lacked energy and reporters tired of his shows. Irish tabloids ran a story titled, "Elvis: Forty, Fat and Fading". Dr. Nick did what he could and suggested for Elvis to be hospitalised when required. The serious health problems were showing, as in a short period of time he had been admitted to Baptist Memorial Hospital on several occasions. One time Linda had woken up to find Elvis struggling for breath and he was immediately taken to hospital.

On release from hospital Dr. Nick helped him refrain from over using the medication. A routine was established to get Elvis healthy and a nurse was assigned to visit Graceland each day. The doctor even spent time playing racquetball with Presley in order to get him active again. Although he agreed to many of the recommendations that were insisted upon him, he did not refuse to drift away from his music and in less than a month he made his way to a new recording session.

In early March 1975 at Hollywood's RCA Studios, Elvis's first song was "Fairytale". From folk ballads to country, up next Elvis recorded the song he had rejected many years previously, "Green, Green Grass Of Home". The song had become a smash hit for Tom Jones almost ten years before. This song has also been covered by the great Irish tenor Frank Patterson.

Frank was born in Co. Tipperary in 1938 and began singing with the Wren Boys at a young age. He relocated to Dublin in 1961 where he studied vocal technique and received top honours at the *Feis Ceoil*. Frank began as a classical singer but gradually turned towards popular tunes. Throughout his career he performed sell out concerts from London's Albert Hall to New York's Carnegie Hall. Frank died in the year 2000.

Like many other Irish tenors, Patterson has recorded several standards of his genre. "Amazing Grace", "How Great Thou Art", "I'll Take You Home Again, Kathleen", "O Solo Mio" and "The Impossible Dream" are classic covers in his collection, which we are also well informed now that Elvis also did. However, Patterson sang some other numbers, uncommon to older traditional tenors and again, recorded by Presley. These include "Can't Help Fallin' In Love", "You'll Never Walk Alone" and the songs Elvis would soon perform live; "America The Beautiful" and "Unchained Melody". In 2005 when Lisa Marie, now aged thirty-seven, paid a visit to Ireland, she arranged that flowers be placed at Patterson's grave.

Elvis finished off the first day of his March 1975 session with "I Can Help" and "And I Love You So". Elvis's version of "I Can Help" became an Irish Top 30 single hit on 1 January 1984. These sessions continued as Elvis glided through "Susan When She Tried" and the country rocker "T-R-O-U-B-L-E". Even though he didn't seem pleased at times with some of his own recordings, RCA pushed their "cash cow" to continue as they needed new material.

So far the majority of the tracks were uptempo country tunes, but the recording session came to a close with "Pieces Of My Life". With a shredded heart in full light this song projected Presley's feelings clearly. For Elvis his deep sense of loneliness, despite all the women, resulted in such songs. This work reflected a man who was deteriorating and a man sorrowfully lamenting, turning into a self-destructive wreck.

Elvis's 1975 session had been mostly country music orientated. Although this genre was always an influence on him, he had rarely cut straight country tracks without combining blues. Despite Elvis having recorded in the country music capital of Nashville, he had never been one to join in with the country or folk scene. However, many great country and folk artists have seen him as an influence. In Ireland some of the most famous performers of this genre have found Elvis an important influence.

Irish folk singer Christie Hennessy, born in 1945 in Co. Kerry, found Elvis to be one of his earliest inspirations in music. Christie first began recording music in the early 1970s and some of his most noted songs are "Messenger Boy" and "I Am A Star".

Other Irish country and folk musicians who also emerged during the 1970s include Foster And Allen. Guitar-playing Tony Allen from Co. Westmeath and Accordion-playing Mick Foster from Co. Kildare first met working in local groups and performing at venues in the early '70s. In 1975 they formed their own group and toured Britain playing easy-listening with a strong hint of Irish traditional. They eventually decided to become a duo act and returned to Ireland, releasing a song called "The Rambles Of Spring". After success in Ireland with this, they then recorded "A Bunch Of Thyme", which hit the Irish charts several times from 1978 onwards. Included in their recordings and live performances are covers of the Elvis hits "Can't Help Fallin' In Love", "Love Me Tender" and "Always On My Mind". They have also covered the classics, "Green, Green Grass Of Home", "Bridge Over Troubled Water", "For The Good Times" and "Spanish Eyes" also done by Presley in his later years.

While Tony and Mick set their sights on success at this point in 1975, Elvis prepared for his latest Vegas shows which had been postponed since January. 18 March saw his return to the Hilton. His record sales were low but Presley was kept as one of the most successful box office draws in show business. During certain gigs he began to joke about his weight as many people were surprised to see him heavy. The self mocking kept him in good cheer for the crowd.

During this Vegas season, actress and singer Barbra Streisand presented Elvis with a deal to star in her new movie, *A Star Is Born*. It was a remake of the original based on success and failure but now involving a burned-out rock star. Elvis got excited about the idea of the movie, which he felt would fulfil his dream of starring in a worthwhile movie. Nevertheless, as usual, Parker interrupted the dream in order to gain what he wanted; a more than generous income. His charge went beyond what she could offer and Elvis lost his chance. Elvis lost out on many projects that could have rid him of the monotony he encumbered from the constant tours around the one country.

Parker insisted that he get the same wages he always had, despite the fact that his career was unsteady. While Presley was sweating it out with show after show, Colonel Parker was sitting back smoking his cigars, sitting in the casino throwing away millions that Elvis earned for him. Due to Parker's many debts at the hotel casino, he knew he had to keep Presley performing there. Elvis had become completely subservient to the power of his management without any hope or idea of how to escape this manipulation.

In the weeks following the first Vegas season of the year, Elvis purchased a Convair 880 Jet, which was the first plane he owned. Naming it after his daughter, Presley furnished it with elaborate decor and the plane gave him a chance to travel in style with his first tour of 1975 just around the corner. The tail of the plane also had printed Elvis's personal trademark which he had created some years previously which included the letters TCB with a lightning bolt, standing for "Taking Care Of Business In A Flash". Elvis's hope lingered on that a world tour would eventually be arranged, something he was stirring towards. Parker often suggested that they would get around to it and this got Elvis enthusiastic.

In May, during an eighteen-concert tour, Elvis gave a charity performance in Mississippi to benefit the victims of a recent tornado disaster and handed a cheque to the state's governor for no less than $100,000. Three weeks after this tour Elvis was back on the road again starting with eight shows over five days. Elvis then went onto appear in his third tour of the year. During some of the shows, Elvis' wild temper was noticed clearly by the audience.

Noticing a lack of enthusiasm from the audience, Elvis began letting them request songs. For an extra lift he threw his guitar into the audience and began giving away $40,000 rings. His mind was in a spin from all the complexities in life, mixed with the pestilent pills. From this came the temper tantrums. On occasion Elvis shot out TV sets for target practice. This anger became dangerous as he shot off his guns into hotel walls and chandeliers. This was rock 'n' roll at its extreme.

Sometimes his generosity matched such excessive behaviour as he began purchasing houses for different people and paid medical bills for others. Nevertheless his finance levels were at an all time low. He had given almost everything away and now relied on a bank loan. After living through enormous amounts of excess between the drugs, bad food and charity, he returned to Vegas on 18 August. Eventually Elvis had to sit down on occasion during shows for the first time in his career. The slender, energetic, karate chopping Elvis who took Vegas by storm at first had made a complete turnaround for the worse. Lacking energy, the power in his shows waned but the ability to sing remained.

Suddenly, after working only three days, in what would normally be a two week engagement, Elvis fell ill, cancelling the rest of his shows and flying back to Memphis where he was hospitalised. Elvis was suffering from fatigue, but his doctor observed that he continued to have intestinal problems, a dangerously high cholesterol level and a bad liver. Dr. Nick also took into account that he suffered from depression.

Elvis's depression sometimes transformed him into a brooding mess of anger, which irritated some members of his entourage. His temper could frighten some people but he was then often thoughtful to the same people. Like any human being he had to let off steam but now he was beginning to run out of life. Some negative critics focus on this brief aspect of his life failing to realise that it was all part of the human condition. Elvis was a human being who exemplified the philosophical axiom of Aristotle that "man is flawed".

In the months following recuperation, Elvis began construction on a racquetball court behind Graceland. He then went to work with a two week schedule in Vegas on 2 December. Dr. Nick suggested he shorten his performances to only one show a night instead of his usual two. With each show a full sell out, the hotel was sold out at a time normally only half the building would be occupied. Finishing up his concerts in mid December, Elvis flew back to Memphis where he tried to relax but could not find comfort due to constant illness.

After Christmas, Elvis was scheduled for a single gig on New Year's Eve. 1975 was a reasonable success as Presley continued to gain chart hits in America and around the world. January of this year saw his track "Promised Land" jump into the Irish charts at number seven and in April, Ireland had made "I've Got A Thing About You Baby" a number twenty. His New Year's Eve performance secured his position as the biggest concert performer in the business but it continued to play havoc with his health.

Elvis could not physically live up to his image. He had done something mammoth for the music industry during the 1950s and he had been the figurehead for all the incredible musicians who broke free to perform the music they wanted to perform. However, trying to fulfil the expectations desired by rock fans and music lovers was becoming life threatening.

Elvis had rushed through life early on and left his mark during a different era. However, the Elvis of the 1970s could not reverse time and keep that era alive to the extent expected by fans. It was a time for new musicians. His time had come and gone and although that didn't mean he had to disappear into the wings, it just meant he needed to settle down and take it easy. However, this was not something he seemed capable of doing. Elvis was withering away as new stars came along in his place.

The 1960s and '70s were the fresh years of experimentation in rock music after the rock revolution of the 1950s. The '70s introduced such talents as David Bowie and Bruce Springsteen who expressed their admiration for Presley. Although he was mainly just a performer now, Elvis was still seen as the creative and revolutionary artist from the '50s and this is why he continued to be admired. The Ireland of 1975 was far more aware of the outside world and was slowly keeping up-to-date on modern issues, especially in music.

1975 in Ireland marked the introduction of Dublin-born Bob Geldof. He started his career in the music industry when he formed the group the Boomtown Rats in Dún Laoghaire. They formed songs made up of the punk sounds of the time. Their punk-pop persona did not last long but Geldof later began his solo career. The most popular songs of his early career were "Rat Trap" and "I Don't Like Mondays" which gave his group a number one hit. Bob Geldof conveyed his respect and understanding of the achievements of Elvis Presley when he explained, "He was an intuitive genius shot across our lives".

Geldof pushed the boundaries on the importance of rock 'n' roll as a positive force. With a massive rock culture behind him, he launched the phenomenal platforms for *Live Aid* and *Live 8* worldwide to highlight the horrific struggles faced by third world countries. Such events brought together the top names in music to perform a historic concert of awareness for the poverty of the third world. Rock culture proved to be a powerful and effective organisation.

The Ireland of the 1970s saw an economy which had not yet reached any exceptional level, even with Ireland's introduction to the European Economic Community in 1973. However the country had broken away on an enormous scale from oppressive censorship. Nonetheless, a truly free Ireland had yet to emerge. Catholicism still held a major place and while it was indirectly challenged by a lean towards the arts which it had condemned, as well as a growth in Feminism, it still clutched onto the masses.

The Ireland of the 1970s still banned contraception and equal and civil rights had a long road ahead. Nonetheless, despite all this, the Irish music scene was far more exciting than ever as Thin Lizzy reached the pinnacle of their careers. Rock concerts in Ireland were not far off those performed in America, with young people now having the freedom to go wild and set themselves free. The heroes of rock in America had paved a way and now Ireland was embracing that path as more and more rock and punk groups set up. While Elvis was fading, Ireland was vastly changing and getting every inch closer to reaching the greatest heights imaginable for the rock 'n' roll industry within its own nation.

CHAPTER TWENTY-TWO

In January of 1976, an article appeared on the front page of Ireland's *Sunday World* with the headline, "Elvis turns to God". The report by Sam Smyth discussed the idea that Elvis was planning to stop his career in entertainment and "resurface as the biggest gospel singing evangelist ever seen in America". The article was not far off one of Elvis's wishes which he once discussed with J. D. Sumner, but it never came to pass.

Shortly after this piece another article surfaced in the same Irish tabloid, this time asking "Is Elvis going blind?" It discussed the fears from fans over Presley's glaucoma and his "hermit existence" due to it, "coming out only to buy cars". While Elvis's legendary status increased, making him more of a mystery for the media across the globe, his reclusive habits were entertained further by the completion of the racquetball court behind Graceland. He began to spend heavily again and presented more expensive gifts to a range of people including a TV presenter who joked about wanting a car too.

Elvis knew his life was like no other and he assumed he could not do things like anyone else. This created the reclusive lifestyle which just grew worse. Regarding the medication intake, nobody could help him other than himself but he began to fade faster. Life had become a nightmare and the real Elvis Presley was nowhere to be found. Here was a body of a man who lived in fear, paranoia and pain.

Elvis had rapidly transformed from the days he was a fast, fit fighter. Unfortunately nobody could entice this man to mend his ways. A once towering, powerful man who had completely lost his way. Nobody could do anything for Presley other than himself, but he was no longer himself anymore. It was not a common task for celebrities to take such measures to help their lives during these years. The Betty Ford clinic which later helped celebrities had not been invented yet and Elvis denied his health problems.

With a new recording session beginning in February 1976,

the songs chosen once again revealed how Elvis was singing tunes of a nature to which he related. For the first time ever, Elvis did the recordings at Graceland instead of a studio. "Bitter They Are, Harder They Fall" was the first track joining the list of haunting and regretful songs. His mind was not fully focused and his attention span was low as he lacked much interest in the session.

The next evening, Elvis began with "Solitaire" which was one of the saddest songs he ever recorded. This number told the story of a lonely man who had lost everything. While many songs displayed such loneliness and anguish, Presley's touching rendition meant something as the story paralleled his life. The following night, the genre changed with Elvis returning to fast paced country rock. Written by Mark James, "Moody Blue" was favoured by Elvis and the session proved his variances again. Although he did complete it, he went back to a song which represented his own pathos with "I'll Never Fall In Love Again". Like "Solitaire" it was a morose story of a man who had failed in love.

Elvis entered his fourth evening of recordings and first on the list was "For The Heart", a soft R&B number. He followed that with a breathtaking version of the song "Hurt". That was the greatest challenge of the time and he pulled it off brilliantly, again establishing himself as a superb vocalist. Elvis concluded the next morning with a song he loved for decades. This song was "Danny Boy" and although he had done informal home recordings of it since his time in Germany and during rehearsals for his '68 comeback special, he now wanted to do a professional version.

Although it has traditionally been considered an Irish song, "Danny Boy" was written by British writer Frederic Weatherly (1848 - 1929) in 1913. Legend has suggested that the tune was originally composed by Rory Dall O'Cahan in the 1600s. However, the first words were set to the music of the song "Londonderry Air". The first appearance of the tune in print occurred in 1855 in *Ancient Music of Ireland* published by George Petrie (1789 - 1866). The untitled melody was supplied to Petrie by Miss Jane Ross of Limavady, Co. Derry (also known as Londonderry) who claimed to have taken it down from the playing of an itinerant piper. This is from where the title of "Londonderry Air" originated. Today "Danny Boy" is what the tune remains to be called and it has become a favourite of Irish tenors and ballad performers.

Presley's version was enchanting as he took the decision to sing it while playing a piano, without any background vocals or additional instruments. Other charming performances have been given by such Irish tenors as John McCormack, John Feeney, Josef Locke, Louis Brown, Frank Patterson, Mark Forrest, the Celtic Tenors and the Irish Tenors. There is also performances by performers Sean Dunphy and Red Hurley plus instrumental versions by James Galway and Johnny Carroll.

Over the last two days which brought the session to a close, the choice of material was all downhearted with "Never Again", "Love Coming Down" and "Blue Eyes Crying In The Rain". From this selection of songs it was obvious that this was a disconsolate man who was grieving.

Just over five weeks after Elvis ended his recordings, he was back performing. St. Patrick's Day saw him commencing his first tour of the year which included eight shows. By now Elvis seemed incapable of giving an exceptional performance and throughout many of the shows he appeared disoriented and began forgetting words to songs. The first tour of the year was quickly completed but not surprisingly, he was back on the road again in late April which then lead straight into his annual Sahara Tahoe engagement.

The single release of "Hurt" reached its peak position of twenty-eight in May. The same Billboard Top 100 chart for that week saw Elvis sharing the U.S. charts for the one and only time with Irish rock group Thin Lizzy, whose song "The Boys Are Back In Town" was currently at fifty.

While Elvis continued to spiral downhill, new tours were booked and at the end of May 1976 Elvis was back on the road. Thirteen concerts over eleven nights proved too much, but he claimed that the only place he was happiest was on stage. It was here he could be seen smiling, joking and having fun which was a rarity for him off stage these days. Performing on stage was the best thing Elvis knew. The stage was his safest territory.

One thing that did bring a smile to his face was the sight of his little girl, Lisa Marie, who stayed at Graceland for a short while after his latest tour. They played and Elvis took her to amusements and spoiled her with gifts but while her presence did delight him, it did not draw a conclusion to his reclusive habits the rest of the time. Much of his free time had him remaining in his bedroom reading books. He eventually came out of his room on 25 June for his fourth tour of 1976.

Shortly after this tour, under Elvis's apparent orders, Vernon informed several of his closest confidants that their positions were all to be terminated within a week. This would lead to a major "tell all" book which would come out within the next year and detailed Elvis's dependency on drugs. From the very thought of this book, Elvis fumed and never failed to release the stress that accumulated, but when he stopped he would fall into a quiet, emotional and despondent phase.

Arguing and losing people made little difference to an Elvis poisoned by medication. All he could do was live for the moment and he tried to do things the way he wanted to. Despite being in constant physical pain, he had no challenge to rise up to. He could lose weight and take care of himself if he had a challenge, like during the movie years or when he did the Hawaiian TV special. Parker was the man with all the power to organise something new but failed to change the pattern of endless tours, despite the fact Presley had never left the country.

With no other project in sight, Parker booked Elvis into his fifth tour of the year with fifteen consecutive daily shows. Critics now took him as a "has been" but his lackeys reassured him that he was fine. One report explained how the fans screamed for what he had done and what he symbolised, rather than what he was now. His glory was only in his past. "I like to think of him" explained Irish novelist Maeve Binchy, "of when he burned bright like a star and made us all terribly happy and sing and dance and dream".

Late August marked the beginning of his sixth tour of the year. It ran for thirteen days with sixteen performances. Some shows were good considering the condition Presley was in but the overall quality gave a mixed feeling. How he performed now was not right for this man's original style and there was no doubt that he should not have been expected to work like this.

Elvis had crossed a line directing him to a danger zone of constant medical problems. These problems included a damaged kidney, glaucoma, a twisted colon, persistent hypoglycaemia, hypertension and severe head, stomach and muscle pains. Despite such problems he persisted to go ahead with shows even when told not to.

"The King" was living up to his image in order to give to all his millions of fans. Being "Elvis Presley" was a severely strenuous job. Irish singer Donna Dunne maintains, "Elvis was the man . . . who was loved to death". The Dublin born performer, who grew up as a teenage Elvis fan in the 1990s recounts, "Elvis has inspired me in so many different ways. Apart from his music, good looks and moves, Elvis had a kind, sincere and loving nature and this is why, in my opinion, the world fell in love with him. Elvis will never be forgotten".

On 15 October 1976, Elvis's 1960 song "Girl Of My Best Friend" had its Irish single release and hit the number seven mark on the charts. Soon after, Elvis's seventh tour of 1976, consisting of fourteen shows, began. Constantly attempting to put his mind at work he followed up the tour with a new but brief recording session at Graceland, starting on 29 October.

The first song was written especially by world famous musical composers Andrew Lloyd Webber and Tim Rice. "It's Easy For You" told the story of a man contemplating his divorce and his incapability of getting over it. His break up from Priscilla had eaten away at him since the day they split. Since his separation in 1972 the music of Elvis Presley had taken on a whole new light. The strife, anguish and conflicts of life were inserted into the majority of his work with depth and honesty.

At various times Elvis fantasised about winning Priscilla back but aborted all efforts, knowing he would not succeed. But it wasn't just Priscilla's departure that left him forlorn but the loss of direction. Linda Thompson, who did her best for him began to distance herself from him, knowing she could never restore his life back to the way it once was. This session, which was ultimately his last, ended with the rock song "Way Down" and the ballad, "He'll Have To Go".

Towards the end of November Elvis began his eight 1976 tour and called his new girlfriend Ginger Alden to join him. The tour went on for seven days before Elvis pursued his next schedule at the Hilton, starting in December. His shows around this time some times presented a fed up man, tired of where he was and what he was doing. While sold out performances went on for almost two weeks, it was obvious to the audience that there was something devastatingly wrong with Elvis. There was no inspiration from these nights as it was the same old thing but these would be his final days in Vegas.

While Vegas was finished with, performing was not and Parker booked another tour to end the year. Although he put on a lot of weight over a short period of time, Elvis never got as obese as has been since exaggerated. Elvis's weight was an easy target for critics. Since he had been the definitive sex symbol, known for extraordinary good looks and stunning features, critics jumped at the first chance to degrade him, even though his appearance was nothing to do with the music. Like such other geniuses of performance as Orson Welles and Marlon Brando, he just got to a point where he didn't care and felt he could succeed without his looks. In such a short time he had changed dramatically. An example of how depression, overwork and being the most famous person in the world could damage the human spirit.

During one of his Vegas shows in the '70s, Irish concert promoter Jim Aiken went to see Elvis perform. Jim had made his way to ask Elvis to come to Ireland, as he was the only major star not to perform in Ireland. Aiken recalled that the show he saw in Vegas was flat and he continued, "This was the person who changed everything in music. To see him singing in Vegas and to think of what he could have done, but the Colonel didn't allow him do the world tours. The music and the person I had imagined didn't match. It was a little bit disillusioning".

Promoters in Australia, Japan and various European countries offered huge amounts to have Elvis come and play but Parker turned all the requests down flat. What is still absolutely fascinating is how Elvis Presley appealed to the entire world without ever leaving his home country to promote himself through public appearances.

Admiration for Elvis had grown considerably in Ireland by 1976, with fans ranging all ages captured by his magnetism. In tribute to him and in interest of the Irish fans the Irish Elvis Taking Care Of Business Fan Club had been set up by Ann Shiels. Irish fans travelled to his Las Vegas engagements and Ann saw him many times in Vegas. She was also most fortunate to have the chance to meet Elvis himself. A number of fan club members went to see Presley during his Vegas run. One fan recalled seeing him at the Hilton and how her friend raced onto the stage to present him with a Connemara marble plaque on behalf of the Irish fan club.

Over the years, there has been several fan clubs organised in Ireland including the Inner Circle of Friends, the Official Elvis fan club of Ireland set up in 1984 and the Irish Elvis Social Club, a division of the official British club, established in 1996. There is also the Wonder Of You Fan Club based in Athlone, Co. Westmeath, established in 2012 and the Official Elvis Fan Club of Northern Ireland set up in 2010. Like many Elvis clubs these too set out to commemorate him and carry on his legacy of beneficence, by donating to charities with money collected from conventions.

Other methods of charity fundraising in Ireland in the name of Presley have included the 1998 tribute album, *Natural Born Elvis*. The project gathered several Irish bands and a few aspiring new groups. The idea was created by the Temple Bar Music Centre in Dublin with the intention of raising donations for Childline. Some of the performers involved in the project included Loyko and Darlene doing "Devil In Disguise", Notch, with King Sativa, covering "As Long As I Have You", Craft performing "Fever" and Yuma singing "Love Me Tender".

CHAPTER TWENTY-THREE

Elvis had usually recorded music reflecting the times and had headed the fashion of the era in his earlier days. However the music changed in the 1970s and especially by 1976. The instrumental styles used were very much the sound of the '70s but this was often due to Jerry Scheff and James Burton. Elvis became an even deeper artist who sang for himself and his own feelings, something for which the mass market scorned. Elvis became a distant figure.

New sounds were coming from all areas and new bands sprung up everywhere reaching for success. One of the new groups which would become a worldwide phenomenon, first formed in 1976 in Ireland. This group was U2 and they went on to define popular music, not only in Ireland but throughout the world. While Elvis became the bridge-head for rock music success across the world, U2 were the cornerstone for Ireland's success in many areas.

It all began in the Autumn of '76 when a young teenage drummer named Larry Mullen put out a notice to begin a group at his school in Dublin. Those who joined were Adam Clayton, Richard Evans, Dave Evans (who became known as the Edge) and Paul Hewson (who became known as Bono). First known as Feedback and then Hype, they eventually settled on U2 and Richard dropped out to study in Trinity College. Each of them expressed musical talent and their first break in the business came along two years later when they won a contest in Co. Limerick.

Through much effort and determination towards their work, U2 became one of the world's most respected bands. Over three decades later they still prove to be as popular as ever. Some of their most memorable songs have included, "Where The Streets Have No Name", "Sunday, Bloody Sunday", "With Or Without You" and "I Still Haven't Found What I'm Looking For". U2 eventually helped change Ireland's view on the importance of entertainment and other forms of show business.

Ireland in 1976 gave little opportunity for people to succeed vastly in entertainment. Once U2 proved what could be done, they became the country's major entertainment export. Since then Ireland has been host to some of the world's biggest music events. U2 were also a liberal group who challenged conventional society. In 1978 they played a gig denouncing Ireland's anti-contraception laws. Bono, like Bob Geldof, became a great humanitarian and made a major impact on raising awareness for the circumstances faced by third world countries.

Like Elvis Presley, Bono is both a supreme pop and rock star and a musician who sustains artistic dedication. U2 have covered music of many genres and commit themselves to music of passion. They are folk heroes, with their stance in music history never to be forgotten and their foothold in Irish society unlikely to be equalled. They have been an impressive influence on musical artists around the globe but they also had important influences too.

Bono proclaimed that Elvis Presley was one of the greatest influences on his career. While many of the biggest popular artists from Ireland or abroad express similar sentiments, Bono's statements hold greater sway as he has reached the pinnacle of his success. His frequent comments about Presley have been positive, expressing his deep understanding of the artist. Bono has noted that Elvis acted on gut instinct and expressed himself by the way he held the microphone and by the way he moved his hips.

For their 1984 album *The Unforgettable Fire* U2 recorded a song titled, "Elvis Presley And America", which confused many people by its unusual wording. However, it is a complex array of lyrics which, in paying tribute to Elvis, can be seen as an understanding of a different and complex man's accomplishments. Such an imaginative and expressive tribute towards Elvis is highlighted through Bono's 1995 poem "American David", which is both a biographical and mythical description of Elvis.

In 1988 the group took a tour of Graceland which was featured in their movie, *Rattle And Hum* and included Larry Mullen being given special permission to pose for a photograph on one of Presley's Harley Davidson motorcycles. Like Bono, Larry has also expressed how much of an enthusiastic Elvis fan he is and named his first son Aaron Elvis. U2 were filmed visiting Sun Studios where they recorded the song "Angel Of Harlem" and Bono explained how delighted he was to be using the same microphone and toilets as Elvis. They also recorded another Elvis themed song titled "A Room At The Heartbreak Hotel".

U2's link to Elvis didn't stop there as they have paid respect to Elvis with covers of his songs, "Are You Lonesome Tonight?", "Can't Help Fallin' In Love", "Little Sister" and "Suspicious Minds", which they did in concert. Also, during their 1992 Zoo TV Tour Bono introduced the character of The Fly from his song of the same name. Bono maintained that the costume he wore was inspired by Elvis's 1968 comeback leather outfit. Bono also recorded a special solo version of "Can't Help Fallin' In Love" for the 1992 movie *Honeymoon In Vegas* and in 1997 narrated an exclusive Elvis documentary. On singing "Can't Help Fallin' In Love", Bono attempted to accentuate the same erotic intensity which Elvis exhibited in his music. These were some of U2's ways of honouring "The King of Rock 'n' Roll".

* * *

With Ireland's ascent into rock superstardom in progress, the original rock superstar approached his forty-second birthday. A new recording session was arranged by Felton Jarvis to take place in Nashville towards the end of January and while Elvis delayed his arrival to the city he was in a discouraged state because he was unable to get Ginger to come with him. Without her presence he did not feel the urge to go ahead with the session and returned to Memphis with the excuse that he had a sore throat. The planned recordings never went ahead.

Having only dated a couple of months Elvis made the sudden decision to propose to Ginger. In late January he had a jeweller quickly make up an eleven and half carat diamond ring. The story goes that he went home to Graceland and headed for his lavish bathroom, which he often used for quietness and privacy to read. He called Ginger in and proposed to her and she accepted.

1977's first concert tour commenced with a total of ten shows.

The tour presented an Elvis, eager to entertain with triumphant displays of such dramatic songs as "How Great Thou Art" and the challenging number, "Hurt". It could be seen in his eyes and expressions that his devotion to gospel music was very true to his soul. He loved the music and when he was on stage, he sang his heart out.

Instinct was his tool. It had made him the success he was and why people still called his name. Commenting on Elvis's overall talent, Irish journalist Eileen Battersby remarked, "The gospel sound, all the catchy rock and roll numbers, the ballads, the love songs, Elvis was, and is, a great singer for many reasons; he had a musical, textured rhythmic voice, that emotional intelligence. Concentrate on his voice, sweet, remorseful, defiant, suggestive. Unlike so many of the superstars of modern popular music, he could sing, that's why he is the King".

Elvis arranged a trip with Ginger to Hawaii and during this particular vacation Elvis stayed away from the medication and was very much clean and sober as he got some good exercise playing football. For a rare moment he enjoyed taking the sunshine, getting a tan which covered up the paleness from too much time indoors. Unfortunately after such good times the trip was cut short as Elvis got an eye irritation and had to return home. After some days recuperating, Presley gave eight performances but three shows had to be cancelled.

For unknown reasons, Presley's most recent attempts to keep healthy failed as he slipped back to his usual ways and in early April he was hospitalised. His health was giving in once again and at times he experienced breathing problems. A few weeks gave him a chance to recover from this and he was then again back out on the road for his third tour of the year. He went for twelve nights straight with twelve concerts.

RCA were bothered that there was little new material to release and it was almost impossible to get him to become committed to a new recording session. They now relied on recording songs from his tour and captured his versions of "Little Darlin' " and "Unchained Melody". His current concert run ended on 3 May but with just a couple of weeks secluded at Graceland, he was put back out on tour again beginning with a show in Tennessee on 20 May. The spirit, attitude and moods varied and so did those of the reports. Most of them were negative, paying more attention to his appearance rather than his continuing ability to sing fantastically. Irish rock musician Steve Wall states, "No matter how bad he got, nobody can discount the fact that he was one of the greatest singers ever and I think that is what wins out in the end".

During these months, Elvis began to get more news coverage. Most interest was turned towards degrading Presley because he now failed to stun music journalists after such a long time at the top. However, the main area of intrigue was based upon the upcoming book by his former bodyguards and reports worldwide discussed its content. Little emphasis was put on how this man could not fail to sell out concert arenas, especially since he was not the artist of the times, but the private information seemed to be more amazing than his magnetism. Then in early June CBS television in America reported that they had negotiated a deal with Presley.

The deal arranged was that he star in a one hour special to be filmed soon and shown the following Autumn. Although it was great to get such attention once again, there had been better times to capture him on film. People worldwide would now be shocked to see such a different man. Although he went by the name 'Elvis Presley' it was as if it was a completely different person to that to which most people were familiar. Pale, bloated, depressed and tired was not what made Elvis popular and compared to the movie made in Vegas only seven years earlier, this was completely surreal.

While he found comfort with Ginger, most of the time she recalled how depressed he could get. A point had come when he lost his way and spiralled into an agonising decline. Each time a new tour came around it was a case of trying to force Elvis out on stage and hope he would remain standing. He was used more as an object now rather than a singer and this contributed to his downfall. Previous concerts saw him failing to be punctual and sometimes cutting short his shows.

In June 1977, in an attempt to help a friend involved in a

federal court case, Elvis attempted to contact U.S. President Jimmy Carter for help. Carter admired Presley and there have been many U.S. Presidents who have expressed their respect for Elvis also. Incidentally what these Presidents share with Elvis are roots tracing back to Ireland. The eight generation Irish descendant Richard Nixon was an admirer and the third generation Irish-American Ronald Reagan encouraged everybody to rejoice in his music as there would never be anybody else like him.

There is also Bill Clinton, a fourth generation Irish-American, who has repeatedly shared his sentiments of admiration for Presley. Among these, Clinton was probably the biggest Presley fan as he collected Elvis memorabilia, even while President. Even his campaign to become President in 1992 took note of his interest in Presley, especially when the song "Don't Be Cruel" was played as background music to his arrival at a function. He even campaigned for the picture of the younger Elvis on a U.S.A. Postal stamp, issued in 1993. This is an American honour that has also been bestowed on the famous Irish tenor John McCormack.

* * *

Elvis's new tour kicked off on 17 June 1977 with a plan of ten performances. CBS TV set up their cameras on 19 June in Omaha, Nebraska to record Elvis's show. Another would be filmed in Rapid City, South Dakota on 21 June. Both would form the one hour special, *Elvis In Concert*.

The first gig was one of the saddest shows Elvis gave as people saw him so distant from himself. He forgot the lines to songs and stuttered and tripped over words. It was heartbreaking for fans to watch a man who had been so powerful and so strong reduced to such weakness, distraction and bewilderment. On stage he appeared to be a nervous wreck in front of the cameras, looking worried and unsettled.

The shows went on until 26 June and even with his show in Indiana, which was considered to be the best of the tour, he had faded further. Over the last several months he had added several different songs to his repertoire and one of these songs was "My

Way". A version that would give him a number six hit in Ireland the following year.

Although he had done the Frank Sinatra ballad many times over the years since 1971, more emphasis was put on it around now. He sang it while CBS were filming him and he sang straight into the camera as if he was stressing the words which reflected a man at the end of his life. While the song has been widely criticised as an unashamedly self-indulgent piece, the ironic thing about Presley covering it was that he had hardly lived much of his life "his way", or without the regrets the song claims.

The last show ended with the usual love song, "Can't Help Fallin' In Love" and Elvis bid farewell to his fans saying, "May God bless you, *Adios*". Did he know if he would be performing again is something nobody will ever know. This show turned out to be the very last performance he would ever give. Only half the year had gone, but for 1977 Elvis would still top the poll for the most sold out concerts. Once the show was over, Elvis accompanied Ginger and his entourage back to Graceland.

It was around this time more than ever that Elvis recalled his days visiting Germany and France. His need to get to new places grew essential as he had now worn out America. Entourage members recalled that Elvis often discussed travelling to places like UK and Ireland and it was something he became extremely enthusiastic about, but it was not to be. Elvis reminisced over the past and worried about the future, but mainly worried about how he would be remembered in time. He often would speak softly and sadly, repeating how he felt that nobody was going to remember him for anything worthwhile when he was gone.

For almost the entire month of July Elvis remained in his bedroom with hardly anyone other than Ginger and his doctor seeing him. He kept himself engrossed, studying his books on philosophy and spirituality. He was troubled with questions that seemed to have no answers, which concerned him. He searched the Bible, wearing out the pages looking for something, looking for any clue or meaning on where to turn. Constantly reading it over and over he couldn't seem to find that of which he was in search.

At times he slipped into a formidable impasse and completely fell apart.

Lisa Marie came for a two week visit in early August and Elvis took her and her friends to the local fairgrounds which he had rented. Over the next few days he spent time with Ginger motorcycling around the city and attending the movies where they saw the latest James Bond film, *The Spy Who Loved Me*.

Around this time too, the book by his former bodyguards was released and there was nothing Elvis could do about it. He remained unsure, depressed and so lonely on the issue, falling into a plight of anxiety and trepidation. This was combined with his repeating nightmares where he had lost everything. These ever persistent dreams had been going on for a long time and he would often wake up in a panic, convinced that he had really lost everything. Presley symbolised his country by fully living the "American Dream" but he also lived the rarely spoken of "American Nightmare". As Bono wrote in his poem "American David": "Elvis ate America before America ate him".

Chapter Twenty Four

By the summer of 1977, the year so far had seen Elvis gain an Irish number five hit in February, with his 1961 song "Suspicion". This was followed by his more recent "Moody Blue", taking a place at number seven in April. "Way Down" was soon to be released, which would give Presley his first Irish number one hit in seven years.

After twenty-three years as a professional singer his popularity had no intention of vanishing, even in a country he had never visited. While Ireland didn't look like it was going to see Elvis walk upon its shores, the only option for Irish fans, was to head for America and hope to see him anywhere there, which many had done during the 1970s. On 15 August Elvis was set for his next twelve show concert tour to begin in Maine two days later.

The night before departure Elvis headed for a dental appointment. After getting a few cavities filled he returned to Graceland after 2 A.M. He requested painkillers to stop a toothache and needed some prescriptions to be filled. Before taking his regular dosage of medicine Elvis decided to play a light-hearted game of racquetball. He followed this by playing some piano. He placed his fingers on the keys as he began to sing one of his latest recordings, "Blue Eyes Crying In The Rain". Shortly thereafter in the early hours of the morning, Elvis walked upstairs, said goodnight to Lisa Marie and headed into his bedroom, where Ginger was lying in bed. He told Ginger that he was going into the bathroom to read and as she told him not to fall asleep, he replied that he wouldn't and headed on in with some new books to read.

The following afternoon Ginger awoke to discover that Elvis was not in bed. After a while she decided to go check on him and headed into the bathroom. She found him lying on the ground with a book clutched tightly in his hands. She immediately called an entourage member downstairs who raced up. At that moment, time froze as if a million candles were all blown out at once, to a world in slow motion. A vibe of fear and horror struck aloud as everybody tried to come to grips with the reality of the moment.

An ambulance was called immediately and the room crowded with people including Vernon who cried out for his son. Lisa Marie, through all the panic and commotion, called out to know what was wrong with her daddy, but she was kept back. Paramedics did what they could to try and resuscitate him as he was taken to Baptist Memorial. On arrival at the hospital he was rushed into the trauma room where the final attempts to save him took place, but at about 3.30 P.M. it was officially confirmed that Elvis was dead.

Dr. Nick broke the news to Elvis's friends. The Colonel was also quickly informed of the news and after a brief moment of silence he went to work, beginning with the cancellation of the concerts. Reporters already began to gather outside the hospital but an official statement could not be given until Dr. Nick had informed Vernon personally of the tragic news. As the doctor walked into Graceland with Elvis's personal belongings, he saw Lisa crying and once Vernon saw the bag, he broke down in tears. After a short while of consoling, a large group of people had gathered outside the house.

News cameras and microphones flooded the hospital which was already packed with people from everywhere and the statement was made that Elvis Presley had died that afternoon. The news was so tragic that the world stopped in its tracks. Nobody could believe that a man of this stature could die. Every media outlet in the world covered this breaking news interrupting other broadcasts to inform people. It was a day the world stood still. Elvis Presley's death was a sincere shock for he had emotionally touched millions of lives. The news hit Thin Lizzy's Phil Lynott very hard as he indulged in bottles of wine and replayed his old Presley records.

An autopsy was underway but as Elvis had suffered many medical problems it was complex to determine how his death had been brought on. While this was underway it was announced that Elvis had died from cardiac arrhythmia. Elvis Presley suffered an agonising decline due to his various health problems and his death took him away from such indescribable pain. How his death had come about was not what was essential to music fans but mourning this loss was.

When Elvis died, a huge part of the world went with him. Thousands of his admirers felt they had to get to Memphis and flights into the city were sold out in a flash, with the world showing up at the gates of Graceland. Irish broadcaster Martin King remembered hearing the news when he was fourteen. King recalled, "I have been an Elvis fan all my life and was on holidays in the Isle of Man when he died. I couldn't get an armband so I took the black laces out of my shoes and tied them around my arm as a mark of respect".

Although Ireland had gained a large fan base, the country's only television station did not react to the news in any hurry. *The Irish Independent* wrote an article declaring, "Elvis who? That was the RTÉ reaction". Unlike the majority of countries in the modern world who interrupted programmes to make the announcement, RTÉ continued their regular scheduling and told the country this disturbing news at the end of the evening's transmissions.

UTV in Northern Ireland told the viewers that there was speculation that Presley had died towards the end of their *News at Ten* broadcast and then cut into the follow up programme to confirm that he had in fact died. Radio listeners in Ireland did catch the news as it was first confirmed however, on *The Larry Gogan Show* on RTÉ Radio. The news had just come in as Larry told listeners in the first few seconds of his broadcast.

Tony Prince of Radio Luxembourg, the first radio station to bring the music of Presley to Ireland, who had met Presley on occasion, was reluctant to begin his show due to his despair. However, Tony eventually revealed the news, crying over and over that "The King" was dead. Radio Luxembourg cancelled all commercials in order to play the music of Elvis and according to reports lost out on £10,000 in advertising revenue.

RTÉ radio presenter John Creedon looked back at the time of Elvis's death and recalled, "Like JFK's assassination, everyone who was around at the time of Elvis's passing will remember where they were. I was on air at a Cork pirate station, ABC, when fellow DJ Rocky Stone popped his head around the door and said

'The King is dead' ". Presley's death was a sudden shock as it was possibly the first time the world had lost an internationally known icon. What made his death more tragic was that he had died at the young age of forty-two. Like his mother he had died in his forties and coincidentally there were only two days between each other's death dates. In fact, at the time of Gladys' death when she was forty-six, her family suspected that she was actually forty-two, the same age Elvis was now.

On 17 August every newspaper across the world reported the unfortunate passing on the front page. Fan clubs worldwide remembered Elvis in their own special ways. Church services were organised for fans to honour him and in Ireland, fans got together at the St. Mary of the Angels Church on Church Street in Dublin. Many singers also displayed their respect for "The King" with tribute songs including Brendan Bowyer who made his arrival back to the Irish charts with the song, "Thank You Elvis" which became a number four hit in September. Irish singer Cahir O'Doherty also honoured Presley with "Salute To Elvis", reaching number six in October.

Presley's funeral was set for 18 August and fans who congregated outside Graceland got a chance to see Elvis one last time as his open coffin was placed on view. Enormous crowds gathered outside and police were on guard as the street, flooded with fans, began to get out of control. Thousands of fans filed past in the heat to catch a last glimpse of the great performer. A gathering of the closest associates and family attended the service which began with a performance of the song "Danny Boy" on the organ.

Presley's coffin was placed in a white hearse which was followed by a stretch of white cadillacs carrying his family and associates. A slow drive to the Forest Hill Cemetery met with specially blocked off streets with pavements that were blanketed for miles with mourners who still cried and grieved over the loss. Flags were flown at half mast across the nation and guards put their hands over their hearts out of respect, while many also saluted this former U.S. army sergeant. Several women had to be pulled back as they ran out and flung themselves towards the car. It was an extraordinarily sad, depressing and truly moving moment but the fans did what they could to honour him and emphasise how much this man was loved. It was the biggest outpouring of public grief ever seen at that time.

On arrival to Forest Hill, Elvis's body was laid to rest in a mausoleum not far from his mother. Tons of flowers were stacked around the building, which had been sent in from all around the globe. Many former acquaintances turned up and the Colonel was also present, wearing a baseball cap and ready to sell some profitable merchandise in the following days to come.

In Ireland on 21 August 1977 out of respect, one minute of silence for Presley took place at Dalymount Park, Dublin, during the day-long rock concert which attracted 10,000 music fans, with Thin Lizzy and the Boomtown Rats performing. Over the following few weeks the shock naturally faded but it was only the beginning of the tributes and honours that would keep his memory alive.

Many people literally could not believe that he was dead and therefore some over eccentric fans claimed he may still be alive, thus beginning one of the biggest trashy tabloid tales. A few brought it a step too far, as at the end of August there was an attempted kidnap of his body from the cemetery. Those who tried were arrested and failed to disturb the resting place but to stop any chances of this ever happening again, Elvis's body was moved with Gladys's to the meditation garden beside Graceland, which would remain their final resting place.

Once the body of Elvis was placed in the grounds of Graceland, Vernon had an honour to his son inscribed on his tombstone. It includes the lines, "He was admired not only as an entertainer but as the great humanitarian that he was, for his generosity and his kind feelings for his fellow man. He revolutionised the field of music and received its highest awards. He became a living legend in his own time, earning the respect and love of millions. God saw that he needed some rest and called him home to be with him".

3 October 1977 saw the premiere of *Elvis In Concert* and ended with a sombre message from Vernon Presley who thanked

everybody for their cards and flowers and expressed his grief over the loss of his son. On the first anniversary of his death, a small group of fans gathered at Graceland to remember him with a candlelit vigil. Each year that passed, this group got larger reaching to tens of thousands and his grave site was eventually opened to the fans. From that moment on, the biggest commemorations in history for one entertainer began. Elvis's legacy is so phenomenal to ever be surpassed. As Irish journalist and former Senator Eoghan Harris explained, "Presley is one of the few great artists of the twentieth century who will outlast all the little guys".

Elvis's death took an immense effect on a lot of his fans. Irish broadcaster Páidí Ó Lionáird recounted:

> Elvis was huge in our house. I was born in 1968, the youngest of 12 and I remember one brother in particular, Mickey was devastated at the news of The King's death. He wailed at the shocking news and seemed to be gripped by the grief that ensued. Mickey was also a musician, played concert flute to a very high standard. Unfortunately Mickey also passed away in 1979 aged 17 and due to a tragic motorcycle accident and though he was one of 12 the chain was broken and breached for the first time. Each year Elvis' anniversary is commemorated, Mickey's reaction to his death always comes to mind. It's not a bad thing however, its a good grounder from the daily grind of 'me, me and I'. It keeps me thinking about the real things in life at least one day every year! For that I'm grateful.

Elvis Presley's death was a result of the pressures of super-stardom as the surroundings of such a position used and abused him, chewing him up and spitting him out. Elvis was an unfortunate victim and he was an example of how sensitivity can destroy a human life. Remove the diminutive details of drugs, bad food and a life of excess as it was sadness, loneliness and overwork that did the worst damage. Nonetheless, the respect he still receives since his untimely departure remains remarkable.

Irish artist and writer Don Conroy remembered vividly hearing the news:

> The day Elvis died, I overheard the sad news while sitting in Bewley's Cafe in Grafton St., Dublin. Next to my table sat two men with tidy hairstyles and tidy suits. They shared a newspaper, looking at a picture of 'The King'. Their remarks were anything but flattering with phrases like 'he ended up a pathetic fat fuck'. As I watched the two men leave, one carefully folding up the newspaper, both clutching twin briefcases, like proper young business men, the words of the English poet, artist and mystic William Blake came to me; 'More people die of caution than from excess'. Elvis did end up a tragic figure. Yet like all great talents could make life beautiful for others, but could not make his own beautiful. When we lose remarkable people from the world, we are so much more impoverished. Yet, in the case of Elvis we have a remarkable legacy. The music, record performances and some enjoyable movies. Today, there is a billion dollar industry living off this remarkable talent. Some achievement for a poor boy from Tennessee.

On 21 August 1977, Irish TV Personality, Gay Byrne, wrote in his weekly *Sunday World* column that he first heard the news of Elvis's passing, on a boat on his way back from Tory Island. Byrne explained that he felt very sorry that such a young man with so much died alone. He added, "Elvis is going to be an even almightier industry dead than alive and its going to go on for a long, long time". Truer words couldn't be spoken as Parker continued to devise plans on how to make money, but with Presley's estate left to Lisa, Vernon arranged that Priscilla take care of everything. She invested every cent into the corporation that became the multi-million dollar Elvis Presley Enterprises (EPE). Parker no longer had the rights to Elvis and he would later die in 1997.

On 26 June 1979 after many years of illness, Vernon Presley passed away at the age of sixty-three and was also buried in the meditation garden. Then the following year Elvis's grandmother, Minnie Mae Presley died on 8 May aged eighty-six and she was the last to be placed in the meditation garden. As an adult Lisa Marie has made regular visits to Ireland visiting friends in a castle in Co. Tipperary and searching for a property of her own in the Irish countryside.

In June 1982, the doors of Graceland were opened for the first time to the public and that was when the big money began rolling in from an enormous amount of asinine merchandise. Merchandise which sees Elvis's image and name used on anything from dinner plates to bath towels. In Ireland on the 25th anniversary of his death, the Irish National Lottery even issued a special Elvis Presley scratchcard. Nonetheless, with people ignoring this mass commercialisation and just keeping focused on why Elvis was an important asset to the music industry is something essential. Dublin-born actor Marc Bannerman realised, "Elvis was a fantastic entertainer, a generous man, very good looking, with a gift".

Of his enduring legacy Steve Wall said, "I don't think anybody like Elvis will come along again. I noticed with my godson, when he was a toddler, the minute Elvis came on the TV he was just riveted. So for someone who had never even heard of Elvis, like a child, the minute Elvis came on, you could see through them there was something about the guy that got people's instincts. I think that's the beginning with people's fascination with Elvis. He just exuded music".

The memory of Elvis continues on with the creation of many documentaries and an intemperate string of compilation albums. In the weeks after Elvis died in 1977, Irish producer Noel Pearson, presented a stage show called *The King*, written by Shay Healy and Niall Tóbín, about the life of Presley. Showband singer Cahir O'Doherty played the earlier Elvis, while the great Irish actor Donal McCann portrayed the later years of the legend. In 2009 Shay Healy also won second prize at the "P. J. O'Connor Awards" for his play, *Elvis Is Dead* about an Elvis tribute performer.

In 1997 EPE created, *Elvis: The Concert* to mark the 20th anniversary of his death which presented a virtual reality show. Selected footage of Elvis's performances were projected on a huge screen with many of his original 1970s band playing live to his singing voice. The show became a hit and it was the best way for people who never saw Elvis live to try and grasp hold of that spectacular experience.

In 1998 the show began a nationwide tour of America and made its first world tour in 1999 but it wasn't until 20 March 2000 that Irish fans got to see it at the Point Theatre in Dublin and the previous night at Kings Hall in Belfast. It then made a return on 7 March 2001 to a completely sold out house again at the Point and again on 28 May 2003. It also performed at the Odyssey Arena, Belfast on 2 March 2010 and 13 March 2012 as well as at the O2 Arena, on the former Point Theatre location, on 3 March 2010 and 14 March 2012.

Elvis's greatest success has possibly been his longevity. He has had a string of chart-topping hits spanning thirty years since his death. In 2005 all of Presley's most successful hits (based on British charts) got their first consecutive release in Ireland. Elvis Presley has had no less than fifty-five Irish chart hit entries since 1962. This excludes the even greater chart success he would have had, if charts had been compiled in Ireland at the height of his career between the years 1954 to 1962. For a man who died this long ago, there remains to be many signs of life. As Irish Radio/TV Presenter, Ronan Collins, simply said, "Elvis! - That's the way it was and still is!"

Elvis's level of superstardom can never be eclipsed. New generations are realising from where modern music first leaped. Elvis is someone who will always last forever as he was new, different and unlike a lot of performers who come and go rapidly, he defined originality. Elvis was all about individuality. He symbolised the ability to stand up, pushing aside establishments to do what he wanted to do. Irish musician Eamonn Campbell maintains, "I often think to myself if I hadn't heard Elvis on that Saturday night in '55 I'd probably have become an accountant who played the accordion . . . Thank you Elvis for inspiring me to get a guitar and stick with it".

What remains to be the legacy of this singer is a young boy who gained inspiration in music from vast areas. He was a young poor child who received a guitar for his birthday and made a dream become a reality. He was a poor country boy who became a worldwide icon. He was a raw, energetic, intuitive and passionate singer who formed a new sound and transcended races, languages, classes and religions.

Elvis has become a mythical figure who easily challenges the parables of Greek gods for how he is viewed and followed. Drawing on a quote from the English poet Coventry Patmore, the Irish poet W. B. Yeats explained, "The end of art is peace and the following of art is little different from the following of religion in the intense preoccupation it demands". Elvis Presley was an artist who has become followed much like a religion. There will always be unending mysteries surrounding Elvis in the search for how he was so much more than just a singer. The most important area of Presley's credentials as a musician is the emotion he injected into all his music.

The covers of Elvis songs by contemporary Irish bands and soloists in tribute to him indicate how Elvis's popularity lives on. His stance in music is solid due to these performers covering the songs he made famous, just because he did them. His influence on music is carried forward by many thousands of fantastic new artists, mixing, adding, contributing and creating a new array of sounds to identify emotion and be the voice of a generation. Ironically, in the year of Elvis's death, Ireland had realised and adopted music as a cherished industry, with the formation of U2, the publication of the major music magazine, *Hot Press* and the country's first open stadium rock concert at Dalymount Park, Dublin.

Elvis coincidentally died shortly after Ireland found its first epitome of international rock superstardom in the shape of U2. Since then many further fantastic artists of rock have emerged in Ireland. These are artists who have been mentioned throughout this story, not only on the basis that they have recorded Elvis songs but because most are important assets to the Irish rock industry. Elvis is one of the finest examples of how one culture can reach another.

Today, Ireland is respected for its variances of popular music, which has not only helped its economy but its artistic placement in the world music scene by bringing together diverse tastes. It is this kind of unconventional creativity that connects with Presley. Most individual rock bands have begun in music the same way Elvis did. Although often unknown to them, most of today's young rockers represent the teenage Elvis, playing the beat music they adore with friends anywhere they can. For Elvis it was a secluded spot outside Lauderdale Courts, today it's usually somebody's garage. This was not a regular scene in America during Elvis's time and would have been frighteningly alien to an Irish teenager in the 1950s. However this pastime is now quite prevalent in Ireland and stems from Elvis's time.

Elvis will also always be linked to sex for it being the natural root of passion in his music. An activity which once openly discussed and accepted, helped to free Ireland. Entertainment and sex have now become an openly accepted optional pleasure for mature consenting young adults. Through rock music, it was the first time youth took little notice of religion and what it had to dictate.

The Ireland of the early twenty-first century made the move towards hosting vibrant and cosmopolitan cities. Crawling through a nation of conservatism proved a long struggle to see the light and the rush of blood in popular rock 'n' roll music played its part. Elvis rose up from America's depression and this is something Ireland, arguably a victim of more extensive periods of depression and repression, could not fail to witness and admire. Elvis was and always will be an inspiration and he certainly left his mark on the souls of many creative Irish artists and Irish people. Making Elvis and his Irish connections an essential part of Ireland's history.

NOTES

1) Bono and Elvis, "The Immortals: Elvis Presley", *Rolling Stone*, 15 April 2004.
2) "He tapped into the spirit of gospel music...": Joe Jackson, *Joe Jackson's Essential Music Collection*, 5 July 2006.
3) "Up until the age of nine ...": Interview with Eamonn Campbell, 2012 and all subsequent quotes from Eamonn Campbell.
4) "When I became interested in ...":Interview with Charlie McGettigan, 2011.
5) "That's not a criticism at all ...": B. P. Fallon, *The Last Word with Matt Cooper*, Today FM, 16 August 2007.
6) "The most famous Southern ...": John Kelly, "Elvis was no highway robber across colour line", *The Irish Times*, 7 October 2000.
7) "What Elvis was doing was ...": John Kelly, *Who Was Elvis Presley?* (Dir. Gerald Heffernan), Frontier Films, 2002.
8) Bono, Elvis, politics "The Immortals: Elvis Presley". *Rolling Stone*, 15 April 2004.
9) "The landscape of popular culture ...": Barry Egan, 'Why Heartbreak Elvis is always on our minds', *Analysis, The Sunday Independent*, p.18
10) "He was very sexually provocative ...": Jonathan-Rhys Meyers, *The Late Late Show*, RTÉ, 20 May 2005
11) "it was like nothing I had heard before ...": Interview with P. J. Curtis, 2011 and all subsequent quotes from P. J. Curtis.
12) Mary Coughlan memories of Elvis: 'Touched By Elvis', Weekend, *The Irish Times*, 10 August, 2002, p.1.
13) "If he was just a good looking singer ...": David Trimble in interview with Claire McNeilly, 'The Elvis Film That Left Me All Shook Up', *Belfast Telegraph*, 14 August 2007
14) June Juanico and Elvis: *Mary Kennedy Show*, RTÉ, 16 August 1997.
15) Pat Rabbitte memories of Elvis: 'In My Life', *The Irish Times*, 12 February 2007, p.12
16) "Rock 'n' roll, which started life as a precocious child ...": *The Irish Times*, 28 December 1956.
17) "This is hysteria ...": *The Irish Times*, 20 October 1956.
18) "I think he did have a kind ...": Niall Stokes, Ireland AM, TV3, 16 August 2002
19) "he could slide so easily from gospel to rhythm and blues ...": Joe Jackson, *Joe Jackson's Under The Influence*.
20) "If God means all good and sex comes from God ...": Joe Jackson, *Joe Jackson's Under The Influence*.
21) "Elvis was like a force of ...": Interview with Don Conroy, 2007.
22) "Elvis is a real decent fine boy ..." Ed Sullivan, *The Ed Sullivan Show*, CBS Television, 3 January 1957.
23) "When he sings 'One Night' ...": Barry Egan, 'Why Heartbreak Elvis is always on our minds', Analysis, *The Sunday Independent*, p.18
24) A nun told a student "her soul was condemned to hell": Alan Hanson, *Elvis '57: The Final Fifties Tours* (iUniverse, 2007) p.81
25) Archbishop John Charles McQuaid investigations: John Cooney, *John Charles McQuaid: Ruler of Catholic Ireland* (O'Brien Press, 1999) p.308
26) Flanagan and Elvis: Eamonn McCann, *McCann: War & Peace In Northern Ireland* (Hot Press Books, 1998) p.78
27) Elvis has been, 'unmasked ...': Eamonn McCann, *Dear God: The Price Of Religion in Ireland* (Larkham, 1999)p.137
28) Censorship views of Beckett and O'Flaherty: Julia Carlson, *Banned In Ireland: Censorship & the Irish Writer* (Routledge London, 1990) p.13
29) Bishops in Maynooth warned, 'The evil one is ...': Julia Carlson, *Banned In Ireland: Censorship & The Irish Writer* (Routledge London, 1990) p.9
30) "Art is the most ...": Oscar Wilde, *The Soul of Man Under Socialism*, 1895
31) 'Elvis was young ...': Shay Healy, RTÉ, *Elvis Night*, 10 August 2002.

32) "In Cork, like everywhere else ...": George Hook, *Time Added On* (Penguin Ireland, 2005) p.30
33) 'a terrible judgement must await ...': W.J. McCormack & Patrick Gillan, *The Blackwell Companion to Modern Irish Culture* (Wiley-Blackwell, 2001) p.482
34) Priest on Elvis: Interview with Mullingar Historian Leo Daly, 2007.
35) "Is Presley human?": *The Irish Times*, January 1957.
36) "the famous frenetic 'wiggle'...": *The Irish Times*, 4 February 1957.
37) "Presley sings a song or two ...": *The Irish Independent*, February 1957
38) "I don't think Elvis needed ...": Interview with Steve Wall, 2005.
39) "when he sang 'Baby I Don't Care' ...": Interview with Shay Healy, 2011
40) "I was a greaser ...": Victoria Mary Clarke, Shane MacGowan, *A Drink With Shane MacGowan* (Sidgwick & Jackson, 2001), P.51
41) "lots of people can sing but ...": Interview with Jim Fitzpatrick, 2005.
42) "for me it was his voice ...": Interview with Steve Wall, 2005.
43) "*Jailhouse Rock* was the first time ...": Interview with Shay Healy, 2011.
44) "giving us the ineffable Elvis Presley": *The Irish Times*, March 1958.
45) Review of *Jailhouse Rock*: *The Irish Independent*, March 1958.
46) Review of *Jailhouse Rock*: *The Evening Press*, March 1958.
47) 13 year old fan and Elvis dream: *The Irish Times*, 23 March 1958.
48) "this picture is a tough one ...": Liam O'Hora, Film Censor Notes, National Archives, Dublin.
49) "the Elvis of Ireland": Sinéad O'Connor, *The Late Late Show*, RTÉ
50) "I thought he was an angel ...": Sinéad O'Connor, *100 Greatest No.1 Singles*, Producer: John Piper, Channel 4, 2001.
51) Dáil debates 1959-60: Thaddeus Lynch, Copyright Houses of the Oireachtas.
52) Dáil debates 1959-60: James Dillon, Copyright Houses of the Oireachtas.
53) Dáil debates 1959-60: James Dillon, Copyright Houses of Oireachtas.
54) "In the tight key with his vibrato ...": Rick O'Shea, *Evening Herald*, April 1959.
55) "I'm gonna visit Ireland": Bryan Kelly, *Sunday World*, August 1977.
56) "With Elvis's hip wiggling ...": Interview with Dermod Lynskey, 2004.
57) Dr. Iognáid G. Ó Muircheartaigh, Memories: "In My Life", *The Irish Times*, 24 April 2007, p.12
58) "priests flipping their lid": RTÉ Radio, 1997.
59) "this picture will be ...": Liam O'Hora, Film Censor Notes, National Archives, Dublin.
60) "most cold-blooded ...": Liam O'Hora, Film Censor Notes, National Archives, Dublin.
61) "See and hear the new Elvis ...": *The Irish Times*, January 1961.
62) "His voice was ...": Interview with John Spillane, 2011.
63) "There are millions who argue ...": Bob Geldof, *Music of the Millennium*, Channel 4, 13 November 1999.
64) "Music for the young": Letters to the editor, *Evening Press*, December 1960.
65) "After three years, rock 'n' roll ...": *Evening Press*, 12 February 1958.
66) "Some modern dances are ...": Kim Bielenberg, *'From Polygamy and orgies to the Late, Late Scandals'*. *Irish Independent*, 29 December 2001.
67) "which piece do you want me to take off?": Tony Farmer, *Ordinary Lives: Three Generations of Irish Middle Class Experience* (Gill & Macmillan Ltd., 1991) p.192.
68) "most cold-blooded": Film Censor Notes, National Archives, Dublin.
69) "Ninety-nine per cent of ...": Kevin Rockett, *Irish Film Censorship: A Cultural Journey from Silent Cinema to Internet Pornography* (Four Courts Press, 2004) p.151.
70) "My teenage years were filled with his magic ...": Interview with Maxi, 2003.
71) "even Elvis Presley's nearest and ...": *The Irish Times*, 16 August 1963.
72) "Elvis the Pelvis' enjoys an income ...": James Dillon, Copyright Houses of Oireachtas.
73) "Elvis was of primary ...": Interview with Shay Healy, 2011.
74) Brendan Bowyer on Elvis, *Evening Press*, January 1964.
75) "I hold that virtually every ...": Dickie Rock, *Evening Press*, January 1964.
76) Elvis said "Love is the bottom line": Kanai Seanoa, *The Definitive Elvis: The Spiritual Soul of Elvis* (Passport Productions, 2002)

77) "Elvis Helped in Success of Burton-O'Toole Movie": Peter Guralnick, *Careless Love: The Unmaking of Elvis Presley* (Little, Brown, 1999) p.171.
78) "When I was growing up and ...": Rory Gallagher in interview with Joe Breen, *The Irish Times*, 12 October 1976.
79) "A wise man ...": Jonathan Swift, *The Works of Jonathan Swift: Volume 1*, 1843.
80) "this guy's a really good singer ...": Eileen Battersby, An Irishwoman's Diary, *The Irish Times*, 8 August 2002.
81) Leonard Bernstein: "Elvis is the greatest cultural force in the 20th century...": Gene L. Landrum, *Paranoia & Power: Fear and Fame Of Entertainment Icons*, p.63
82) The Late Late Show incidents of 1966: Fergal Tobin, *The Best of Decades: Ireland in the 1960s* (Gill and Macmillan Ltd, 1984) p.141.
83) "I love the Elvis movies ...": Larry Mullen, *U2: Rattle and Hum* (Dir. Phil Joanou) Paramount Pictures, 1988.
84) "one thing that can be said for Elvis Presley ...": Fergus Linehan, *The Irish Times*, 11 September 1967.
85) "It's a known fact that if you ask ...": Brendan O'Connor, 'A Boy's Own Book', Life, *The Sunday Independent*, 14 March 2004, p.31
86) "I like Elvis because ...": Eamonn Holmes, *Essential Elvis UK*, Issue 20, January / February 2002. www.essentialelvis.com.
87) "is the Irish nation slowly going mad?": *The Irish Times*, 22 December 1969.
88) "the performance with much shaking and swivelling ...": Ken Grey, *The Irish Times*, 5 January 1970.
89) "He was not afraid to ...": Interview with Nuala Holloway, 2011.
90) "Early Elvis Presley...": Phil Lynott, *The Rocker: A Portrait of Phil Lynott* (Dir: Shay Healy) Safinia Productions, 1996.
91) "He had a great voice ...": Christy Dignan, *Elvis: Burning Love* (Dir. Brian Reddin) Adare Productions 2002.
92) "Pop, rock, white soul ...": Antony Farrell, Vivienne Guinness, Julian Lloyd, *My Generation. Rock 'n' Roll Remembered: An Imperfect History* (Lilliput Press, 1996) p.171
93) "He was the King of America ...": Joseph O'Connor, *Sweet Liberty: Travels in Irish America*, (Picador, 1996)
94) "Elvis had the wisdom ...": Bono, (Flanagan 1987) borrowed from Gilbert B. Rodman, *Elvis After Elvis. The Posthumous Career of A Living Legend* (Routledge 1996) p.78.
95) "Brendan Bowyer used to do an impression of me ...": Elvis Presley, as recounted by Brendan Bowyer in *The Man Who Would Be King*, The Sunday Independent, 16 September 2001.
96) Elvis and Tom Dunphy, recounted in '*The Man Who Would Be King*', The Sunday Independent, 16 September 2001.
97) "He had it all ...": Eamonn Holmes, *Essential Elvis UK*, Issue 20, January / February 2002. www.essentialelvis.com.
98) Colm Wilkinson and Elvis: *The Daniel O'Donnell Show*, RTÉ, 2005.
99) "Elvis was simply an incredible singer ...": Paul Brady interview, Antony Farrell, Vivienne Guinness, Julian Lloyd, *My Generation. Rock 'n' Roll Remembered: An Imperfect History* (Lilliput Press, 1996) p.11
100) "Drawing together sundry musical influences ...": Eamon Carr, 'Elvis Is Back In The Building Again', *The Evening Herald*, 19 February 2001.
101) "What amazes me is his voice ...": Jack L, *Elvis: Burning Love* (Dir. Brian Reddin) Adare Productions 2002.
102) "Elvis was a deity ...": B. P. Fallon, 'Touched By Elvis', Weekend, *The Irish Times*, 10 August, 2002, p.1.
103) "Elvis was the original star ...": Aonghus Ralston, *Elvis: Burning Love* (Dir. Brian Reddin) Adare Productions 2002.
104) "Elvis is a Fraud": Kevin Marron, *Sunday World*, 25 March 1973.
105) Daniel O'Donnell memories of Elvis: Eddie Rowley, *Daniel O'Donnell: My Story* (Virgin Books, 2005)
106) "He was an intuitive genius ...": Bob Geldof, *There's Only One Elvis* (Dir. Karina Brennan) BBC Television Manchester, 2002.

107) "Elvis turns to God": *Sunday World*, January 1976.
108) "Is Elvis going blind?": *Sunday World*, January 1976.
109) "I like to think of ...": Maeve Binchy, Elvis Night, RTÉ Two, 10 August 2002.
110) "Elvis is the man ...": Interview with Donna Dunne, 2012
111) "This was the person ...": Jim Aiken, 'Touched by Elvis', Weekend, *The Irish Times*, 10 August, 2002, p.1.
112) "'I'll never forget his concert ...": *Irish Independent*, 18 August 1977.
113) "The gospel sound, all the catchy rock and roll numbers ...": Eileen Battersby, *An Irishwoman's Diary, The Irish Times*, 8 August 2002.
114) "No matter how bad he got ...": Interview with Steve Wall, 2005.
115) "Elvis Ate America ..." Bono, *American David*. 1995.
116) "I have been an Elvis fan ...": Interview with Martin King, 2004.
117) "Elvis who? ...": *The Irish Independent*, 18 August 1977.
118) "Like JFK's assassination ...": Interview with John Creedon, 2003.
119) "Presley is one of the few ...": Interview with Eoghan Harris, 2002.
120) "The day Elvis died ...": Interview with Don Conroy, 2007.
121) Elvis and Gay Byrne, *Sunday World*, 21 August 1977.
122) "Elvis was a fantastic entertainer ...": Marc Bannerman, *Essential Elvis UK*, Issue 15, March / April 2001. www.essentialelvis.com.
123) "I don't think anybody like Elvis ...": Interview with Steve Wall, 2005.
124) "Elvis! ...": Interview with Ronan Collins, 2003.
125) "The end of art is peace ...": W. B. Yeats, *Samhain*, 1905.

BIBLIOGRAPHY

Brown, Peter Harry & Broeske, Pat H. *Down at the End of Lonely Street: The Life and Death of Elvis Presley* (EP Dutton, 1997)
Clarke, Victoria Mary & MacGowan, Shane, *A Drink with Shane MacGowan* (Sidgwick & Jackson, 2001)
Coghe, Jean-Noel, *Rory Gallagher: A Biography* (Mercier Press, 1997)
Collins, M.E., *History in the Making: Ireland 1868-1966* (The Educational Company of Ireland, 1993)
Cooney, John, *John Charles McQuaid: Ruler of Catholic Ireland* (O'Brien Press, 1999)
Carlson, Julia, *Banned in Ireland: Censorship & the Irish Writer* (Routledge London, 1990)
Dillon-Malone, Aubrey, *Rise and Fall and Rise of Elvis* (Leopold Publishing, 1997)
Doggett, Peter, *The Complete Guide to the Music of Elvis Presley* (Omnibus, 1994)
Dundy, Elaine, *Elvis and Gladys*, (University Press of Mississippi, 1985)
Farmer, Tony, *Ordinary Lives: Three Generations of Irish Middle Class experience* (Gill & Macmillan, 1991)
Farrell, Antony & Guinness, Vivienne and Lloyd, Julian, eds., *My Generation: Rock 'n' roll Remembered: An Imperfect History* (Lilliput Press, 1996)
Flippo, Chet, *Graceland: The Living Legacy of Elvis Presley* (Hamlyn, 1994)
Gordon, Robert, *Elvis: King On The Road* (Hamlyn, 1996)
Guralnick, Peter, *Careless Love: The Unmaking of Elvis Presley* (Little Brown, 1999)
Guralnick, Peter, *Last Train to Memphis: The Rise of Elvis Presley* (Abacus, 1995)
Guralnick, Peter & Ernst Jorgensen, *Elvis: Day By Day* (Ballantine Books, 1999)
Hanson, Alan, *Elvis '57: The Final Fifties Tours* (iUniverse, 2007)
Jorgensen, Ernst, *Elvis Presley: A Life In Music* (St. Martin's Press, 2000)
Kirkland, K.D. *Elvis* (Bdd Promotional Book Co., 1990)
Marsh, Dave, *Elvis* (Thunder Mouth's Press, 1993)
Matthews, Rupert, *Elvis: King of Rock 'n' Roll* (Gramercy, 1998)
McCann, Eamonn, *Dear God: The Price of Religion in Ireland* (Larkham, 1999)
McCann, Eamonn, *McCann: War & Peace in Northern Ireland* (Hot Press, 1998)
McCormack, W.J. & Gillan, Patrick, *The Blackwell Companion to Modern Irish Culture* (Wiley-Blackwell, 2001)
O'Connor, Joseph, *Sweet Liberty: Travels in Irish America* (Picador, 1996)
O'Halloran, Daragh, *Green Beat: The Forgotten Era of Irish Rock* (Brehon Press Ltd., 2006)
O'Keefe, Finbar, *Goodnight, God Bless and Safe Home: The Golden Showband Era*, (O'Brien Press, 2002)
Prendergast, Mark J., *Irish Rock: Roots, Personalities, Directions* (O'Brien Press, 1987)
Presley, Priscilla & Presley, Lisa Marie, *Elvis by The Presleys* (Century 2005)
Putterford, Mark, *Phil Lynott: The Rocker* (Omnibus Press, 2002)
Rockett, Kevin, *Irish Film Censorship: A Cultural Journey from Silent Cinema to Internet Pornography* (Four Courts Press, 2004)
Rodman, Gilbert B., *Elvis After Elvis: The Posthumous Career of a Living Legend* (Routledge, 1996)
Schroer, Andreas, et al, *Private Elvis: Elvis in Germany* (Boxtree, 1993)
Simpson, Paul, *Rough Guide to Elvis Presley* (Rough Guides, 2004)
Smyth, Gerry, *Noisy Island: A Short History of Irish Rock* (Cork University Press 2005)
Tobin, Fergal, *The Best of Decades: Ireland in the 1960s* (Gill & Macmillan Ltd, 1984)
Tunzi, Joseph A., *Elvis No.1: The Complete Chart History of Elvis Presley* (JAT Productions, 2000)

FILMOGRAPHY

Classic Albums: Elvis Presley, Dir. Jeremy Marre, EagleVision, 2001
Early Elvis, Hughes Leisure Group, 1994
Elvis '56, Dir. Alan Raymond, Lightyear Entertainment, 1987
Elvis 'Aran' Presley, Dir. Ciarán Gallagher, TG4, 2005
Elvis by the Presleys, Dir. Rob Klug, EPE, 2005
Elvis: Burning Love, Dir. Brian Reddin, Adare Productions, 2002
Elvis: He Touched Their Lives, Dir. David Green, ITV, 1980
Elvis in Hollywood, Dir. Frank Martin, BMG Video, 1993
Elvis in Vegas, Dir. Jeremy Marre, BBC TV, 2010
Elvis: King of Entertainment, Good Times Video, 1997
Elvis Lives, Producer: Mary Wharton, BMG, 2002
Elvis On Tour, Dirs. Robert Abel & Pierre Adidge, MGM/UA, 1972
Elvis Presley's Graceland, Ross Productions, 2001
Elvis: Private Moments, Brentwood Communications, 1997
Elvis: Return to Tupelo, Dir. Michael L. Rose, Michael Rose Productions, 2008
Elvis: That's The Way It Is, Dir. Dennis Sanders, MGM/UA, 1970
Elvis: The Great Performances, Dir. Andrew Solt, Wienerworld, 1992
Elvis: The Last 24 Hours, Dir. Mike Parkinson, Phase 4 Films, 2007
Famous Families: The Presleys, Producer: Kevin Burns, Glen Avenue Films, 1998
Mr. Rock 'n' Roll: Col. Tom Parker, Dir. Christopher Bruce, Channel 4, 1999
Music of the Millennium, Channel 4, 13 November 1999
Presley: I Don't Sing Like Nobody, Producer: Ann Freer, BBC TV, 1987
Presley: Cut Me and I Bleed, Producer: Ann Freer, BBC TV, 1987
Remembering Elvis, Dir. Richard Bluth, IMC Vision, 2000
Sun Days with Elvis, Dir. Bernard Roughton, Hughes Leisure Group, 1992
Sun Days with Elvis Vol.2, Dir. Bernard Roughton, EPFC Video Workshop, 1995
The 100 Greatest No.1 Singles, Producer: John Piper, Channel 4, 2001
The Day Elvis Died, Visual Corporation Limited, 1997
The Definitive Elvis Collection, Passport Productions, 2002
The Gospel Music of Elvis Presley, Vol.1, Dir. Michael Merriman, Coming Home Music, 1999
The Gospel Music of Elvis Presley, Vol.2, Dir. Michael Merriman, Coming Home Music, 1999
The Ed Sullivan Show, CBS Television, 3 January 1957
The Elvis I Knew, Dir. Dale Hill, Decker Television & Video Productions, 1994
The Elvis Mob, Dir. Jeremy Marre, Leopard Films, 2002
The Last Days of Elvis: E! True Hollywood, Dir. Big Boy Medlin, E! Entertainment Television, 1999
The Rocker: A Portrait of Phil Lynott, Dir: Shay Healy, Safinia Productions, 1996.
There's Only One Elvis, Dir. Karina Brennan, BBC Television Manchester, 2002
This is Elvis, Dirs. Malcolm Leo & Andrew Solt, Warner Bros., 1981
U2: Rattle and Hum, Dir. Phil Joanou, Paramount Pictures, 1988
Who Was Elvis Presley?, Dir. Gerald Heffernan, Frontier Films, 2002
Young Elvis in Colour, Dir. Alexander Marengo, Darlow Smithson, 2007

INDEX

The Acoustic Motorbike, 94
Aiken, Jim, 204
"Ain't That Loving You Baby", 62, 110
Alden, Ginger, 204, 208-210, 212-214
"All Shook Up", 41, 42, 101, 138, 153
Allen, Tony, 193
Aloha From Hawaii, 179, 181, 182, 184, 186, 202
"Also Sprach Zarathustra", 165
"Always On My Mind", 177, 184, 194
"Amazing Grace", 167, 192
"America, The Beautiful", 193
"American David", 207, 213
"An American Trilogy, 175
An Emotional Fish, 60
Ancient Music of Ireland, 200
"And I Love You So", 193
"And The Grass Won't Pay No Mind", 144
Andress, Ursula, 103
"Angel Of Harlem", 208
Ann-Margret, 104, 132, 166
"The Answer To Everything", 149
"Any Way You Want Me", 33
Apple Cart, the, 38
"Apple Of My Eye", 177
"Are You Lonesome Tonight?", 77, 82, 83, 96, 186, 208
"Are You Sincere?", 187
Arnold, Eddy, 24
"As Long As I Have You", 205
Ash, 54
Aslan, 159
"Baby I Don't Care", 53, 54
"Baby Let's Play House", 24
Bachelors, the, 88
Ball, Chris, 170
Bannerman, Marc, 221
Bass Odyssey, 142
Bassey, Shirley, 153
Battersby, Eileen, 122, 209
Beach Boys, the, 122
Beatles, the, 106, 107, 125, 127, 134, 153, 162, 163, 174
Becket, 109
Beckett, Samuel, 46, 133
Behan, Brendan, 46
Belew, Bill, 136, 151, 156
"Believe Me If All Those Endearing Young Charms", 38
Bell X1, 159
Bellefire, 77
Bernstein, Leonard, 125

Berry, Chuck, 75, 135, 188
The Best Of Everything, 82
Big 8, the, 166
"Big Boss Man", 133, 137
The Big Cube, 34
"A Big Hunk O' Love", 62, 72
Binchy, Maeve, 202
Binder, Steve, 135, 136, 138
"Bitter They Are, Harder They Fall", 200
Black Aces Showband, the, 88
Black Eagles, the, 149
Black Romantics, the, 59
Black, Bill, 15, 16, 23, 25, 75
Blackman, Joan, 94, 98
Blackwell, Otis, 101
Blackwood Brothers, the, 65
Blink, 30
Bloom, Luka, 94
"Blue Christmas", 56
"Blue Eyes Crying In The Rain", 201, 214
Blue Hawaii, 94, 96-98, 105
"Blue Moon Of Kentucky", 17, 22, 23
"Blue Moon", 22, 37
"Blue Suede Shoes", 28, 30, 153
Bluesville, 119
Bono (Paul Hewson), 7, 21, 50, 146, 165, 206-208, 213
Bonzo Goes To College, 124
Boomtown Rats, the, 197, 218
Boone, Pat, 34, 75
"Bossa Nova Baby", 103
Bowie, David, 197
Bowyer, Brendan, 87, 105, 128, 157, 166, 175, 183, 217
Boyd, Stephen, 82
"The Boys Are Back In Town", 150, 201
Brady, Paul, 173
Brando, Marlon, 204
Brel, Jacques, 59
Brennan, Stephen, 108
"Brewing Up A Storm", 59
"Bridge Over Troubled Water", 158, 194
Brosnan, Pierce, 101
"Brown Eyed Girl", 106
Brown, Louis, 169, 201
Brown, Roy, 20
Brown, W. Earl, 138
Browne, Dave, 179
Browne, Michael, 126
"Bullfrog Blues", 120
"A Bunch Of Thyme", 194
"Burning Love", 176, 180
Burton, James, 104, 152, 206
Burton, Richard, 109

231

Bye Laws, the, 148
Byrne, Eamonn, 99
Byrne, Gabriel, 95
Byrne, Gay, 90, 220
Byrne, T .J., 87
Cairns, Andy, 156
Campbell, Barry, 30
Campbell, Eamonn, 17, 18, 24, 29, 49, 222
"Can't Help Fallin' In Love", 94, 95, 149, 157, 193, 194, 208, 212
Capitol Showband, the, 88
Caravelles, the, 106
Carr, Eamon, 173, 174
Carrigan, Ben, 104
Carroll, Johnny, 157, 170, 201
Carter, Jimmy, 211
Caruso, Enrico, 13, 52
Casablanca, 31, 60
Cash, Johnny, 39
Celtic Tenors, the, 201
Change Of Habit, 144, 145
Charles, Ray, 26
Charro!, 139
Chessmen, the, 119
Chieftans, the, 19, 106, 107, 134
Christopher, Mic, 143
Clambake, 131, 134
Clancy Brothers, the, 19, 107, 108
Clarke, Dave, 143
Clayton, Adam, 206
Clinton, Bill, 96, 211
Clipper Carlton, the, 87
Cochran, Eddie, 28
Colgan, Maureen, 92
Colgan, Maurice, 92
Collins, Ronan, 222
"Come Back To Sorrento", 81, 170
The Commitments, 95, 143
Commodores, the, 171
Como, Perry, 30
Conroy, Don, 40, 220
Coppinger, Michael, 87
Corrs, the, 137
Coughlan, John, 103
Coughlan, Mary, 26
Coulter, Phil, 189
Craft, 205
Cranberries, the, 142
"Crawfish", 59
Creatures, the, 119
Creedon, John, 216
Crosby, Brian, 159
The Crowd Roars, 53
Crudup, Arthur, 15

"Crying In The Chapel", 81, 124
Cult, the, 173
Curtis, P. J., 25, 29, 35, 49, 172
Curtiz, Michael, 60
Daly, Leo, 50
"Danny Boy", 69, 200, 201, 217
Dark Victory, 31
"Datin' ", 124
Davis Jr., Sammy, 76
Day, Dennis, 37
Dean, James, 56
Deasy, Conor, 104
DeBurgh, Chris, 177
DeCordova, Frederick, 124
Dempsey, Damien, 177
"Devil In Disguise", 103, 108, 205
Devlin, Barry, 20, 173, 174
"Didn't We", 142
Dignam, Christy, 159
Dillon, Eoin, 176
Dillon, James M., 70, 71, 102
"Dirty Old Town", 167
"Dirty, Dirty Feeling", 77
"Do You Wanna Do It", 37
"A Dogs Life", 124
Dolan, Joe, 88, 149, 156, 177
Domino, Fats, 20, 153
Domino", 162
"Don't Be Cruel", 33, 36, 40, 101, 186, 211
"Don't Cry Daddy", 141, 157, 163
"Don't Think Twice, It's All Right", 168
"Don't", 62
"Doncha' Think It's Time", 60
Dorsey Brothers Stage Show, 27, 28
Dorsey, Jimmy, 27
Dorsey, Tommy, 27
Double Trouble, 130-132
"Down In The Alley", 129, 130
Downey, Alan, 159
Doyle, Rory, 59
Doyle, Tony, 108
Dr. No, 103
Drifters, the, 88, 149
"Dublin Town", 177
Dubliners, the, 19, 107, 167, 189
Dundy, Elaine, 10
Dunne, Donna, 203
Dunne, Philip, 82
Dunphy, Sean, 201
Dunphy, Tom, 87, 166, 183
Dylan, Bob, 97, 129, 168
Easy Come, Easy Go (1947), 130
Easy Come, Easy Go, 130, 131
Eat the Peach, 108

The Ed Sullivan Show, 35, 38, 40, 107
Edge, The (Dave Evans), 206
Edgery, Peter, 58
Egan, Barry, 21, 41
Egan, Richard, 34
Eire Apparent, 148
Elvis (1956 album), 37
Elvis (1973 album), 186
Elvis (1979 TV movie), 102
Elvis (2005 Miniseries), 160
Elvis 'Aran' Presley. 53
Elvis and The Beauty Queen, 160
Elvis In Concert, 211, 218
Elvis Is Back, 76
Elvis Is Dead (2009 play), 221
Elvis Now, 176
Elvis On Tour, 177, 178, 180
Elvis Presley (1956 album), 31
"Elvis Presley And America", 207
The Elvis Presley Show (Radio Luxembourg), 85
Elvis Sails, 67
Elvis: Burning Love, 176, 179
Elvis: On Stage, 156
Elvis: That's The Way It Is, 158, 160
Elvis: The Concert, 221, 222
Elvis' Christmas Album, 55, 58
Elvis' Golden Records, 62
Emerald Society Pipe Band, the, 36
Engine Alley, 99
Eurovision, 119, 165, 189
Evans, Richard, 206
"Everybody Loves My Girl", 179
"Evil Elvis", 156
Ewing, Fyfe, 156
"Faded Love", 158
"Fairytale Of New York", 43
"Fairytale", 192
Fallon, B.P., 21, 178
"Fame And Fortune", 76, 77
Father Ted, 96
Fean, Sean, 173
"Feel No Shame", 159
Feeney, John, 169, 170, 201
"Fever", 77, 205
Field, the, 101
"The First Noel", 168
"The First Time Ever I Saw Your Face", 166
Fitzgerald, Barry, 36, 130
Fitzgerald, Geraldine, 82
Fitzpatrick, Jim, 57
Fitzsimons, Charles B., 160
The Flame Of Araby, 34
Flaming Star, 80, 81, 83, 94, 139, 166
"The Fly", 208

Fog, Seanie, 60
Follow That Dream, 97, 101
Fontana Showband, the, 88, 120
Fontana, D. J., 24, 75, 135, 136, 152
"A Fool Such As I", 72, 185
"Fool", 176, 186, 187
"For Ol' Times Sake", 185
"For The Good Times", 176, 194
"For The Heart", 200
"For The Millionth And The Last Time", 97
Forrest, Mark, 129, 167, 169, 201
Foster and Allen, 170, 193, 194
Foster, Mick, 193
Frames, the, 143
Francois, Charles, 189
Frankie and Johnny, 124
Franklin, Aretha, 152
Frew, David, 60
Friel, Brian, 98
Friendly Sons of St. Patrick, the, 36
"From A Jack To A King", 185
"From Galway To Graceland", 173
Fun In Acapulco, 103, 108
G.I. Blues, 77, 78, 80-84, 94
"G.I. Blues", 77
Gallagher, Rory, 90, 119-121, 141, 173
"Galway Bay", 128, 170
Galway, James, 201
Gamblers, the, 106
Geldof, Bob, 83, 197, 207
"Gentle On My Mind", 141
"Georgie Boy", 59
"Ghost of Elvis", 143
Gilmartin, Thomas, 49
Girl Happy, 110, 121
"Girl Of My Best Friend", 186, 203
Girls! Girls! Girls!, 100, 101
"Give Me The Right", 93
Gina, Dale Haze and the Champions, 36
"Gloria", 106
"Go, Move, Shift", 167
Gogan, Larry, 216
"Going To Nepal", 30
"Good Luck Charm", 97, 99, 157
"Good Rockin' Tonight", 22
"Good Time Charlie's Got The Blues", 188
Good Times, 190
Gorham, Scott, 149
"Got A Lot O' Livin' To Do", 41, 43
"Got My Mojo Working", 158
Graft Jr. George, 63
Granny's Intentions, 148
Gray, Ken, 140
"Green, Green, Grass Of Home", 192, 194

233

Greenbeats, the, 34, 106
Greene, Angela, 110
Guercio, Joe, 159, 165
"Guitar Man", 133, 136, 137
Haley, Bill, 20, 43, 46, 48, 75, 88
Hamilton, Mark, 54
"Hard Headed Woman", 59, 63
Hardin, Glen D., 152
"Harem Holiday", 121
Harms, Carl, 59
Harrington, Paul, 119
Harris, Eoghan, 219
Harris, Richard, 107, 124, 142, 155, 189
Harry Boland Danceband, the, 87
Hart, Dolores, 64
Harum Scarum, 121, 124
Hassett, Colm, 143
Hatherly, Charlotte, 54
Hawaii, 124
"Hawaiian Wedding Song", 105
Hayes, Isaac, 171, 185
"He Touched Me", 169
Healy, Shay, 48, 54, 61, 103, 221
"Hear My Song", 170
"Heartbreak Hotel", 26, 28, 30, 31, 120
"He'll Have To Go", 204
"Help Me Make It Through The Night", 168
Hendrix, Jimi, 150
Hennessey, Christie, 193
"Here Comes Santa Claus", 56
"Here Comes The Night", 124
"Hey Jude", 153
Higgins, Michael D., 96
His Hand In Mine, 81, 93
"His Latest Flame", 97
Hodge, Charlie, 81, 136, 152
Hogan, Mike, 142
Hogan, Noel, 142
Holloway, Nuala, 147
"Holly Leaves And Christmas Trees", 168
Holly, Buddy, 75
Holmes, David, 137
Holmes, Eamonn, 136, 168
"Homes Of Donegal", 173
Honeymoon In Vegas, 208
Hook, George, 48
Horan, Kevin, 104
Horslips, 149, 171, 173, 174
"Hot Digity", 30
Hothouse Flowers, 142
"Hound Dog", 32-34, 36, 52, 138, 148
"How Great Thou Art", 129, 185, 192, 209
Hurley, Red, 165, 170, 201
"Hurt", 200, 201, 209

"I Am A Star", 193
"I Believe In Elvis Presley", 21
"I Believe In The Man In The Sky", 81
"I Believe", 55, 129
"I Can Help", 193
"I Don't Like Mondays", 197
"I Got A Feeling In My Body", 188
"I Got A Woman", 26, 153
"I Got Stung", 62, 71
"I Just Can't Help Believin' ", 159, 176
"I Love You Because", 15
"I Love You More And More Everyday", 149
"I Miss You", 187
"I Need Somebody", 104
"I Need You So", 41
"I Need Your Love Tonight", 62, 72
"I Still Haven't Found What I'm Looking For", 206
"I Was The One", 26
"I'll Be Home For Christmas", 56, 129
"I'll Get Home On Christmas Day", 168
"I'll Never Fall In Love Again", 200
"I'll Never Stand In Your Way", 14
"I'll Remember You", 130
"I'll Take You Home Again, Kathleen", 69, 169, 170, 192
"I'm Leavin' ", 169
"I'm Left, You're Right, She's Gone", 25
"I'm Movin' On", 141
"I'm Yours", 105
"I've Got A Thing About You Baby", 196
"I've Lost You", 163
"If Everyday Was Like Christmas", 130
"If I Can Dream", 138, 141, 142
"If That Isn't Love", 188
"If You Talk In Your Sleep", 188
Impact Showband, the, 120
Imperials, the, 130, 171
"The Impossible Dream", 165, 167, 192
"In The Ghetto", 141, 142, 153, 157
"Indescribably Blue", 130
"Indian Summer", 97
"Infamy", 99
"Inherit The Wind", 141
Ireland, John, 82
"Ireland's Call", 189
The Irish In Us, 130
Irish Steppers, the, 36
Irish Tenors, the, 167, 169, 201
Irvine, Andy, 173
"It Feels So Right", 124
It Happened at the World's Fair, 102
"It Hurts Me", 137
"It Is No Secret", 55

"It Won't Seem Like Christmas", 168
"It Wouldn't Be The Same Without You", 14
"It's All Good", 177
"It's Easy For You", 203
"It's Impossible", 174
"It's Not My Fault", 30
"It's Now Or Never", 77, 79, 83, 96, 170
"It's Only Love", 169
"It's Over", 175
"It's Playing For Keeps", 92
Jackson, Joe, 17, 39
"Jailbreak", 150
Jailhouse Rock, 53-55, 61, 103, 132
"Jailhouse Rock", 54, 120, 138
James, Mark, 200
Jarvis, Felton, 128, 208
Jewell, Joe, 159
Johnson, Don, 160
Johnstons, the, 173
Jones, Carolyn, 64
Jones, Norah, 77
Jones, Tom, 156
Jordanaires, the, 41, 81, 152, 186
Joyce, James, 134
Juanico, June, 31
Juniper, 143, 159, 177
Juno and the Paycock, 60
"Just Call Me Lonesome", 133
"Just For Old Times' Sake", 105
Kanter, Hal, 40
Keane, John B., 101
Kearns, Anthony, 167
Keisker, Marion, 14
Kelly, Bryan, 73
Kelly, John, 21
Kelly, Luke, 52
Kenealy, Brian, 99
Kenealy, Canice, 99
Kenny, Tony, 177
"Kentucky Rain", 144, 163
Keogh, John, 34, 49, 106, 107
Kid Galahad, 97, 101
Kila, 176
The King (1977 play), 221
King Creole, 58-60, 63, 64, 68, 83, 91
"King Creole", 59
King Jr., Martin Luther, 138
King, Martin, 216
"King's Call", 150
Kingbees, the, 119
Kirkham, Millie, 81, 152
"Kiss Me Quick", 97, 100
Kissin' Cousins, 104, 108
Kitt, David, 176

"Known Only To Him", 81
Kristofferson, Kris, 168
"Kung Fu", 54
L., Jack, 59, 175, 177
"Lace Virginia", 60
"Lady In Red", 177
"Lakes Of Pontchartrain", 173
Lambert, Dermot, 30
Lange, Hope, 82
Lansbury, Angela, 94
Lanza, Mario, 13
Last Of The High Kings, 95
The Late Late Show, 22, 90, 103, 126
Laughton, Charles, 36
"Lawdy, Miss Clawdy", 28
Lawler, Fergal, 142
The Lawnmower Man, 101
Lawrence of Arabia, 110
Led Zeppelin, 21
Leiber, Jerry, 52, 53, 103
Lemass, Sean, 86
"Let Yourself Go", 137
Lewis, Jerry Lee, 39, 75, 106
Linehan, Fergus, 152
"Linger", 142
"Little Cabin On The Hill", 185
"Little Darlin' ", 209
Little Gaelic Singers, the, 38
"Little Less Conversation", 135, 137
"Little Sister", 97, 208
Live 8, 198
Live a Little, Love a Little, 135
Live Aid, 198
Locke, Josef, 170, 201
Lockhart, Jim, 173
Logan, Johnny, 189
"Londonderry Air", 200, 201
"The Loneliest Man In Town", 143
Lonely Hearts, 148
"Long Black Limousine", 141
"Long Tall Sally", 37
"Looking For Jude", 143
"Lord's Prayer", 168
"Love Coming Down", 201
"Love Letters", 129
Love Me Tender, 35, 36, 38, 48, 52
"Love Me Tender", 34, 36, 160, 186, 194, 205
"Love Me", 34, 36
"Loving Arms", 188
Loving You, 40, 41, 54, 58
"Loving You", 54
Loyko and Darlene, 205
The Luck Of The Irish, 82
Lynch, Joe, 108

235

Lynch, Thaddeus, 70
Lynott, Phil, 149, 215
Lynskey, Dermod, 75
"MacArthur Park", 155
Mac Con Iomaire, Colm, 176
MacGill, Moyna, 94
MacGowan, Shane, 43, 56, 103, 159
Magee, Jimmy, 100
Major Barbara, 36, 133
"Make Me An Island", 149
"Make Me Know It", 75
"Make The World Go Away", 158
Maken, Tommy, 107, 108
Mancini, Henry, 153
Mansell, Richard, 10
Mansell, William, 10
Marron, Kevin, 182
Martin, Bill, 189
Martin, Dean, 13, 52
"Mary In The Morning", 158
Mary Janes, the, 143
Matthau, Walter, 60, 64
Maxi, 99
May, Imelda, 28
McCalla, Irish, 32
McCann, Donal, 221
McCann, Eamonn, 45
McColl, Ewan, 167
McColl, Kirsty, 167
McCormack, John, 13, 67, 169, 170, 201, 211
McDermott, John, 167
McDonnell, Myles, 143
McGahern, John, 126
McGeegan, Pat, 105
McGettigan, Charlie, 17, 119
McGuinness, Billy, 159
McGuinness, Tony, 159
McHugh, Frank, 130
McKee, Fearghal, 143
McLoughlin, Brian, 30
McMahon, Padraic, 104
McMurray, Rick, 54
McNiff Irish Dancers, the, 36
McQuaid, John Charles, 44, 126
"Mean Woman Blues", 41
Meany, Colm, 95
"Memphis, Tennessee", 103
Meredith, Burgess, 133
"Merry Christmas Baby", 168
"A Mess of Blues", 76
"Messenger Boy", 193
Meyers, Jonathan-Rhys, 22, 160
Miami Showband, the 88, 105
Midnight Cowboy, 139

Mildred Pierce, 110
"Minnie Minnie", 37
"Milkcow Blues Boogie", 23
"Milky White Way", 81
The Milton Berle Show, 28, 32, 41
"Miracle Of The Rosary", 168
Monarchs, the, 106
"Money Honey", 26, 28
Monroe, Marilyn, 147
"Moody Blue", 200, 214
Moore, Bobby, 152
Moore, Christy, 148, 167, 173
Moore, Gary, 149
Moore, Mary Tyler, 145
Moore, Scotty, 15-17, 19, 23, 25, 75, 136, 152
Morgan, Dermot, 96
Morning Dove White, 10
Morrison, Van, 90, 106, 161, 180
Morrissey, Eamon, 108
Movement, the, 148
Mulhare, Edward, 107
Mullen, Larry, 131, 206, 207
Mundy, 179
Munroe, Bill, 17
Munroe, Marilyn, 147
Murphy, Ann B., 61
Murphy, Martin, 60
"My Baby Left Me", 28, 59
"My Boy", 189
"My Happiness", 14
"My Way", 170, 212
"My Wish Came True", 60
"Mystery Train", 25, 59
Natural Born Elvis, 205
NBC Television Special ('68 Comeback), 135-140, 155, 200
Neal, Bob, 23, 24
Nevada Showband, the, 165
"Never Again", 201
The New Gladiators, 191
Nichopoulos, Dr. George, 131, 188, 190, 192, 196, 215
Nirvana, 137
Nixon, Richard, 162, 163, 211
"No More", 105
"Nobody Knows", 173
Noonan, Paul, 159
Norton, Graham, 103
Notch, 205
"Nothing Compares To You", 67
Ó Braonáin, Fiachna, 143
Ó Lionáird, Páidí, 219
Ó Maonlaí, Liam, 142
Ó Muircheartaigh, Dr. Iognáid G., 79

Ó Snodaigh, Rónán, 176
Ó Snodaigh, Rossa, 176
"O Solo Mio", 77, 170, 192
Ó Suilleabháin, Tom, 53
O'Brien, Kate, 46
O'Cahan, Rory Dall, 200
O'Casey, Sean, 8, 60, 98, 107
O'Connor, Brendan, 133
O'Connor, Charles, 173
O'Connor, Frank, 46
O'Connor, Joseph, 164
O'Connor, Sinéad, 67
O'Doherty, Cahir, 217, 221
O'Donnell, Daniel, 185, 186
O'Faolain, Sean, 46
O'Flaherty, Liam, 46
O'Hara, Maureen, 34, 36
O'Herlihy, Dan, 34
O'Hora, Liam, 63, 64, 80, 96, 98
O'Malley, Kevin, 62
O'Riordan, Dolores, 142
O'Shea, Rick, 71
O'Sullivan, Camille, 103
O'Sullivan, Maureen, 124
O'Toole, Peter, 107, 109
Ocean's Eleven, 137
Odlum, Dave, 176
Odlum, Karl, 176
"Oh How I Love Jesus", 128
Ohio Showband, the, 88
Olcott, Chauncey, 63
"Old Shep", 12
"On A Snowy Christmas Night", 168
"One Broken Heart For Sale", 102
"One Night Of Sin", 41
"One Night With You", 41, 71
"Only Believe", 158
Orange Machine, 148
Page, Paul, 143
Paget, Debra, 32
Paradise: Hawaiian Style, 124
Parker, 'Colonel' Tom, 24, 25, 31, 32, 54, 57, 63, 68, 72, 78, 83, 93, 96, 102, 104, 107, 108, 110, 121, 122, 128, 132, 134, 135, 138-141, 152, 153, 155, 157, 161, 171, 174, 177-179, 182, 184, 186, 187, 190, 194, 195, 202, 204, 215, 220
Parker, Ed, 168, 184
"Party", 41
"Passing Through", 59
"Patch It Up", 158
Patmore, Coventry, 223
Patterson, Frank, 167, 169, 192, 193, 201
Pavarotti, Luciano, 52
"Peace In The Valley", 40, 41, 55

Pearson, Noel, 221
Perkins, Carl, 39, 75
Petrie, George, 200
"Petrol", 54
Philadelphia, Here I Come, 98
Philips, Dewy, 19
Philips, Dominic, 159
Phillips, Sam, 14-16, 18, 19, 22, 25, 27, 39
Picturehouse, 179
"Pieces Of My Life", 193
"Pizza And Wine", 97
Planxty, 148, 173
The Playboy of the Western World, 98, 133
"Playing For Keeps", 34, 54
"Pocketful of Rainbows", 77, 78
Poems that Touch the Heart, 66
Pogues, the, 43
"Polk Salad Annie", 156, 186
"Power Of My Love", 144
Prendergast, Peter, 103
Prendergast, Philip, 103
Presley, Gladys, 9, 11, 31, 42, 43, 60, 64, 65, 68, 74, 175, 217
Presley, Jesse Garon, 9, 11
Presley, Lisa-Marie, 135, 144, 175, 193, 202, 214, 215, 220, 221
Presley, Minnie Mae, 9, 220
Presley, Priscilla Beaulieu, 72-74, 84, 101, 104, 130-133, 135, 156, 165, 167, 169, 172, 175, 177, 178, 180, 187, 203, 220
Presley, Vernon, 8, 11, 31, 43, 64, 65, 171, 202, 215, 218-220
Pressley, Andrew, 9
Pressley, David, 9
Prince, Tony, 216
"Promised Land", 188, 196
"Proud Mary", 156
"Put The Blame On Me", 93
The Quiet Man, 14
Rabbitt, Eddie, 141, 144, 158
Rabbitte, Pat, 33
"Rags To Riches", 161
"Rain", 60
"Raised On Rock", 185
Ralston, Aonghus, 179
"Rambles Of Spring", 194
"Rat Trap", 197
Rattle and Hum, 131, 207
"Reach Out To Jesus", 170
Reagan, Ronald, 211
"Reconsider Baby", 77
Recorded Live On Stage In Memphis, 190
"Reddy Teddy", 37
Redmond, Liam, 98

"Redwood Tree", 180
Reed, Jerry, 133, 135
Reed, Lou, 29
The Reno Brothers, 31, 34
"Return To Sender", 101, 108
Rhee, Master Kang, 167
Rice, Damien, 143, 159, 177
Rice, Tim, 203
Richard, Little, 62, 75, 106
"Rip It Up", 37
Robertson, Brian, 149
"Rock 'n' Roll Kids", 119
Rock Around The Clock, 20, 43, 46
"Rock Around The Clock", 20
Rock, Dickie, 88, 105, 106
"Rock-A-Hula-Baby", 94
Rockhouse, 173
Rolling Stones, the, 122, 127, 134
"A Room At The Heartbreak Hotel", 208
Ross, Jane, 200
Roustabout, 104, 108, 109, 184
Royal Irish Showband, the, 87, 88, 100, 105, 107, 166
"Rubberneckin' ", 142
"Run On", 129
Russell, Kurt, 102, 160
Ryan, Daniel, 104
Ryan, Dr. Thomas, 126
Salamanca, J. R., 82
"Salute To Elvis", 217
"Santa Bring My Baby Back", 56
"Santa Claus Is Back In Town", 58
"Santa Cruz", 104
"Santa Lucia", 170
Scheff, Jerry, 152, 206
"Screamager", 156
The Sea Wolf, 31
"See See Rider", 156, 181
Sellers, Peter, 110
"Sentimental Me", 93
"Separate Ways", 176
Sexton, Robbie, 30
"Shadow Play", 120
Shaft, 185
"Shake, Rattle and Roll", 28
Shaw, George Bernard, 36, 38, 46
"She Didn't Dance The Day", 38
"She Wears My Ring", 188
"She's Not You", 99, 100
Shiels, Ann, 205
Sholes, Steve, 26, 54, 63, 68, 128
"Sick Bed Of Cúchulainn", 43
The Silver Tassie, 98
Sinatra, Frank, 38, 52, 76, 78, 134, 140, 170, 212

Sinatra, Nancy, 74, 76, 132
"Singing Tree", 133
Skid Row, 149
Slate, Jeremy, 101
Smyth, Sam, 199
The Snapper, 95
"Snowbird", 161
"So Much For The City", 104
"Soldier Boy", 75
"Solitaire", 200
"Something Blue", 99
Something For Everybody, 93, 97
"Something", 159
"Soulmate", 179
"Spanish Eyes", 188, 194
Speedway, 132, 137, 139
Spillane, John, 83
Spinout, 128, 132
Springfield, Dusty, 158
Springsteen, Bruce, 29, 197
The Spy Who Loved Me, 213
St. Elvis, 10
Stamps Quartet, the, 171
A Star Is Born, 194
Stay Away, Joe, 133, 134
"Steamroller Blues", 182
The Steve Allen Show, 33
Stokes, Niall, 38
Stoller, Mike, 52, 53, 103
Stone, Mike, 175, 184
Stone, Rocky, 216
"Stranger In My Own Home Town", 144
"Stranger In The Crowd", 158
Strangers, the, 119
Streisand, Barbara, 194
"Stuck On You", 76, 77
Stunning, the, 59
"Such A Night", 77, 96, 110
"Such An Easy Question", 124
Sullivan, Ed, 36, 38, 40
Sumner, J. D., 171, 199
"Sunburst", 179
"Sunday, Bloody Sunday", 206
"Surrender", 81, 170
"Susan When She Tried", 193
"Suspicion", 99, 105, 214
"Suspicious Minds", 142, 143, 149, 153, 155, 157, 208
Sweet Inspirations, the, 152, 153
Swift, Jonathan, 122
"Switch", 99
Sykes, John, 149
"Sylvia", 158
Synge, John Millington, 98

"Take Good Care Of Her", 185
"Take My Hand, Precious Lord", 41, 55
"Taking Care Of Business", 143
"Talk About The Good Times", 188
Tarzan, 53
Taste, 120
Taurog, Norman, 101
"Teddy Bear", 41, 55, 174
"Teethgrinder", 156
Ten North Frederick, 82
"Thank You, Elvis", 217
"That's All Right", 15-17, 19, 28, 179, 186
"That's Something You Never Forget", 97
"That's When Your Heartaches Begins", 14, 41
Them, 106, 124
Therapy?, 156
"There Goes My Everything", 158
"There Is No God But God", 170
"There's A Guy Who Works Down The Chip Shop Swears He's Elvis", 167
Thin Lizzy, 57, 149-151, 171, 173, 174, 198, 201, 215, 218
"Thirty Foot Trailer", 167
This is Elvis, 160
"This Is The Story", 141
"This Is", 159
Thompson, Linda, 179, 180, 184, 185, 187, 191, 192, 203
Thompson, Richard, 173
Thorpe, Richard, 103
Three Cheers For The Irish, 31
Thrills, the, 104
Thunder Road, 139
Tickle Me, 110, 124
'Til We Meet Again, 31
"To The Bright And Shining Sun", 59
"To You I Bestow", 179
Tóbín, Niall, 108, 221
"Today, Tomorrow And Forever", 104
"Tomorrow Is A Long Time", 129, 130
"Tomorrow Never Comes", 158
"Tomorrow Night", 22
Ton Ton Macoute, 67
"Too Much Monkey Business", 135
"Too Much", 34
Toomey, Regis, 145
"Treat Me Nice", 53
Trevaskis, Brian, 126, 127
Trimble, David, 27
The Trouble with Girls, 139
"T-R-O-U-B-L-E", 193
"Trouble", 59, 137
"True Love Travels On A Gravel Road", 144
"Trying To Get To You", 24

Turner, Big Joe, 20
Turner, Juliet, 97
Tutt, Ronnie, 152
"Tutti Frutti", 28
"Twenty Days And Twenty Nights", 158
"Twinkle", 143
Tynan, Ronan, 167
"U.S. Male", 135
U2, 21, 97, 131, 206-208, 223
Ulysses, 134
"Unchained Melody", 193, 209
The Unforgettable Fire, 207
"Until It's Time For You To Go", 169
Van, the, 95
Victors, the, 88
Vincent, Gene, 28
Viva Las Vegas, 103, 104, 110, 170
"Viva Las Vegas", 104, 110
The Voice of Ann Boyle, 53
Waiting for Godot, 133
"Walk A Mile In My Shoes", 157
Wall, Steve, 52, 59, 210, 221
Wallis, Hal B., 31, 60, 104, 110
Walls, the, 52, 59
"Way Down", 204, 214
"We Call On Him", 133
"We Can Make The Morning", 169
"We Don't Need Nobody Else", 143
"Wear My Ring Around Your Neck", 60
Weatherly, Frederic, 200
"Weatherman", 159
Webber, Andrew Lloyd, 203
"Welcome To My World", 182
Welles, Orson, 204
West Side Story, 139
Westendorf, Thomas P., 169
"The Westmeath Bachelor", 149
Westmoreland, Kathy, 152
Wharton, Darren, 149
"What Now My Love", 182
What's New Pussycat?, 110
Wheeler, Tim, 54
Whelan, Gerard, 60
"When Irish Eyes Are Smiling", 62, 78, 135
"When It Rains, It Really Pours", 25
"When", 165
"Where Did They Go Lord?", 161
"Where The Streets Have No Name", 206
Whipping Boy, 143
Whitaker, T. K., 86
Whitcomb, Ian, 119, 124, 152
"White Christmas", 56
White, Barry, 79
White, Snowy, 149

239

Whitfield, Frederick, 128
Who Was Elvis Presley?, 21
Wild in the Country, 81, 82, 93, 96
Wilde, Oscar, 47
Wilkinson, Colm, 155, 169
Wilkinson, John, 152
Williams, Paul, 106
"Winter Wonderland", 129
"With Or Without You", 206
"Without Him", 129
Witnesses, the, 155
"The Wonder Of You", 157, 163
"Wooden Heart", 77, 185
Wyatt, Enda, 60
Yeats, W. B., 7, 223
"Yesterday", 153
"You Can't Have It All", 54
"You Don't Have To Say You Love Me", 158, 161, 165
"You Gave Me A Mountain", 175
"You Turn Me On", 119, 124
"You'll Be Gone", 99
"You'll Never Walk Alone", 129, 133, 193
"You're A Heartbreaker", 23
"You've Lost That Lovin' Feelin' ", 159
"Young And Beautiful", 53
Young, Gig, 98
"Your Cheatin' Heart", 60
Yuma, 205

Made in the USA
Charleston, SC
12 February 2013